新文科英语系列教程

Academic English for Business
商务学科英语

主　编　田力男
副主编　王　敏　张文娟
编　者　张卓娟　高　静　杜洁敏
　　　　李　丹　徐新燕　李　昕

清华大学出版社
北京

内 容 简 介

本教材共十个单元，每个单元包括搜索背景信息、视听说、课文A和课文B、练习、影视和技能培养六个部分，旨在培养学生用英语进行商学专业学习和从事商务活动的能力，从而实现学生专业学习能力与英语应用能力双赢的培养目标。本教材以商学相关热点话题为依托，涵盖经济、管理、生产、营销、金融等多个领域；以原文输入真实语料为媒介，选取第一手的阅读和视听材料，并配有词汇手册供学生学习使用。本教材相关的视听材料，读者可通过扫描正文对应的二维码进行学习，也可通过点击http://www.tup.com.cn/index.html下载使用。

本教材可供具有一定大学英语基础的商学及相关专业的本科生和研究生使用。

版权所有，侵权必究。举报：010-62782989，beiqinquan@tup.tsinghua.edu.cn。

图书在版编目（CIP）数据

商务学科英语 / 田力男主编. — 北京：清华大学出版社，2019（2021.12重印）
（新文科英语系列教程）
ISBN 978-7-302-53289-7

Ⅰ.①商… Ⅱ.①田… Ⅲ.①商务—英语—教材 Ⅳ.①F7

中国版本图书馆CIP数据核字（2019）第142103号

责任编辑：刘细珍
装帧设计：陈国熙
责任校对：王凤芝
责任印制：宋 林

出版发行：清华大学出版社
网　　址：http://www.tup.com.cn, http://www.wqbook.com
地　　址：北京清华大学学研大厦A座　　邮　　编：100084
社 总 机：010-62770175　　邮　　购：010-62786544
投稿与读者服务：010-62776969, c-service@tup.tsinghua.edu.cn
质量反馈：010-62772015, zhiliang@tup.tsinghua.edu.cn

印 装 者：三河市科茂嘉荣印务有限公司
经　　销：全国新华书店
开　　本：185mm×260mm　　印　张：18　　字　数：410千字
版　　次：2019年8月第1版　　印　次：2021年12月第3次印刷
定　　价：68.00元

产品编号：083396-01

前言 Preface

本教材秉承国家培养大批具有国际视野、通晓国际规则、能够用英语直接参与国际事务和国际竞争的国际化人才的指导思想，旨在培养学生用英语进行商学专业学习和从事商务活动的能力，从而实现学生专业学习能力与英语应用能力双赢的培养目标。本教材编写的主要特色如下：

一、以学术能力培养为导向

不同于其他商务实务英语教材，本教材着重提高学生用英语进行商学专业学习的能力，具体包括：1）学生听专业讲座记笔记的能力；2）搜索和阅读综述性专业文献，抓住主要事实和有关细节的能力；3）就商学领域重要议题准确表达个人观点、进行专业探讨、汇报科研成果的演示陈述能力；4）按照学术规范撰写专业论文的英文摘要和英语学术小论文的能力；5）翻译专业英语文献资料的能力等。

二、以综合能力拓展为目标

本教材按照项目研究方法设计教学任务。每个教学单元要求学生围绕单元主题撰写总结性小论文，以小组为单位组织辩论和开展相关课题研究，并将研究结果在课堂上以英语口头报告的形式呈现出来。本教材希望通过以上活动培养学生的英语应用能力、自主学习能力、团队合作能力、批判思维能力、分析解决问题等综合能力。

三、以商学相关热点话题为依托

本教材选取与商学学科相关的话题，包括全球化、企业社会责任、众筹、外包、零售业变革、贸易战、脱欧、人工智能、共享经济、比特币等。以上话题基本上是经济、管理、生产、营销、金融等领域当前的热门话题，在激发学生英语学习积极性的同时，将语言学习和专业学习有效结合起来，从而有利于将学生培养成为既懂英语又通晓商学专业的复合型人才。

四、以原文输入真实语料为媒介

本教材输入性阅读和视听材料均选自当今主流期刊及网络媒体，除个别材料的长度根据教材需要有所裁剪外，所选取的材料基本没有其他改动，以期通过原汁原味的语料输入来增强学生的英语语言感知力，培养学生用英语学习商学概念、了解商学领域信息的能力，并激发学生用英语表达相关话题的批判性观点。

本教材使用对象包括但不限于具有一定大学英语基础的商学及相关专业的本科生、研究生。本教材编写的宗旨不在于系统介绍商学学科专业知识，而是通过商学及相关领域具有争议性的热门话题来引导学生进行英语学习，使其逐渐掌握用英语学习商学专业知识的能力以及从事商务、金融、经济、贸易等涉外业务的沟通交往能力。

商务学科英语

本教材共十个单元，每个单元包括搜索背景信息、视听说、课文 A 和课文 B、练习、影视和技能培养六个部分。具体如下：

搜索背景信息：该部分列出了涉及单元话题的关键商学术语和背景知识点，并提供了相关网址供学生在课前进行自主学习，了解相关背景知识。

视听说部分：包含与单元话题相关的视听和口语练习。视听练习总长度在五分钟左右，取材于权威平台，既可以作为学生课前热身练习，也可以作为语言和知识点的输入应用于课堂教学过程中。除视听练习外，该部分还包括口语练习，锻炼学生语言输出能力。

课文部分：每单元包括两篇关于同一话题，但观点相对的课文，即课文 A 和课文 B。在学习课文的过程中，学生能够通过练习提高其用英语归纳段落大意、锁定具体信息、总结全文、形成观点进行批判讨论的口头和笔头能力。课文最后设置辩论任务，学生可以在学完课文后对辩论话题展开讨论。

练习部分：包括语义、句法、语篇等方面的不同题型，帮助学生掌握和夯实语法、翻译和写作技能。

影视部分：包括影片的基本信息、故事梗概、根据影片中地道的语言素材编写的语言练习，旨在营造完整的语言情境，从而培养学生语感，扩大其知识面，提高其文化素养、语言运用能力和跨文化交际能力。

技能部分：每单元集中介绍一项学术研究相关技能，如口头报告技能、转述技能、学术论文写作技能、文献引用技能、辩论技能等。

此外，本教材还附有词汇手册供学生学习使用。

本教材参编人员为长期从事高校英语教学与研究的一线教师。编写人员的分工如下：张卓娟负责第一单元和第十单元的编写工作；高静负责第二单元和第七单元；李丹负责第三单元；杜洁敏负责第四单元和第九单元；徐新燕负责第五单元；李昕负责第八单元；张文娟负责第六单元的编写工作，以及第一至第五单元技能部分的编写和单元统稿工作；王敏负责影视部分的编写，以及第六至第十单元技能部分的编写和单元统稿工作；田力男负责本教材的策划、选题、统稿和出版联络工作；张清负责本教材的审阅工作。

此外，感谢中国政法大学商学院巫云仙、宏结、张巍、王玲、胡继晔等教授和刘克凡、李鸣等同学对本教材选题和选材的指导和帮助。所选材料均已注明出处，但因时间和距离限制无法联系到作者进行授权，在此对其深表感谢。

书中如有失误或不妥之处，还望广大读者批评指正，以便不断改进和完善。

编者
2019 年 5 月 12 日

目录
Contents

01 — **Unit 1** Globalization
1. Search for Background Information 02
2. Discuss the Words' Meaning.................................03
3. Watch the Video 07
4. Read for Information 08
5. Practice for Enhancement 16
6. Movie Exploration: *Wall Street* (1978) 20
7. Reading Skills 23

27 — **Unit 2** Workplace Automation
1. Search for Background Information 28
2. Discuss the Words' Meaning.................................29
3. Watch the Video 32
4. Read for Information 34
5. Practice for Enhancement 43
6. Movie Exploration: *The Big Short* (2015) 46
7. Presentation Skills..50

55 — **Unit 3** Crowdfunding
1. Search for Background Information 56
2. Discuss the Words' Meaning.................................57
3. Watch the Video 61
4. Read for Information 62
5. Practice for Enhancement 71
6. Movie Exploration: *Inside Job* (2010)...................75
7. Listening Skills 78

81 — **Unit 4** Brexit
1. Search for Background Information 82
2. Discuss the Words' Meaning.................................83
3. Watch the Video 86
4. Read for Information 87
5. Practice for Enhancement 96
6. Movie Exploration: *Margin Call* (2011)................99
7. Paraphrasing Skills..103

107 — **Unit 5** Outsourcing
1. Search for Background Information 108
2. Discuss the Words' Meaning...............................109
3. Watch the Video 113
4. Read for Information 115
5. Practice for Enhancement 125
6. Movie Exploration: *Too Big to Fail* (2011) 128
7. Debating Skills..132

商务学科英语

137 Unit 6 Sharing Economy

1. Search for Background Information 138
2. Discuss the Words' Meaning 139
3. Watch the Video 142
4. Read for Information 144
5. Practice for Enhancement 153
6. Movie Exploration: *Barbarians at the Gate* (1993) 156
7. Note-Taking Skills 159

163 Unit 7 Corporate Social Responsibility

1. Search for Background Information 164
2. Discuss the Words' Meaning 165
3. Watch the Video 169
4. Read for Information 171
5. Practice for Enhancement 179
6. Movie Exploration: *Rouge Trader* (1999) 182
7. Summarizing Skills 185

187 Unit 8 Retailing

1. Search for Background Information 188
2. Discuss the Words' Meaning 189
3. Watch the Video 192
4. Read for Information 194
5. Practice for Enhancement 202
6. Movie Exploration: *Boiler Room* (2000) 205
7. Debating Skills 209

213 Unit 9 Bitcoin

1. Search for Background Information 214
2. Discuss the Words' Meaning 215
3. Watch the Video 218
4. Read for Information 220
5. Practice for Enhancement 228
6. Movie Exploration: *Wall Street 2: Money Never Sleeps* (2000) 231
7. Writing Skills 235

239 Unit 10 Trade War

1. Search for Background Information 240
2. Discuss the Words' Meaning 241
3. Watch the Video 244
4. Read for Information 246
5. Practice for Enhancement 254
6. Movie Exploration: *Jerry Maquire* (1996) 258
7. Referencing Skills 261

265 Appendix 词汇表

ACADEMIC ENGLISH FOR BUSINESS

Unit 1
Globalization

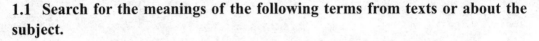

1 Search for Background Information

1.1 Search for the meanings of the following terms from texts or about the subject.

1) globalization: _____
2) the anti-globalization movement: _____
3) free trade: _____
4) open economy: _____
5) closed economy: _____
6) neoliberalism: _____
7) punitive tariff: _____
8) IMF: _____
9) trade protectionism: _____
10) FDI: _____
11) Smoot-Hawley Tariff Act: _____
12) subprime mortgage crisis: _____
13) arbitrage: _____
14) dumping: _____
15) anti-dumping duty: _____

Web Resources

https://en.wikipedia.org/wiki/Globalization
https://en.wikipedia.org/wiki/Anti-globalization_movement
http://www.globalissues.org/issue/38/free-trade-and-globalization
http://www.wisegeek.com/what-is-the-difference-between-an-open-and-closed-economy.htm
https://en.wikipedia.org/wiki/Neoliberalism
http://dictionary.cambridge.org/dictionary/english/punitive-tariff
http://www.imf.org/en/About
http://www.economicsonline.co.uk/Global_economics/Trade_protectionism.html
https://www.investopedia.com/terms/f/fdi.asp
https://www.investopedia.com/terms/s/smoot-hawley-tariff-act.asp
http://marginalrevolution.com/marginalrevolution/2015/04/is-globalization-going-in-

Unit 1   Globalization

reverse.html
https://en.wikipedia.org/wiki/Subprime_mortgage_crisis
https://www.thebalance.com/what-was-the-asian-financial-crisis-1978997
https://www.investopedia.com/ask/answers/04/041504.asp
https://en.wikipedia.org/wiki/Dumping_(pricing_policy)
https://www.investopedia.com/terms/a/anti-dumping-duty.asp

1.2   Present what you've found to the class orally with or without PowerPoint in three minutes.

2   Discuss the Words' Meaning

2.1   Define the following underlined words. An example is given for you.

e.g. They tend to visualize themselves going through their routine in preparation for their actual performance.
   visualize: form a picture of something in the mind.

1) The general consensus is that global warming is a bad thing.
   consensus: _____

2) Kindle FreeTime, is a free, personalized tablet experience just for kids and exclusively available on Kindle Fire.
   exclusively: _____

3) Once we have, through analytic meditation, come to an insight or a deeper understanding, then we should cease our analysis and begin the practice of calm abiding.
   cease: _____

4) At the same time, however, CEOs, particularly in financial services, have grown concerned about government regulation.
   regulation: _____

5) He also said the British press risked a backlash from the public if they published them.
   backlash: _____

6) European farmers are planning a massive demonstration against farm subsidy cuts.
   subsidy: _____

7) Moreover, big powers would further exploit such fears to heighten <u>hostility</u> between rival camps.
   hostility: _____
8) Advertisers will see this and I can imagine the <u>emergence</u> of a new advertising technique.
   emergence: _____
9) How would people react when this cultural icon had done something that people <u>perceive</u> as immoral?
   perceive: _____
10) The key conclusion of this theory is that <u>transitory</u>, short-term changes in income have little effect on consumer spending behavior.
    transitory: _____
11) Uganda's President Yoweri Museveni said he backed economic <u>integration</u> but Africa was too diverse for one government.
    integration: _____
12) Not only did she <u>exceed</u> our expectations, but she added tremendous value to the team.
    exceed: _____
13) With Steve Jobs gone, they will not get to <u>dominate</u> any market for too long.
    dominate: _____
14) Humans are tool builders and we build tools that can dramatically <u>amplify</u> our innate human abilities.
    amplify: _____
15) Several other vehicles were involved in <u>subsequent</u> collisions after the crash in which he died.
    subsequent: _____
16) The carbon market works like any other <u>commodity</u> market: companies trade and the market sets prices.
    commodity: _____
17) Instead, he realized, he was fascinated by the dynamics of change and <u>innovation</u> in the market.
    innovation: _____
18) Protesting workers in Belfast and Enfield have staged factory sit-ins to <u>highlight</u> their plight.
    highlight: _____
19) But for those looking for something a bit different, several <u>alternative</u> events are also starting to pop up.
    alternative: _____
20) And that created enormous challenges, of our capability and systems and process to deal with this tremendous growth and <u>expansion</u>.
    expansion: _____

Unit 1 Globalization

21) The mystery is starting to clear around how diverse species with an array of features evolve.
    diverse: _____
22) Some merger investors make bets on potential acquisition targets before any deal is announced.
    acquisition: _____
23) Danica has been hard at work sorting out a mixed and varied set of songs.
    varied: _____
24) The General laid down a few strategic targets on the map.
    strategic: _____
25) Madame Curie was the physicist with expertise in chemistry that, in 1898, discovered the radioactive substances of radium and polonium in Paris, France.
    expertise: _____
26) Many other industrial giants have developed their own power generation capacity over the years.
    capacity: _____
27) We can offer advice, but ultimately, the decision rests with the child's parents.
    ultimately: _____
28) The importance of livability in Danish culture is exemplified in the sustainable infrastructure of its capital city.
    sustainable: _____
29) Competition would then do what it has done elsewhere: generate productivity, innovation, and better prices.
    generate: _____
30) The number and severity of cyber incidents is not likely to diminish in the near future.
    diminish: _____

2.2 Fill in the following blanks with various forms of each word. An example is given for you.

No.	Base form	Variations in the word family
e.g.	consist	consistency, consistent, consistently, inconsistency, inconsistent
1)	migrate	
2)	exclude	
3)	transit	
4)	commit	

(Continued)

No.	Base form	Variations in the word family
5)	content	
6)	affect	
7)	benefit	
8)	perceive	
9)	equal	
10)	globe	
11)	ample	
12)	integral	
13)	credit	
14)	export	
15)	acquire	

2.3 **Explain the meaning of the following roots or affixes. Add at least five similar derivatives with their Chinese definitions. An example is given for you.**

No.	Roots/Affixes	Meaning	More derivatives with Chinese translation
e.g.	hydro-	water	hydro-bomb鱼雷；hydro-airplane水上飞机；hydro-electric水力发电的；hydro-lab水下实验室；hydro-pathic水疗法的
1)	sent/sens		
2)	it		
3)	cred		
4)	clud		
5)	sist		
6)	fact/fac		
7)	rupt		
8)	viv		

Unit 1 Globalization

3 Watch the Video

Difficult Words and Expressions

★ cutting-edge /ˌkʌtɪŋˈedʒ/ *adj.* 先进的，尖端的
★ simmering /ˈsɪmərɪŋ/ *adj.* 沸腾的；升温的
★ disproportionally /ˌdɪsprəˈpɔːʃənəli/ *adv.* 不均衡地；不成比例地
★ rhetoric /ˈretərɪk/ *n.* 辞令，言辞；修辞
★ per capita /pə ˈkæpətə/ *adj.* 人均的
★ dispersed /dɪˈspɜːst/ *adj.* 分散的
★ exacerbate /ɪɡˈzæsəbeɪt/ *v.* 使加剧；使恶化

3.1 Watch the first part of the video and answer the following questions.

1) What is the debate about?
2) What is the controversy around this topic based on?
3) How does the speaker describe the language used by both sides?
4) What do supporters think of globalization?
5) What do opponents think of globalization?

3.2 Watch the second part of the video and take notes according to the questions in the left column.

No.	Questions	Notes
1)	What was devised to measure the overall effect of interconnection?	
2)	What does the speaker think of the results of the study?	
3)	What did one point rise in the globalization index result in?	
4)	Which countries benefited much more than others?	
5)	What does the study mean?	

3.3 Watch the whole video again and write a short summary of it according to your answers and notes.

3.4 Work in groups and give a report to the class on "Globalization" according to the following clues in five minutes.

1) What views do supporters and opponents have on globalization?
2) What should be done to ensure a bright future for globalization?

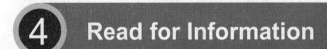

4 Read for Information

An Open and Shut Case[1]

*The **consensus** in favor of open economies is cracking, says John O'Sullivan. Is globalization no longer a good thing?*

❶ The Revolution Mill in Greensboro, North Carolina, was established in 1900. It was a **booming** time for local enterprise. America's cotton industry was moving south from New England to take advantage of lower wages. By 1938, the Revolution Mill was the world's largest factory **exclusively** making flannel. The mill **ceased** production in 1982, an early warning of another revolution on a global scale. The textile industry was starting a fresh **migration** in search 5 of cheaper labor, this time in Latin America and Asia. The Revolution Mill is a monument to an industry that lost out to globalization.

❷ North Carolina **exemplifies** both the promise and the **casualties** of today's open economy. Yet even thriving local businesses there grumble that America gets the raw end of trade deals, and that foreign rivals benefit from unfair **subsidies** and lax **regulation**. In places that have found it 10 harder to adapt to changing times, the **rumblings** tend to be louder.

❸ A **backlash** against freer trade is reshaping politics. Donald Trump has clinched an unlikely nomination as the Republican Party's candidate in November's presidential elections with the

---

1 Adapted from An open and shut case (2016, October 01). *The Economist* (Special Report): The world economy, 45–48.

Unit 1　Globalization

support of blue-collar men in America's South and its rustbelt. These are places that lost lots of manufacturing jobs in the decade after 2001, when America was hit by a surge of imports from China (which Mr. Trump says he will keep out with punitive tariffs). Free trade now causes so much **hostility** that Hillary Clinton, the Democratic Party's presidential candidate, was forced to disown the Trans-Pacific Partnership (TPP), a trade deal with Asia that she herself helped to negotiate. Talks on a new trade deal with the European Union, the Transatlantic Trade and Investment Partnership (TTIP), have stalled. Senior politicians in Germany and France have turned against it in response to popular opposition to the pact.

Keep-out signs

❹ The **commitment** to free movement of people within the EU has also come under strain. In June, Britain, one of Europe's stronger economies, voted in a **referendum** to leave the EU after 43 years as a member. Support for Brexit was strong in the north of England and Wales, where much of Britain's manufacturing used to be; but it was firmest in places that had seen big increases in migrant populations in recent years. Since Britain's vote to leave, anti-establishment parties in France, the Netherlands, Germany, Italy, and Austria have called for referendums on EU membership in their countries too. Such parties favor closed borders, caps on migration, and barriers to trade. Mr. Trump, for his part, has promised to build a wall along the border with Mexico to keep out immigrants.

❺ There is growing **disquiet**, too, about the **unfettered** movement of capital. More of the value created by companies is **intangible**, and businesses that rely on selling ideas find it easier to set up shop where taxes are low. America has clamped down on so-called tax **inversions**, in which a big company moves to a low-tax country after agreeing to be bought by a smaller firm based there. Europeans grumble that American firms engage in too many clever tricks to avoid tax.

❻ Free movement of debt capital has meant that trouble in one part of the world quickly spreads to other parts. The **fickleness** of capital flows is one reason why the EU's most ambitious cross-border initiative, the euro, which has joined 19 of its 28 members in a currency union, is in trouble. In the euro's early years, countries, such as Greece and Italy, enjoyed **ample** credit and low borrowing costs, thanks to floods of private short-term capital from other EU countries. When crisis struck, that credit dried up and had to be replaced with massive official loans. The conditions attached to such support have caused relations between creditor countries such as Germany and debtors such as Greece to sour.

❼ Some claim that the growing **discontent** in the rich world is not really about economics. After all, Britain and America, at least, have enjoyed reasonable GDP growth recently, and unemployment in both countries has dropped to around 5%. Instead, the argument goes, the **revolt** against economic openness reflects deeper anxieties about lost relative status. Some arise from the **emergence** of China as a global power; others are rooted within individual societies. For example, in parts of Europe, opposition to migrants is prompted by the Syrian refugee crisis. It stems less from worries about the effect of immigration on wages or jobs than from a **perceived** threat to social **cohesion**.

⑧ **Nevertheless**, there is a material basis for discontent because a **sluggish** economic recovery has bypassed large groups of people. In America, one in six working-age men without a college degree is not part of the workforce, according to an analysis by the Council of Economic Advisers, a White House think-tank. Most other rich countries are in the same boat. A report by the McKinsey Global Institute, a think-tank, found that the real incomes of two-thirds of households in 25 advanced economies were flat or fell between 2005 and 2014, compared with 2% rise in the previous decade. The few gains in a sluggish economy have gone to salaried gentry.

⑨ This has fed a widespread sense that an open economy is good for small **elite** but does nothing for the broad mass of people. Even academics and policymakers who used to welcome openness unreservedly are having second thoughts. They had always understood that free trade creates losers as well as winners, but thought that the disruption was **transitory** and the gains were big enough to compensate those who lost out. However, a body of new research suggests that China's **integration** into global trade has caused more lasting damage than expected to some rich-world workers.

⑩ It is not easy to establish a direct link between openness and wage inequality, but recent studies suggest that trade plays a bigger role than **previously** thought. Large-scale migration is increasingly understood to conflict with the welfare policy needed to shield workers from the disruptions of trade and technology.

⑪ The consensus in favor of unfettered capital mobility began to weaken after the East Asian crises of 1997–1998. As the scale of capital flows grew, the doubts increased. A recent article by economists at the IMF entitled "Neoliberalism: Oversold?" argued that in certain cases the costs to economies of opening up to capital flows **exceed** the benefits.

Multiple hits

⑫ How far is globalization, defined as the free flow of trade, people, and capital around the world, responsible for the world's economic ills and whether it is still, on balance, a good thing? A true **reckoning** is trickier than it might appear, and not just because the main elements of economic openness have different **repercussions**. Several other big **upheavals** have hit the world economy in recent decades, and the effects are hard to **disentangle**.

⑬ First, jobs and pay have been greatly affected by technological change. Much of the increase in wage inequality in rich countries stems from new technologies that make college-educated workers more valuable. At the same time companies' profitability has increasingly **diverged**. Online platforms, such as Amazon, Google, and Uber, that act as matchmakers between consumers and producers or advertisers rely on network effects: The more users they have, the

Unit 1 Globalization

more useful they become. The firms that come to **dominate** such markets make spectacular returns compared with the **also-rans**. That has sometimes produced **windfalls** at the very top of the income distribution. At the same time the rapid decline in the cost of automation has left the low- and mid-skilled at risk of losing their jobs. All these changes have been **amplified** by globalization, but would have been highly disruptive in any event.

❹ The second source of **turmoil** was the financial crisis and the long, slow recovery that typically follows banking blow-ups. The credit boom before the crisis had helped to mask the problem of income inequality by boosting the price of homes and increasing the spending power of the low-paid. The **subsequent** bust destroyed both jobs and wealth, but the college-educated bounced back more quickly than others. The free flow of debt capital played a role in the build-up to the crisis, but much of the blame for it lies with lax bank regulation. Banking busts happened long before globalization.

❺ Some of the concerns about economic openness are **valid**. The strains **inflicted** by a more integrated global economy were underestimated, and too little effort went into helping those who lost out. But much of the criticism of openness is misguided, underplaying its benefits and blaming it for problems that have other causes.

(1441 words)

Notes

North Carolina:（美国）北卡罗来纳州。It is a state in southeastern United States and one of the original 13 colonies.

Rustbelt: 铁锈地带（指从前工业繁盛今已衰落的发达国家一些地区）。Rustbelt, also known as the Rust Belt, is the informal description for a postindustrial region straddling the upper Northeastern, the Great Lakes, and the Midwest States, referring to economic decline, population loss, and urban decay due to the shrinking of its once powerful industrial sector.

Trans-Pacific Partnership (TPP): 跨太平洋伙伴关系。The Trans-Pacific Partnership is a trade agreement between Australia, Brunei, Canada, Chile, Japan, Malaysia, Mexico, New Zealand, Peru, Singapore, Vietnam, and the United States signed on February 4, 2016, which was not ratified as required and did not take effect. After the United States withdrew its signature, the agreement could not enter into force. The remaining nations negotiated a new trade agreement called Comprehensive and Progressive Agreement for Trans-Pacific Partnership, which incorporates most of the provisions of the TPP.

Transatlantic Trade and Investment Partnership (TTIP): 跨大西洋贸易与投资伙伴关系协定。The Transatlantic Trade and Investment Partnership is a proposed trade agreement between the European Union and the United States, with the aim of promoting trade and multilateral economic growth. TTIP is considered by the U.S. a companion agreement to the Trans-Pacific

Partnership (TPP). The negotiations were halted indefinitely following the 2016 United States presidential election, but by mid-2017, representatives of both the U.S. and the EU expressed willingness to resume the negotiations.

Brexit: 英国脱欧。Brexit is the prospective withdrawal of the United Kingdom (U.K.) from the European Union (EU). In a referendum on June, 23 2016, 51.9% of the participating U.K. electorate voted to leave the EU.

GDP: 国民生产总值。Gross Domestic Product means the total value of all goods and services produced in a country, in one year, except for income received from abroad.

the Syrian refugee crisis: 叙利亚难民危机。Syrians have poured across their borders since anti-government protests in 2011 spiraled into a full-blown war between rebels, government troops, and foreign backers. The Syrian refugee crisis remains one of the largest humanitarian crises since the end of World War II. The number of refugees who have fled the country now exceeds five million, including more than 2.4 million children, and millions more have been displaced internally, according to the United Nations.

credit boom: 信贷繁荣。Episodes in which credit to the private sector rises significantly above its long-run trend (i.e. "credit booms") are often associated with periods of economic turbulence.

4.1 Read Text A and answer the following questions.

1) Why does the author say North Carolina exemplifies both the promise and the casualties of today's open economy?
2) What attitude do Donald Trump and some senior politicians in Europe take to free trade?
3) What are the keep-out signs in global economy?
4) Why is there growing discontent in the rich world?
5) According to this passage, is globalization to blame for the world's economic problems?

4.2 Read Text A again and write a summary.

Summary (about 100 words): _____

_____

_____

_____

TEXT B

America Must Resist Protectionism Because Globalization Benefits Us All[1]

Alexis Crow

America's prosperity depends on turning outwards to the rest of the world.

① U.S. financial markets have staged a stunning rally since Donald Trump's surprise election victory. However, some observers remain **wary** of Trump's promised trade protectionism and its long-term impact. Many fear a return to the disastrous, protectionist, nationalist U.S. policies of the 1930s.

② As we **transition** into a digital age, the free flow of goods, services, technology, capital, education, and **innovation** remains vital to our **prosperity**. A quick look at the numbers **highlights** a powerful, **alternative** narrative to the emotional and popular anti-globalization messages currently being **proclaimed** in developed economies. These facts need to inform the next generation of financial, political, and business leaders on the world stage. Here are four major ways that global commerce benefits us all.

Way 1: There is a direct correlation between growth and trade.

③ GDP growth rises with the volume of global exports. The production and trading of physical **assets**, such as agriculture and **commodities**, combined with faster transaction times and processes **fueled** by globalization, resulted in extraordinary global economic **expansion** during the 1990s.

④ Even as that flow of physical assets has slowed, countries in Southeast Asia are still growing rapidly. Young populations in the region are benefiting from higher incomes due to exports. And those increased wages **boost** demand for goods from "new economy" sectors, such as health care, services, and technology, much of which originates in the U.S. and Europe. Chinese demand for American blockbuster movies is just one example of "old economy" jobs (such as in manufacturing) in developing economies fueling "new economy" jobs (such as in digital media) in advanced economies.

Way 2: Global commerce provides diverse sources of funding and enables international public-private partnerships.

⑤ Beyond the free flow of physical assets, a look at foreign direct investment and cross-border mergers and **acquisitions** reveals a very different storyline from the protectionist message. Last year, 1.89 million jobs were created globally by greenfield foreign direct investment (that is,

---

1 Adapted from Crow, A. (2017, December 01). *America must resist protectionism because globalization benefits us all*. Retrieved from https://www.huffingtonpost.com/entry/globalization-protectionism_us_587 54ff3e4b03c8a02d3b82b?section=us_world

investing in a foreign country in a project or operations from the ground up).

❻ In Arkansas, a Chinese manufacturer is creating jobs by building factories in the retail and consumer space. In Ohio, a Chinese billionaire is **reviving** a closed auto plant to create 3,000 jobs. In Egypt, the European Bank for Reconstruction and Development recently announced it will work with a local bank to fund small and medium enterprises to tackle energy efficiency. As these examples show, goods produced in one country meet the demand of workers in another, and capital to fund business growth often comes from diverse sources around the globe.

❼ These creative cross-border structures are essential to solve some of the world's complex problems. As Trump's advisors put forward their **infrastructure** plan, we should remember that no man and no infrastructure plan is an island in a globalized world. Successful large-scale projects often rely on **varied** funding sources and global **strategic** partnerships around the world. The Panama Canal, funded and created by the Panama Canal Authority and a **consortium** of international banks, is a case in point. Moreover, diversified capital sources can beneficially spread risk across investors.

Way 3: Nowhere are cross-border bridges more important than in education.

❽ In the U.S. and Great Britain, higher tuition fees paid by foreign students have helped **counterbalance** decreased public funding. And America has much to learn from other countries, including France, Germany, and Mexico, about vocational training. Perhaps knowledge from well-regarded foreign programs can be adapted and **piloted** in Pennsylvania, where old-economy steelworkers need to be transitioned into new-economy jobs, such as IT and data analysts. Looking farther ahead, the U.S. vocational **expertise** could then be exported to China, as the Chinese government seeks to upgrade its manufacturing **capacity** through digitization.

Way 4: Supporting innovation and incubating ideas across borders has a multiplier effect.

❾ As our economies shift from computers to digitization and the Internet of things and onward to whatever comes next, free exchange will be central to growth—globally, regionally, nationally, provincially, municipally, and at the community level. A Chinese company is currently making significant inroads in developing 5G mobile technology, and its advancements will **ultimately** benefit Western counterparts. This kind of cross-pollination benefits us all.

❿ The private sector has a role to play in solving global problems—whether it is in the form of a publicly owned corporation, a family office, an institutional investor or a start-up company with a **vision** and a purpose. These structures may take on the character of specific **advocacy**—such as for the environment. The deepening preference of millennials for social-impact investing and **sustainable** development goals is a case in point. But the private sector can't go it alone—governments and public-private partnerships form part of the mix. Mutual **collaboration** to solve common problems—**incentivized** by a rate of return—is not a bad thing.

Unit 1 Globalization

⓫ Global commerce does not have to mean **rampant** capitalism or unfettered financial markets. Instead, our debate should focus on the **singular** role that the private sector can play in advancing the needs of humanity within and across communities and in enabling individuals to directly contribute to **generating** income, value, and growth.

⓬ Because they are based in economic reality, the trade winds will continue to **prevail**—at least in the long term—against the current protectionist gasps of hot air. That protectionism **diminishes** the livelihood of the very people whom it is supposed to protect. The appeal of turning inwards during tough times is understandable. But our prosperity depends on our doing just the opposite: turning outwards to the rest of the world, with the trade winds in our sails.

(942 words)

Notes

new economy:（依赖计算机、现代科技和高素质员工的）新经济体系。New economy is an economic system that is based on computers and modern technology, and is therefore dependent on educated workers.

old economy:（以老式工业如钢铁、能源和机械制造为基础的）老式经济体系。Old economy is an economic system that is based on older types of industry, such as steel, energy, and machinery.

greenfield foreign direct investment: 对外直接投资建立新厂。It means the foreign direct investment in a structure in an area where no previous facilities exist.

millennials: 千禧一代。Millennials (also known as the Millennial Generation or Generation Y) are the demographic cohort following Generation X. There are no precise dates when the generation starts and ends. Researchers and commentators use birth years ranging from the early 1980s to the early 2000s.

4.3 Read Text B. Write a summary in the following form and take notes according to the table below.

Subject: _____
Key words: _____
Organization types: _____
Thesis statement (or main ideas): _____
_____
_____
Conclusion (or major findings): _____
_____
_____

No.	Paragraph(s)	Structure	Content
1)		Argument	
2)		Benefit 1	
3)		Benefit 2	
4)		Benefit 3	
5)		Benefit 4	
6)		Closing statement	

4.4 Read Text B again and answer the following questions.

1) How does Text B differ from Text A in its attitude towards globalization?
2) How does Text B differ from Text A in its description of the anti-globalization phenomenon?
3) How does Text B differ from Text A in its discussion of protectionism?
4) What aspect of globalization does Text A mention which Text B fails to take into account?
5) What's your view on globalization based on the comparison of the two texts?

UNIT PROJECT

Read Text B and Text A again, form two groups, and hold a debate on the topic "Globalization is no longer a good thing". Give evidence to support your arguments and refute your opponents'.

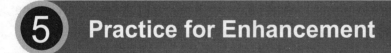

5 Practice for Enhancement

5.1 Read the four words in each group and cross the word which is not a synonym for the bold word. An example is given for you.

e.g. **reckoning**
   × majority   ☐ calculation   ☐ estimate   ☐ evaluation

1) **fickleness**
   ☐ rigidity   ☐ changeability   ☐ inconstancy   ☐ variability

Unit 1　Globalization

2) **ample**

☐ plenty　　☐ sufficient　　☐ efficient　　☐ abundant

3) **disquiet**

☐ concern　　☐ worry　　☐ anxiety　　☐ disbelief

4) **cohesion**

☐ cease　　☐ solidarity　　☐ unity　　☐ consistency

5) **proclaim**

☐ announce　　☐ declare　　☐ state　　☐ prosper

6) **boost**

☐ increase　　☐ improve　　☐ enhance　　☐ boom

7) **singular**

☐ remarkable　　☐ rampant　　☐ outstanding　　☐ extraordinary

8) **prevail**

☐ triumph　　☐ conquer　　☐ provide　　☐ succeed

9) **turmoil**

☐ chaos　　☐ disorder　　☐ confusion　　☐ hostility

5.2 Match the word in the box with the words in each column that regularly go together. An example is given for you.

balance, labor, stage, economy, correlation, assets, credit, status, tax, impact			
e.g. labor	1) _____	2) _____	3) _____
-shortage	high-	social-	get-
-saving	income-	diplomatic-	-boom
-market	-avoidance	enjoy a high-	-risk
unskilled-	impose-	-quo	give-
4) _____	5) _____	6) _____	7) _____
great-	on-	tangible-	negative-
full-	strike a-	gross-	direct-
have an-	a healthy-	invaluable-	-between
soften the-	a delicate-	net-	have-
8) _____	9) _____		
first-	booming-		
at a-	global-		
-a comeback	regulate-		
-a protest	boost-		

5.3 Paraphrase the following sentences. An example is given for you.

e.g. Because of the rapid evolution of technology, we are now able to trap the sun's rays into solar cells.
Our ability of trapping the sun's rays into solar cells is attributed to the rapid evolution of technology.

1) North Carolina exemplifies both the promise and the casualties of today's open economy.

2) Since Britain's vote to leave, anti-establishment parties in France, the Netherlands, Germany, Italy, and Austria have called for referendums on EU membership in their countries too.

3) Nevertheless, there is a material basis for discontent because a sluggish economic recovery has bypassed large groups of people.

4) This has fed a widespread sense that an open economy is good for small elite but does nothing for the broad mass of people.

5) A true reckoning is trickier than it might appear, and not just because the main elements of economic openness have different repercussions.

6) The strains inflicted by a more integrated global economy were underestimated, and too little effort went into helping those who lost out.

7) A quick look at the numbers highlights a powerful, alternative narrative to the emotional and popular anti-globalization messages currently being proclaimed in developed economies.

Unit 1　Globalization

8) The deepening preference of millennials for social-impact investing and sustainable development goals is a case in point.

_____

_____

5.4 Translate the following sentences into Chinese.

1) A backlash against freer trade is reshaping politics. Donald Trump has clinched an unlikely nomination as the Republican Party's candidate in November's presidential elections with the support of blue-collar men in America's South and its rustbelt.

_____

_____

2) Talks on a new trade deal with the European Union, the Transatlantic Trade and Investment Partnership (TTIP), have stalled. Senior politicians in Germany and France have turned against it in response to popular opposition to the pact.

_____

_____

3) Yet even thriving local businesses there grumble that America gets the raw end of trade deals, and that foreign rivals benefit from unfair subsidies and lax regulation.

_____

_____

4) How far is globalization, defined as the freer flow of trade, people, and capital around the world, responsible for the world's economic ills and whether it is still, on balance, a good thing?

_____

_____

5) The production and trading of physical assets, such as agriculture and commodities, combined with faster transaction times and processes fueled by globalization, resulted in extraordinary global economic expansion during the 1990s.

_____

_____

6) As our economies shift from computers to digitization and the Internet of things and onward to whatever comes next, free exchange will be central to growth—globally, regionally,

nationally, provincially, municipally, and at the community level.

6 Movie Exploration: *Wall Street* (1978)

Cast

Directed by: Oliver Stone
Starring: Michael Douglas as Gordon Gekko
                 Charlie Sheen as Bud Fox
                 Terence Stamp as Lawrence Wildman

Plot

- Bud Fox, a junior stockbroker in New York City at Jackson Steinem & Co., wants to work with his hero, Gordon Gekko, a legend in Wall Street. He calls Gekko's office 59 days in a row trying to land an appointment.
- Bud finally gets the opportunity to visit Gekko who is unimpressed by him until he offers secret information on Bluestar Airlines where his father works as the union leader.
- Gekko agrees to offer Bud a chance to work with him by asking Bud to spy on Lawrence Wildman, a British CEO.
- Through Bud's spying, Gekko makes big money and forces Wildman to buy his shares of a steel company.
- Bud continues to use his friends to maximize information and gets both himself and Gekko rich. And he is given a corner office at his stock company.
- Bud starts to break rules and pulls his father and Bluestar Airlines into a scheme.
- Bud finds out he is used by Gekko and decides to disrupt Gekko's plan to dissolve Bluestar Airlines.
- Bud is arrested for insider trading.
- Bud confronts Gekko in the park and gives the recordings of their conversation to the authorities as the evidence against Gekko. He goes to the Supreme Court with his parents.

Unit 1 Globalization

6.1 Search for the meanings of the following terms from the movie.

1) gold standard: _____
2) bull market: _____
3) bear market: _____
4) subordinated debt: _____
5) break-up value: _____
6) marketing strategy: _____
7) bear raid: _____
8) insider trading: _____

> **Web Resources**
>
> https://en.wikipedia.org/wiki/Gold_standard
> http://www.businessdictionary.com/definition/bull-market.html
> http://www.businessdictionary.com/definition/bear-market.html
> https://en.wikipedia.org/wiki/Subordinated_debt
> https://www.investopedia.com/terms/b/breakup-value.asp
> https://en.wikipedia.org/wiki/Marketing_strategy
> https://www.davemanuel.com/investor-dictionary/bear-raid/?from=singlemessage
> https://sevenpillarsinstitute.org/case-studies/insider-trading-what-would-rawls-do/

6.2 While watching, listen to the conversation between Bud and Gekko and complete it by filling in the blanks.

> In this conversation, Bud (B for Bud) confronts Gekko (G for Gekko), asking him why he has to dissolve Bluestar Airlines after he finds out he's used by Gekko.

B: Why do you need to wreck this company?

G: Because it's wreckable, all right? I took another look. I changed my mind.

B: If these people lose their jobs, they got nowhere to go! My father has worked there for 24 years! 1)_____!

G: It's all about bucks, kid. The rest is conversation. Buddy, you'll still be president, all right? When the time comes, you'll 2)_____ a rich man. With the money you'll make, your dad's never got to work another day in his life.

B: Tell me, Gordon, when does it all end, huh? How many yachts can you water-ski behind? How much is enough?

G: It's not a question of enough, pal. It's a 3)_____ game. Somebody wins; somebody loses. Money itself isn't lost or made. It's simply transferred from one perception to another, like magic. This painting here. I bought it ten years ago for $60,000. I could sell it today for six hundred. 4)_____. And the more real it becomes, the more desperate they want it. Capitalism 5)_____.

B: How much is enough?

G: The richest 1% of this country owns half our country's wealth, five trillion dollars. One third of that comes from hard work, two thirds comes from inheritance, interest on interest 6)_____ widows and idiot sons and what I do, stock and real estate speculation. It's bullshit. You got 90% of the American public out there with little or no 7)_____. I create nothing. I own. We make the rules, pal. The news, war, peace, famine, upheaval, the price of a paper clip. We 8)_____ while everybody wonders how the hell we did it. Now you're not naive enough to think we're living in a 9)_____, are you, buddy? It's the free market, and you're a part of it. You've got that killer instinct. 10)_____ pal, I've still got a lot to teach you.

6.3 After watching, cross the word or phrase that is closest in meaning to the bold one in each of the following sentences from the movie. An example is given for you.

e.g. We got all these new computers and young men that are **edging** me **out** here.
　　☐ complaining about　　✗ displacing　　☐ beating up

1) He lost all his equity when the firm went **belly-up**.
　　☐ flourished　　☐ isolated　　☐ bankrupt

2) I'm asking for a **modest** 20% across-the-board wage cut.
　　☐ significant　　☐ moderate　　☐ limited

3) If we're **in the black**, I'll return part of the givebacks.
　　☐ profitable　　☐ losing　　☐ challenged

4) We **initiate** an employee profit-sharing program with stock.
　　☐ suggest　　☐ contemplate　　☐ start

5) You will **get axed**. No two ways about it. You and the whole airline are going down the tubes.
　　☐ get caught　　☐ get fired　　☐ get replaced

6) Tell them I want **ziplock** mouths on the Bluestar deal.
　　☐ running　　☐ shut　　☐ secret

7) Don't **cross** Gordon. He will crush you.
　　☐ humor　　☐ force　　☐ irritate

Unit 1 Globalization

8) Buyers ran for cover and the stock **plummeted** to 16.5 before closing at 17.

☐ tumbled ☐ ascended ☐ complicated

9) If you make an enemy of Gordon Gekko, I can't be there to **stand by** you.

☐ represent ☐ support ☐ wait for

6.4 Work in groups and discuss the following questions.

1) To what extent do you agree with the saying that money talks?
2) What should be given priority, honesty or profits in the business world?

How to Guess Meaning from Context[1]

When we read, we often meet some new words, and we can guess and deduce the word meanings by means of the context clues or word formation with the exception of consulting a dictionary. Guessing meaning from context or word formation is a necessary skill that helps us read efficiently.

A context is a sentence or paragraph in which a word or phrase appears. The precise meaning of a word or a phrase always depends on the context in which it is used. We can make full use of context clues to extract the right meanings. Moreover, our knowledge of word formation could also help. Recognizing affixes (both prefixes and suffixes) and knowing their usual meanings can be valuable to infer the meanings of unfamiliar words. Many academic words built up from roots which are Greek or Latin in origin often provide clues to understand their meaning. Hence a better knowledge of common word roots and their meanings will help us figure out the meanings of unfamiliar academic words. The following are some useful techniques for guessing the meaning from context.

Technique 1: Use collocation knowledge, that is, guessing the word meaning from its neighboring words which occur regularly with it.

- Opponents **equate** execution and murder, believing that if two acts <u>have the same ending or result</u>, then those two acts are morally <u>equivalent</u>.
- A recent article in the *New York Times* described new computer software that in an instant sifts

---

[1] Adapted from Cai, Z. J. (2012). How to guess meaning from context. *21st Century EAP Series*. Shanghai: Fudan University Press.

through thousands of legal documents looking for a few **litigable** items, replacing hundreds of hours spent by lawyers reading the documents.
- A player can use threats and promises to alter other players' expectations of his future action, and thereby **induce** them to take action favorable to him or **deter** them from making moves that harm him.

Technique 2: Use restatement or synonym clues, such as "in other words", "that is", "also known as", "sometimes called as".
- The **incapacitation** effect saves lives—that is, by executing murderers, you prevent them from murdering again and do, thereby, save innocent life.
- Asteroids, also known as "minor planets", are numerous in the outer space.
- Now a new **paradigm**, or a new model, is created because companies have realized that employees don't do their best work without appropriate example to follow.

Technique 3: Use antonym or contrast clues, such as "but", "however", "unlike", "in contrast", "instead of", "while".
- Fire trucks occasionally kill innocent pedestrians while racing to fires, but we accept these losses as justified by the greater good of the activity of using fire trucks. We judge the use of automobiles to be acceptable even though such use causes an average of 50,000 traffic **fatalities** each year.
- For decades, ages before personal computers, learned observers wrote about how machines were going to replace humans—for better or for ill. But the mass job **shrinkage** that these observers all expected did not come.
- In contrast to the **linear** chain of reasoning for sequential games, a game with simultaneous moves involves a logical circle.

Technique 4: Use definition clues, such as "is defined as", or an appositive phrase.
- Are kidnapping and legal **incarceration** the same? Both involve imprisonment against one's will.
- Another way to make threats credible is to employ the adventuresome strategy of **brinkmanship**—deliberately creating a risk that if other players fail to act as one would like them to, the outcome will be bad for everyone.
- **Sedentary** individuals, people who are not very active, often have diminished health.

Technique 5: Use explanation clues, such as "because", "as a result", "consequently".
- Is there something about the defendant that diminishes moral responsibility or in some way **mitigates** against the imposition of death for the defendant in this case, which may lessen the probability of the jury imposing death?

- Others suggested introducing people to **uplifting** hobbies, <u>since we would have so much more leisure time on our hands</u>.
- The **immune** system is the system in our bodies that <u>fights diseases, and defends the body against things that may harm us</u>.

Technique 6: Use example or anecdote clues, such as, "for example", "such as", "like".

- An African American with an IQ indicating that he was **retarded**, <u>for example, he could not describe the victim or identify where or how he had killed her</u>, but had "quickly" confessed to the crime.
- <u>For example, Cortés burned his own ships upon his arrival in Mexico</u>. He purposefully eliminated **retreat** as an option.
- <u>Two players decide how to split a pie. Each wants a larger share, and both prefer to achieve an agreement sooner rather than later. When the two take turns making offers, the principle of looking ahead and reasoning back</u> determines the **equilibrium** shares.

Technique 7: Use word formation clues, such as the root or affix of a word.

- There were more traffic accidents in the past year because safety rules were <u>disregarded</u>.
- As there is no court in the U.S. with more authority than the U.S. Supreme Court, a Supreme Court ruling cannot be <u>overturned</u> by any other court.
- The risk of executing the innocent is not a <u>justification</u> for the abolition of death penalty.

ACADEMIC ENGLISH FOR BUSINESS

Unit 2
Workplace Automation

1 Search for Background Information

1.1 Search for the meanings of the following terms from texts or about the subject.

1) Alexa: _____
2) active management: _____
3) passive management: _____
4) capital allocation: _____
5) machine learning: _____
6) product line: _____
7) human capital: _____
8) mentorship: _____
9) cash cow: _____
10) Luddites: _____
11) fissured workplace: _____
12) independent contractor: _____
13) gig economy: _____
14) comparative advantage: _____
15) STEM worker: _____

Web Resources

https://developer.amazon.com/zh/alexa
https://www.investopedia.com/terms/a/activemanagement.asp
https://www.investopedia.com/terms/p/passivemanagement.asp
https://www.investopedia.com/terms/c/capital_allocation.asp
https://www.forbes.com/sites/bernardmarr/2016/09/30/what-are-the-top-10-use-cases-for-machine-learning-and-ai/#504fdece94c9
http://www.wisegeek.com/what-is-a-product-line.htm
http://www.businessdictionary.com/definition/human-capital.html
http://smallbusiness.chron.com/types-mentoring-programs-11597.html
https://www.investopedia.com/terms/c/cashcow.asp#ixzz5EPe7TccN
https://en.wikipedia.org/wiki/Luddite
http://www.astronsolutions.net/the-fissured-workplace-and-employee-misclassification/

Unit 2　Workplace Automation

https://www.investopedia.com/terms/i/independent-contractor.asp
https://whatis.techtarget.com/definition/gig-economy
https://encyclopedia.thefreedictionary.com/comparative+advantage
https://en.wikipedia.org/wiki/Science,_technology,_engineering,_and_mathematics

1.2 Present what you've found to the class orally with or without PowerPoint in three minutes.

2 Discuss the Words' Meaning

2.1 Define the following underlined words. An example is given for you.

e.g. Sometimes doctors have to base a diagnosis on intuition as much as on scientific tests.
   intuition: feelings you have that something is true even when you have no evidence or proof of it.

1) Please do not hesitate to contact me here via the e-mail above if you have any other queries or concerns.
   query: _____

2) Most market professionals agree that the new tax policy is a major force behind the exponential growth in stock prices.
   exponential: _____

3) It's clear that the company has a bias against women and minorities.
   bias: _____

4) They will be sent details of their share allocation and will receive a minimum of 550 shares each.
   allocation: _____

5) It is shown that the theoretical conclusions can be used to interpret and predict experiments.
   interpret: _____

6) I can perceive a connection between these apparently disparate topics.
   disparate: _____

7) To compensate for the fast-shrinking labor force, the country would need large numbers of immigrants from overseas.
   compensate: _____

8) John made it clear that he had no intention of withdrawing from the political arena.
   arena: _____
9) Traffic police intend to eliminate congestion caused by illegally parked vehicles.
   eliminate: _____
10) As some scholar said, issues on dormant partnership are obsolete, and even not worth a study.
    obsolete: _____
11) Many people had a feeling of inertia in a summer in the afternoon.
    inertia: _____
12) Government initiatives to help young people have been inadequate.
    initiative: _____
13) Many insurers tout the tax-free investment benefits of cash-value policies.
    tout: _____
14) There will be some disruption to traffic while the construction work is in progress.
    disruption: _____
15) The mother's behavior has a profound impact on the developing child.
    profound: _____
16) Substitutions of one gesture for the other often create not only humorous but also embarrassing moment.
    substitution: _____
17) This problem is outside the domain of medical sciences.
    domain: _____
18) One of the most pressing problems was a stagnant economy.
    stagnant: _____
19) The corporation that owns the spa is hoping to franchise this treatment nationally.
    franchise: _____
20) It was an article in the local newspaper which finally spurred him into action.
    spur: _____
21) She is clearly a dynamic young woman with big ambitions.
    dynamic: _____
22) Such items are obviously subject to wear and tear and require periodic replacement.
    periodic: _____
23) The full rate is the same for all clinical specialists and for general medical practitioners.
    practitioner: _____
24) The troops would not deploy without the consent of the General.
    deploy: _____
25) The government was determined to proceed with the election.
    proceed: _____

Unit 2 Workplace Automation

26) The computer and the human mind have different but <u>complementary</u> abilities.
complementary: _____
27) His landing was <u>cushioned</u> by the fresh snow that had fallen.
cushion: _____
28) The doctor will ask you about the <u>duration</u> and frequency of your headaches.
duration: _____
29) Students on a part-time course are not <u>eligible</u> for a loan.
eligible: _____
30) And at that level of implementation, the <u>aggregate</u> benefits to the enterprise start to become very apparent.
aggregate: _____

2.2 Fill in the following blanks with various forms of each word. An example is given for you.

No.	Base form	Variations in the word family
e.g.	interpret	interpreter, interpretation, interpretable, interpretably, interpretability
1)	automate	
2)	corporate	
3)	fraction	
4)	infer	
5)	profit	
6)	partial	
7)	manufacture	
8)	transit	
9)	code	
10)	project	
11)	extend	
12)	anticipate	
13)	suffice	
14)	produce	
15)	supplement	

2.3 Explain the meaning of the following roots or affixes. Add at least five similar derivatives with their Chinese definitions. An example is given for you.

No.	Roots/Affixes	Meaning	More derivatives with Chinese translation
e.g.	un-	not	unconscious无知觉的；unbiased无偏见的；unfair不公平的；unhappy不高兴的；unfortunately不幸地
1)	mini-		
2)	auto-		
3)	inter-		
4)	ced/cess		
5)	re-		
6)	con-/com-		
7)	ex		
8)	post-		

 Watch the Video

Difficult Words and Expressions

★ advent /'ædvent/ n. 到来；出现
★ churn /tʃɜːn/ v. 搅动
★ rebound effect 反跳作用
★ redeployment /ˌriːdɪ'plɔɪmənt/ n. 调换；重新部署
★ enhancement /ɪn'hɑːnsm(ə)nt/ n. 提高，促进
★ augment /ɔːg'ment/ v. 增加；增大
★ segregate /'segrɪgeɪt/ v. 隔离；分开
★ pharmaceutical /ˌfɑːmə'sjuːtɪkəl/ adj./n. 制药的 / 药物
★ TurboTax 特波税务软件
★ algorithm /'ælgərɪð(ə)m/ n. 算法

★ data-crunching 数据处理
★ molecule /'mɒlɪkjuːl/ n. 分子；微粒
★ biochemist /'baɪəʊ'kemɪst/ n. 生物化学家
★ viability /ˌvaɪə'bɪlətɪ/ n. 可行性
★ cue /kjuː/ n. 暗示；线索
★ adaptability /əˌdæptə'bɪlətɪ/ n. 适应性；可变性
★ nuance /'njuːɑːns/ n. 细微差别
★ complexity /kəm'pleksətɪ/ n. 复杂，复杂性
★ inadvertently /ˌɪnəd'vɜːtəntlɪ/ adv. 非故意地，无心地
★ niche /niːʃ/ adj./n. 针对特定客户群的 / 合适的职位；凹陷处

Unit 2 Workplace Automation

- ★ encyclopedic /enˌsaɪklə(ʊ)'piːdɪk; ɪn-/ adj. 渊博的；知识广博的
- ★ preservationist /prezə'veɪʃ(ə)nɪst/ n. 保护主义者
- ★ analyst /'æn(ə)lɪst/ n. 分析师
- ★ torrent /'tɒr(ə)nt/ n. 急流
- ★ entrepreneurship /ˌɒntrəprə'nɜːʃɪp/ n. 企业家精神
- ★ flourish /'flʌrɪʃ/ v. 繁荣；活跃

3.1 Watch the first part of the video and answer the following questions.

1) What is predicted to be the net number of jobs lost to AI from 2015 to 2020?
2) What kind of jobs will be affected most?
3) In which fields will jobs be added with the advent of AI?
4) What is AI able and unable to do in the field of medicine?
5) In what way can the programs such as TurboTax help users?

3.2 Watch the second part of the video and take notes according to the given information.

What can individuals do to stay in the AI era?	Examples given and (or) the reasons why these jobs cannot be replaced by AI
Increase educational level, by _____.	
Develop skills that _____.	
Learn to spot and correct _____.	
Develop extreme specialization in _____.	
Find a job in the data-related industry.	
What can the government do to ensure citizen employment?	
1)	
2)	

3.3 Watch the whole video again and write a short summary of it according to your answers and notes.

_____
_____
_____
_____

3.4 Share your summary with your partner and present it to the class.

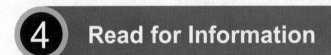

4　Read for Information

AI May Soon Replace Even the Most Elite Consultants[1]

Barry Libert and Megan Beck

❶ Amazon's Alexa just got a new job. In addition to her other 15,000 skills like playing music and telling knock-knock jokes, she can now also answer economic questions for **clients** of the Swiss global financial services company, UBS Group AG.

❷ According to *The Wall Street Journal (WSJ)*, a new partnership between UBS Wealth Management and Amazon allows some of UBS's European wealth-management clients to ask　5 Alexa certain financial and economic questions. Alexa will then answer their **queries** with the information provided by UBS's chief investment office without even having to pick up the phone or visit a website. And this is likely just Alexa's first step into offering business services. Soon she will probably be booking appointments, analyzing markets, maybe even buying and selling stocks. While the financial services industry has already begun the shift from active management　10 to passive management, artificial intelligence will move the market even further, to management by smart machines, as in the case of BlackRock, which is rolling computer-driven **algorithms** and

---

1　Adapted from Libert, B., & Beck, M. (2017, July 24). AI may soon replace even the most elite consultants. *Harvard Business Review*. Retrieved from https://hbr.org/2017/07/ai-may-soon-replace-even-the-most-elite-consultants

Unit 2   Workplace Automation

models into more traditional actively managed funds.

❸ But the financial services industry is just the beginning. Over the next few years, artificial intelligence may **exponentially** change the way we all gather information, make decisions, and connect with **stakeholders**. Hopefully this will be for the better and we will all benefit from timely, comprehensive, and **bias**-free insights (given research that human beings are prone to a variety of cognitive biases). It will be particularly interesting to see how artificial intelligence affects the decisions of corporate leaders—men and women who make the many decisions that affect our everyday lives as customers, employees, partners, and investors.

❹ Already, leaders are starting to use artificial intelligence to **automate mundane** tasks, such as **calendar** maintenance and making phone calls. But AI can also help support more complex decisions in key areas, such as human resources, budgeting, marketing, capital **allocation**, and even **corporate** strategy—long the **bastion** of **bespoke** consulting firms, such as McKinsey, Bain, and BCG, and the major marketing agencies.

❺ The shift to AI solutions will be a tough pill to swallow for the corporate consulting industry. According to recent research, the U.S. market for corporate advice alone is nearly $60 billion. Almost all that advice is high cost and human-based.

❻ One might argue that corporate clients prefer speaking to their strategy consultants to get high priced, custom-tailored advice that is based on small teams doing expensive and time-consuming work. And we agree that consultants provide **insightful** advice and guidance. However, a great deal of what is paid for with consulting services is data analysis and presentation. Consultants gather, clean, process, and **interpret** data from **disparate** parts of organizations. They are very good at this, but AI is even better. For example, the processing power of four smart consultants with Excel **spreadsheets** is **miniscule** in comparison to a single smart computer using AI running for an hour, based on continuous, non-stop machine learning.

❼ In today's big data world, AI and machine learning applications already analyze massive amounts of structured and unstructured data and produce insights in a **fraction** of the time and at a fraction of the cost of consultants in the financial markets. Moreover, machine learning algorithms are capable of building computer models that make sense of complex phenomena by detecting patterns and **inferring** rules from data—a process that is very difficult for even the largest and smartest consulting teams. Perhaps sooner than we think, CEOs could be asking, "Alexa, what is my product line **profitability**?" or "Which customers should I target, and how?" rather than calling on elite consultants.

❽ Another area in which leaders will soon be relying on AI is in managing their human capital. Despite the best efforts of many, mentorship, promotion, and compensation decisions are undeniably political. Study after study has shown that deep biases affect how groups like women and minorities are managed. For example, women in business are described in less positive terms than men and receive less helpful **feedback**. Minorities are less likely to be hired and are more likely to face bias from their managers. These inaccuracies and imbalances in the system only hurt organizations as leaders are less able to nurture the talent of their entire workforce and to appropriately recognize and reward performance. Artificial intelligence can help bring **impartiality** to these difficult decisions. For example, AI could determine if one group of employees is **assessed**, managed, or **compensated** differently. Just imagine: "Alexa, does my organization have a gender pay gap?" (Of course, AI can only be as unbiased as the data provided to the system.)

⑨ In addition, AI is already helping in the customer engagement and marketing **arena**. It's clear and well documented by the AI **patent** activities of the big five platforms—Apple, Alphabet, Amazon, Facebook, and Microsoft—that they are using it to market and sell goods and services to us. But they are not alone. Recently, HBR documented how Harley-Davidson was using AI to determine what was working and what wasn't working across various marketing channels. They used this new skill to make resource allocation decisions to different marketing choices, thereby "**eliminating** guesswork". It is only a matter of time until they and others ask, "Alexa, where should I spend my marketing budget?" to avoid the age-old **adage**, "I know that half my marketing **budget** is effective, my only question is—which half?"

⑩ AI can also bring value to the budgeting and yearly capital allocation process. Even though markets change dramatically every year, products become **obsolete** and technology advances, most businesses allocate their capital the same way year after year. Whether that's due to **inertia**, unconscious bias, or error, some business units rake in investments while others starve. Even when the management team has committed to a new digital **initiative**, it usually ends up with the scraps after the declining cash cows are "fed". Artificial intelligence can help break through this budgeting black hole by tracking the return on investments by business unit, or by measuring how much is allocated to growing **versus** declining product lines. Business leaders may soon be asking, "Alexa, what percentage of my budget is allocated differently from last year?" and more complex questions.

⑪ Although many strategic leaders **tout** their keen **intuition**, hard work, and years of industry experience, much of this intuition is simply a deeper understanding of data that was historically difficult to gather and expensive to process. Not any longer. Artificial intelligence is rapidly closing this gap, and will soon be able to help human beings push past our processing capabilities and biases. These developments will change many jobs, for example, those of consultants, lawyers, and accountants, whose roles will evolve from analysis to judgement. Arguably, tomorrow's elite consultants already sit on your wrist (Siri), on your kitchen counter (Alexa), or in your living room (Google Home).

⑫ The bottom line: Corporate leaders, knowingly or not, are on the cusp of a major **disruption** in their sources of advice and information. "Quant Consultants" and "Robo Advisers" will offer faster, better, and more **profound** insights at a fraction of the cost and the time of today's consulting firms and other specialized workers. It is likely only a matter of time until all leaders and

Unit 2 Workplace Automation

management teams can ask Alexa things like, "Who is the biggest risk to me in our key market?", "How should we allocate our capital to compete with Amazon?", or "How should I restructure my board?"

(1230 words)

Notes

UBS Group AG: 瑞银集团。UBS Group AG is a Swiss multinational investment bank and financial services company founded and headquartered in Switzerland. It is the largest Swiss banking institution in the world. Co-headquartered in Zürich and Basel, it maintains a presence in all major financial centers worldwide.

***The Wall Street Journal*:** 华尔街日报。*The Wall Street Journal* is a U.S. business-focused, English-language international daily newspaper based in New York City. The Journal, along with its Asian and European editions, is published six days a week by Dow Jones & Company, a division of News Corp. The newspaper is published in the broadsheet format and online.

BlackRock: 黑石集团（美国一家债券基金管理公司）。BlackRock, Inc. is an American global investment management corporation based in New York City. Founded in 1988, initially as a risk management and fixed income institutional asset manager, BlackRock is the world's largest asset manager with $5.98 trillion in assets under management as of December 2018.

McKinsey: 麦肯锡公司。McKinsey & Company is a worldwide management consulting firm. It conducts qualitative and quantitative analysis in order to evaluate management decisions across the public and private sectors.

Bain: 贝恩（公司名称）。Bain & Company is a global management consultancy headquartered in Boston, Massachusetts. It is one of the "Big Three" management consultancies. The firm provides advice to public, private, and non-profit organizations.

BCG: 波士顿咨询公司。The Boston Consulting Group, Inc. is an American worldwide management consulting firm with 90 offices in 50 countries. The firm advises clients in the private, public, and non-profit sectors around the world, including more than two-thirds of the Fortune 500, and is one of the "Big Three" strategy consulting firms. Considered one of the most prestigious management consulting firms in a branch-internal survey, BCG was ranked third in *Fortune*'s "100 Best Companies to Work for" in 2017.

Apple: 苹果公司。Apple Inc. is an American multinational technology company headquartered in Cupertino, California, that designs, develops, and sells consumer electronics, computer software, and online services.

Facebook: 脸书。Facebook is an American online social media and social networking service company based in Menlo Park, California. Its website was launched on February 4, 2004, by Mark Zuckerberg, along with his Harvard College students and roommates Eduardo Saverin, Andrew

McCollum, Dustin Moskovitz, and Chris Hughes.

HBR: 哈佛商业评论（期刊名）。*Harvard Business Review* is a general management magazine published by Harvard Business Publishing, a wholly owned subsidiary of Harvard University.

Harley-Davidson: 哈雷戴维森（品牌名）。Harley-Davidson, Inc., or Harley, is an American motorcycle manufacturer, founded in Milwaukee, Wisconsin in 1903. One of the two major American motorcycle manufacturers to survive the Great Depression, the company has survived numerous ownership arrangements, subsidiary arrangements, periods of poor economic health and product quality, as well as intense global competition, to become one of the world's largest motorcycle manufacturers and an iconic brand widely known for its loyal following.

Siri: 美国苹果公司开发的手机语音助手。Siri is an intelligent personal assistant, part of Apple Inc.'s iOS, watchOS, macOS, and tvOS operating systems. The assistant uses voice queries and a natural language user interface to attempt to answer questions, make recommendations, and perform actions by delegating requests to a set of Internet services.

Google Home: 谷歌家庭。Google Home is a Wi-Fi speaker that also works as a smarthome control centre and an assistant for the whole family. You can use it to play back entertainment throughout your entire home, effortlessly manage everyday tasks, and ask Google things you want to know.

4.1 Read Text A and answer the following questions.

1) What activities are expected to be changed by AI in the next few years?
2) What advantages does AI have in general in business consulting?
3) How can AI help in managing human capital?
4) Which companies are cited as using AI in marketing?
5) What are problems with capital allocation for most businesses according to the article?

4.2 Read Text A again and write a summary.

Summary(about 100 words): _____

_____

_____

_____

_____

Unit 2　Workplace Automation

TEXT B

The Question with AI Isn't Whether We'll Lose Our Jobs—It's How Much We'll Get Paid[1]

Lori G. Kletzer

❶ The fear that machines will replace human labor is a **durable** one in the public mind, from the time of the Luddites in the early 19th century. Yet most economists have viewed "the end of humans in jobs" as a groundless fear, **inconsistent** with the evidence. The standard view of technical change is that some jobs are displaced by the **substitution** of machines for labor, but that the fear of total displacement is misplaced because new jobs are created, largely due to the technology-fueled increase in productivity. Humans have always shifted away from work suitable for machines to other jobs. This was true in the 1930s, when the shift was away from agriculture, through the 1990s and early 2000s, when the shift was largely out of **manufacturing**.

❷ However, the expansion of what can be automated in recent years has raised the question: Is this time different?

❸ It doesn't have to be. Yes, there are reasons for concern, both technical and political. Machines are now able to take on less-routine tasks, and this transition is occurring during an era in which many workers are already struggling. Nonetheless, with the right policies we can get the best of both worlds: automation without rampant unemployment.

Is this time different?

❹ To date, automation has meant industrial robots and computer hardware and software designed to do predictable, routine, and **codifiable** tasks requiring physical strength and **exertion**, and the repetition of logical tasks, such as calculation. With robotics, artificial intelligence, and machine learning, what we call automation seems poised to take on a greater share of high-productivity jobs and a range of tasks that were previously the **domain** of humans. These are tasks requiring problem solving, decision making, and interaction within a less-than-fully-predictable environment. Automation of this sort includes self-driving cars and **diagnosing** disease.

❺ Automation anxiety is made more acute by a labor market that has tilted against workers over the last 30 years, with increasing income inequality and **stagnant** real wages. Wage growth has not kept up with productivity growth; labor's share of GDP has fallen and capital's share has risen. The social contract established after World War II, where hard work and loyalty to the firm were met with rising wages, benefits, skills training, and economic security from firms, no longer

---

1　Adapted from Kletzer, G. L. (2018, January 31). The question with AI isn't whether we'll lose our jobs—it's how much we'll get paid. *Harvard Business Review*. Retrieved from https://hbr.org/2018/01/the-question-with-ai-isnt-whether-well-lose-our-jobs-its-how-much-well-get-paid

characterizes much of the American workplace. The "**fissured** workplace"—where firms focus on their **core competencies** and contract out everything else—results in low pay, few benefits, and job insecurity for workers. The share of workers in alternative work arrangements, such as independent contractors, **franchisees**, and in the gig economy, is growing substantially, from 10.7% in 2005 to 15.8% in 2015. The old structures of the post-war labor market are not up to the task of the 21st-century wave of automation, particularly for the low- and middle-skill workers already disadvantaged by previous skill-biased technological change and globalization. While technology and globalization have **spurred** competition, efficiency, and **dynamism**, the gains have not been shared by all. The unequal distribution of the gains is not a technical destiny; it is the work of institutions, business, and governments.

Will robots take all the jobs?

❻ Currently, most automation involves routine, structured, predictable physical activities and the collection and the processing of data. Generally, these tasks form the basis of occupations in manufacturing, professional and business services, food service, and retail trade. Looking ahead, these tasks will continue to have the highest potential for advanced automation. Currently, less than 5% of occupations are entirely automated, and about 60% of occupations have at least 30% of tasks that can be automated. Based on these estimates, there is considerable potential for the spread of advanced automation. What is less knowable is how many new jobs will be created by automation-related productivity growth and how humans and machines will work together.

❼ It's likely that humans will continue to dominate machines in a variety of skills, including creativity, interpersonal relations, caring, emotional range and complexity, **dexterity**, mobility. Luckily, we know there will be ample opportunities in these jobs. The Bureau of Labor Statistics issues **periodic** occupational growth **projections**, and in its most recent report, for the time period 2016 to 2026, 11 of the top 25 fastest-growing occupations are health care-related, where human-dominant skills are essential. These occupations include home health aides, personal care aides, physician assistants, nurse **practitioners**, physical therapy assistants and aides. Some of these occupations require a four-year degree and post-**baccalaureate** training (nurse practitioners, physician assistants), but some require on-the-job training and certification with a high school diploma (home health aides, personal care aides, physical therapy aides).

❽ However, even though jobs where humans have absolute advantage may be narrowing, there is little reason to expect an end to human work. The reason stems from a classic idea in economics: comparative advantage.

❾ Even in a world where robots have absolute advantage in everything—meaning robots can do everything more efficiently than humans can—robots will be **deployed** where they have the greatest relative productivity advantage. Humans, meanwhile, will work where they have the smallest disadvantage. If robots can produce 10 times as many automobiles per day as a team of humans, but only twice as many houses, it makes sense to have the robots specialize and focus full-

time where they're relatively most efficient, in order to maximize **output**. Therefore, even though people are a bit worse than robots at building houses, that job still falls to humans.

⑩ That means that the relevant question is "Will the jobs where humans have comparative advantage pay well and have good working conditions?" As we know from displacement due to globalization and increasing international trade, there is nothing that guarantees that humans displaced from jobs will be reemployed in new jobs that pay as well as their old jobs, or even pay well enough to maintain middle-class status.

What we can do

⑪ Though there is still much we don't know about how this wave of automation will **proceed**, there are several areas of action we can identify now.

⑫ Education and training are at the top of the list. Human capital investment must be at the center of any strategy for producing skills that are **complementary** to technology. The current workforce—including the unemployed—needs opportunities for re-skilling and up-skilling, with businesses taking an active role both in determining the skills needed and in providing the skill training. Workers need opportunities for lifelong learning, and employers will be key. An **extensive** research literature documents the high returns to workers and firms from employer-based training. Workplace training helps bridge gaps between school learning and the application of these skills in the workplace and to specific occupations.

⑬ Schools will have to change too. Anticipating future skill needs and demands adds to the urgency of addressing the many challenges in K-12 and higher education, including achievement and opportunity gaps by race and socioeconomic status in K-12 schooling, and improving access, affordability, and success in post-secondary education. The education system must also do more to produce STEM workers and to ensure that workforce is diverse.

⑭ But education alone will not be **sufficient**. Policy makers should focus on **cushioning** the necessary transitions following job loss by strengthening the social safety net. In the U.S., this means strengthening unemployment insurance (ensuring benefit **adequacy**, including **durations** of **eligibility**), Medicaid, Supplemental Nutrition Assistance Program, and Transitional Assistance to Needy Families. A wage insurance program for all displaced workers will help encourage people to remain attached to the labor force.

⑮ In 1966, the final report of the National Commission on Technology, Automation, and Economic Progress stated, "Constant displacement is the price of a **dynamic** economy. History suggests that it is a price worth paying. But the accompanying burdens and benefits should be distributed fairly, and this has not always been the case." The Commission recommended responses that manage the overall health of the economy (managing and strengthening **aggregate** demand), promote educational opportunity, provide public employment, and secure transitional income maintenance. Fifty years later, these areas remain the basic road map for public policy response. The solutions, and any obstacles, are political, not economic or technical.

(1342 words)

Notes

K-12: 从幼儿园到 12 年级的儿童教育。The educational system called K-12 education refers to the combination of primary and secondary education that children receive from kindergarden until 12th grade, typically starting at ages 4–6 and continuing through ages 17–19. The K-12 educational system is used in the United States as well as several other countries in the world, including Canada, Australia, Turkey, and the Philippines. Although the K-12 curriculum varies among states and between nations, the concept of providing students with fundamental knowledge at no cost is universal.

Medicaid:（美国的）医疗补助计划。Medicaid in the United States is a joint federal and state program that helps with medical costs for some people with limited income and resources. Medicaid also offers benefits not normally covered by Medicare, like nursing home care and personal care services. The Health Insurance Association of America describes Medicaid as a "government insurance program for persons of all ages whose income and resources are insufficient to pay for health care". Medicaid is the largest source of funding for medical and health-related services for people with low income in the United States, providing free health insurance to 74 million low-income and disabled people.

4.3 Read Text B. Write a summary in the following form and take notes according to the table below.

Subject: _____
Key words: _____
Organization types: _____
Thesis statement (or main ideas): _____
_____
_____

Conclusion (or major findings): _____
_____
_____

Thesis Questions	Answers	Arguments and evidence
Is this time different?		
Will robots take all the jobs?		
Can we do something?		
Conclusion		

Unit 2   Workplace Automation

4.4 Read Text B again and answer the following questions.

1) What else is mentioned besides technological advancement that has contributed to the public anxiety over automation in Text B?
2) Where will humans continue to dominate machines according to Text B?
3) Does Text B also suggest as in Text A that AI will replace humans where AI has advantages over humans? What are the reasons given in Text B?
4) Do Text A and Text B discuss automation in the same industries?
5) Do Text A and Text B suggest solutions to deal with the threat of automation?

UNIT PROJECT

Read Text B and Text A again, form two groups, and hold a debate on the topic "Will machines replace human labor?". Give evidence to support your arguments and refute your opponents'.

5 Practice for Enhancement

5.1 Read the four words in each group and cross the word which is not a synonym for the bold word. An example is given for you.

e.g. **eligible**
　　☐ entitled　　☐ qualified　　✗ profitable　　☐ suited

1) **mundane**
　　☐ ordinary　　☐ obsolete　　☐ routine　　☐ commonplace

2) **disparate**
　　☐ distinguished　　☐ different　　☐ distinct　　☐ diverse

3) **substitute**
　　☐ replace　　☐ exchange　　☐ swap　　☐ complement

4) **domain**
　　☐ fraction　　☐ arena　　☐ field　　☐ territory

5) **spur**
　　☐ incite　　☐ drive　　☐ infer　　☐ prompt

6) **dynamic**
　　☐ energetic　　☐ spirited　　☐ vigorous　　☐ competent

7) **proceed**

☐ continue ☐ extend ☐ progress ☐ advance

8) **sufficient**

☐ ample ☐ enough ☐ profound ☐ adequate

9) **aggregate**

☐ collective ☐ exponential ☐ combined ☐ cumulative

5.2 Decide what words can go with the following verbs. An example is given for you.

e.g. allocate: resources, time, money, land, funds, etc.

1) interpret:
2) eliminate:
3) tout (for):
4) disrupt:
5) spur:
6) deploy:
7) anticipate:
8) cushion:
9) project:

5.3 Paraphrase the following sentences. An example is given for you.

e.g. The shift to AI solutions will be a tough pill to swallow for the corporate consulting industry. The transition to use AI will be difficult for the consulting industry to accept.

1) In today's big data world, AI and machine learning applications already analyze massive amounts of structured and unstructured data and produce insights in a fraction of the time and at a fraction of the cost of consultants in the financial markets.

2) These inaccuracies and imbalances in the system only hurt organizations as leaders are less able to nurture the talent of their entire workforce and to appropriately recognize and reward performance.

3) Even though markets change dramatically every year, products become obsolete and

technology advances, and most businesses allocate their capital the same way year after year.

4) Artificial intelligence is rapidly closing this gap, and will soon be able to help human beings push past our processing capabilities and biases.

5) Automation anxiety is made more acute by a labor market that has tilted against workers over the last 30 years, with increasing income inequality and stagnant real wages.

6) However, even though jobs where humans have absolute advantage may be narrowing, there is little reason to expect an end to human work.

7) Human capital investment must be at the center of any strategy for producing skills that are complementary to technology.

8) Policy makers should focus on cushioning the necessary transitions following job loss by strengthening the social safety net.

5.4 Translate the following sentences into Chinese.

1) But AI can also help support more complex decisions in key areas, such as human resources, budgeting, marketing, capital allocation, and even corporate strategy—long the bastion of bespoke consulting firms, such as McKinsey, Bain, and BCG, and the major marketing agencies.

2) Moreover, machine learning algorithms are capable of building computer models that make

sense of complex phenomena by detecting patterns and inferring rules from data—a process that is very difficult for even the largest and smartest consulting teams.

_____
_____

3) Although many strategic leaders tout their keen intuition, hard work, and years of industry experience, much of this intuition is simply a deeper understanding of data that was historically difficult to gather and expensive to process.

_____
_____

4) To date, automation has meant industrial robots and computer hardware and software designed to do predictable, routine, and codifiable tasks requiring physical strength and exertion, and the repetition of logical tasks, such as calculation.

_____
_____

5) The old structures of the post-war labor market are not up to the task of the 21st-century wave of automation, particularly for the low- and middle-skill workers already disadvantaged by previous skill-biased technological change and globalization.

_____
_____

6) Anticipating future skill needs and demands adds to the urgency of addressing the many challenges in K-12 and higher education, including achievement and opportunity gaps by race and socioeconomic status in K-12 schooling, and improving access, affordability, and success in post-secondary education.

_____
_____

6 Movie Exploration: *The Big Short* (2015)

Cast

Directed by: Adam McKay

Unit 2 Workplace Automation

Starring: Christian Bale as Michael Burry
Steve Carell as Mark Baum
Brad Pitt as Ben Rickert
Ryan Gosling as Jared Vennett
John Magaro as Charlie Geller
Finn Wittrock as Jamie Shipley
Tony Bentley as Bruce Miller

Plot

- Michael Burry, the eccentric manager of hedge fund, discovers that the United States housing market is extremely unstable, being based on high-risk subprime loans.
- Burry then proposes to create a credit default swap market for profit, but his clients and his employees choose not to believe him.
- Burry refuses major investment and commercial banks that require paying substantial monthly premiums.
- Jared Vennett, a salesman of Deutsche Bank, one of the first to understand Burry's analysis, decides to enter, earning a fee on selling the swaps to firms who will possibly profit.
- Vennett convinces Mark Baum, a hedge fund manager, who has an interest in his plan due to a misplaced phone call to buy swaps.
- Baum's staff investigates the market, discovering that a market bubble is being created.
- Baum realizes that the fraud will completely collapse the global economy after he has had a talk with a CDO manager.
- Two young investors Charlie Geller and Jamie Shipley ask the retired securities trader Ben Rickert to help them get ISDA after they accidentally discover a prospectus by Vennett.
- Ultimately, Geller and Shipley make a profit of $80 million with their faith in the broken system.
- Vennett makes $47 million by selling off the swaps. The value of Burry's fund increases by 489%. Baum's fund reaches $1 billion after he decides to sell his loans until the last minute.

6.1 Search for the meanings of the following terms from the movie.

1) **mortgage-backed securities:** _____
2) **credit rating:** _____
3) **CDO:** _____
4) **overdraft penalties:** _____
5) **ISDA:** _____

6) **subprime loans:** _____
7) **Allan Greenspan:** _____
8) **Morgan Stanley:** _____

> **Web Resources**
>
> https://en.wikipedia.org/wiki/Mortgage-backed_security
> https://en.wikipedia.org/wiki/Credit_rating
> https://en.wikipedia.org/wiki/Collateralized_debt_obligation
> https://en.wikipedia.org/wiki/Overdraft
> https://www.isda.org/
> https://www.investopedia.com/terms/s/subprimeloan.asp
> https://en.wikipedia.org/wiki/Alan_Greenspan
> https://en.wikipedia.org/wiki/Morgan_Stanley

6.2 While watching, listen to the debate between Mark Baum and Bruce Miller and complete it by filling in the blanks.

> In this debate, Mark Baum (B for Baum) and Bruce Miller (M for Miller) express their polarized opinions to the hostess (H for hostess) on the current situation of the market.

M: So as some of you may know, Bear Stearns has just received a loan from JP Morgan. Of course, we're gonna have to wait and see how the markets react. But that should 1)_____ rest any concerns about the bank's health.

H: Now I take it you have no plans to sell your $200 million in Bear stock?

M: No. As a matter of fact, when we're done here, I'll probably go out and buy some more.

H: For the opposing view, Mr. Baum?

B: I got to stand for this. Okay, hi. My firm's thesis is pretty simple. Wall Street took a good idea, Lewis Ranieri's mortgage bond, and turned it into an 2)_____ of 3)_____. That's on its way to 4)_____ the world economy.

M: How do you really feel?

B: I'm glad you still have 5)_____. I wouldn't if I were you. Now anyone who knows me knows that I have no problem telling someone they're wrong. (Bear Stearns is 6)_____ rumors of liquidity problems.)…We live in an era of fraud in America. Not just in banking, but in government, education, religion, food, even baseball. What bothers me isn't that fraud is not nice or fraud is mean. It's that for 15,000 years fraud and 7)_____ thinking had never, ever worked. Not once. Eventually, people got caught,

Unit 2 Workplace Automation

things 8)_____. When the hell did we forget all that? I thought we were better than this, I really did. And the fact that we're not doesn't make me feel all right or superior. It makes me feel…sad. And as fun as it is to watch pompous, dumb Wall Streeters be 9)_____. And you are wrong, sir. I just know at the end of the day, average people are going to be the ones that are gonna have to pay for all this. Because they always, always do. 10)_____. Thank you.

H: Does our bull have a response?

M: Only that in the entire history of Wall Street, no investment bank has ever failed unless caught in criminal activities. So, yes, I stand by my Bear Stearns optimism.

6.3 After watching, cross the word or phrase that is closest in meaning to the bold one in each of the following sentences from the movie. An example is given for you.

e.g. Pretty soon, stocks and savings were almost **inconsequential** when the market collapses.
   ✗ worthless   ☐ significant   ☐ profitable

1) I start **grilling** him about overdraft penalties.
   ☐ broiling   ☐ annoying   ☐ questioning

2) Lawrence, don't **patronize** me. Listen to what I say.
   ☐ interrupt   ☐ talk down to   ☐ laugh at

3) The housing market is **propped up** on these bad loans.
   ☐ flourished   ☐ shored up   ☐ devastated

4) We're doing $30 million right now, but we started four years ago with $110,000. So as you can see that's pretty **phenomenal** returns.
   ☐ huge   ☐ balanced   ☐ minimum

5) The bonuses of those loans **skyrocketed** a few years ago. I made a large fortune out of it.
   ☐ tumbled drastically   ☐ broke even   ☐ increased rapidly

6) The collapse of the **venerable** New York bank follows a tumultuous few months of market volatility.
   ☐ respectable   ☐ unscrupulous   ☐ incompetent

7) I've come to the **sullen** realization that I must close down the fund.
   ☐ sudden   ☐ vigorous   ☐ depressing

8) The housing bubble is on its way to **decimate** the world economy.
   ☐ boost   ☐ impede   ☐ destroy

9) One of the **hallmarks** of mania is the rapid rise in complexity and the rates of fraud.
   ☐ trademarks   ☐ characteristics   ☐ drawbacks

6.4 Work in groups and discuss the following questions.

1) Why does Mark Baum in a dilemma hesitate to sell his loans at the end of the movie?
2) Do you agree or disagree that the business world is a world of fraud?

7 Presentation Skills

How to Make an Oral Presentation[1]

Presenting information clearly and effectively is a key skill in getting your message across. Today, presentation skills are required in almost every field. There are occasions when you may be asked to speak in public or to a group of people. For example, presenting or making a speech at a conference or event, seeking investment or a loan to help you set up a new business, etc. This section is designed to improve your presentation skills if you find it challenging.

Structure of a presentation

1) Title slide

The first slide should have the title of the presentation and the full name(s) of the presenter or presenters if you are giving a team presentation. It will be displayed until the presentation starts and allows the audience to prepare themselves for your talk.

2) Introduction

The introduction is the most important part of your presentation as it sets the tone for the entire presentation. It should last about 10%–15% of the entire presentation time. In the beginning, the audience are busy preparing for your talk. The introduction allows them to listen with one ear and still get most of it. There are many ways you can use to get the audience's attention, for example, asking a question, sharing a fascinating fact or startling statistic, sharing a personal story, or stating a problem. The best introductions are those that are creative and original.

Furthermore, this part has one important function. It provides enough knowledge in a very compact way so the audience can follow the special parts of the talk. Usually, a table of content showing what your presentation will be about is presented before you go to the body.

3) The body

The body is where you explain your topic and where all your information is presented. It

---

1 Adapted from Untergasser, A. (unknown publication date). *How to make the perfect presentation—or at least avoid the biggest pitfalls!* Retrieved from http://www.untergasser.de/lab/howtos/presentation_v1_0.htm

Unit 2　Workplace Automation

should last 70%–80% of the entire presentation time. Illustrated talks or speeches are usually organized by arranging major points and discussing them. Your presentation should be informative but you should limit these major points to three to five. If you have more than five, the audience can get lost and confused. Arrange your points in a logical order and then give information to support each point. The logical order could be problem-effect-solution, or past-present-future, etc. If you present an experimental study, the order could be what-why-how-what, that is, the field of study, why it deserves study, how it's being done and what results or findings it had.

In the body, you can go deep in to details or talk about special cases. But it is important to get back the people you lost during these parts or who started day dreaming. Therefore, you should make a short pause after these special parts and use a change in your voice to signal the start of a new section which may be of interest for the entire audience.

4) Summary

The summary should last 10%–15% of the entire presentation time. Here the main points are mentioned again and presented as a "take-home-message". The speaker should mention again everything he wants the audience to remember forever. It's also the last time to win the audience for your view on the topic.

5) Last slide

On this slide, you should give your references or mention all persons involved in the work or the presentation and signal that you are going to end your presentation. Usually, a question-and-answer period follows.

Tools for presenting

Because very few speakers will be able to memorize an entire talk, we should have a look at invisible helpers.

1) Scripts

Most speakers do have a script which they place at a suitable location before the start of the talk. It is crucial that the script is written in a condensed form and has a reasonable font size, which could support you in case you lose track. But avoid reading the talk from a script.

2) Slides

Slides could be very useful in both reminding you of what you want to say and serving as a visual aid for your audience. It is very challenging to remember the entire talk. Well-structured contents listed in the slides could help you and your audience to follow the presentation smoothly. A good way to structure your content is to show one point a time. While you talk, the points appear on the slide one by one.

A consistent design with harmonious colors that are in contrast to the background should be a reasonable starting point. The background of your slides should be uniform to not distract the audience. It pays off to support your message with pictures.

But be careful: Every element in a presentation should have a function. Avoid unnecessary elements or effects like small cartoons that do not contribute to the message of your talk. Any text on the slides should be short. Text should not be formulated in complete sentences. Big tables or complicated graphics should be avoided in a presentation as the audience will take too much time to get oriented and have no clue of the focus.

Tips on speaking in front of the audience

1) Preparation

Before the presentation, you must make clear the three following things:

- Who are the audience? Are they from the same culture or different academic background? Think beforehand about how to involve your audience which could help you better understood and accepted.
- How much time are you given?
- Where does your presentation take place and what tools do you have? A place with or without a microphone, a computer, a projector, and even a blackboard will influence the way and style of your presentation.

Make a rehearsal before the real presentation. Ask a partner or friend to listen and time you.

2) Body language

You should stand up straight and look at the audience during 95% of your talk. Body language and accentuation should give the impression that you enjoy talking to them and you are happy to talk about this interesting topic. Only if you are enthusiastic, may you spark the fire in the audience. Therefore, you need eye contact with the audience. You should use your hands to support your spoken words and move a bit while presenting, but do not distract the audience.

3) Recapitulation

Repetitive sentences or information plays an important role in talks. It can be used to discriminate the more important information from the less important. Nevertheless, it makes sense to use a different phrasing so that people unable to understand your first attempt can get a second chance to get it right.

4) Articulation

Articulation may be the most important way to control the talk. You should not speak too fast so the audience can keep up and have enough time to think about what is said before the talk continues. The slower and the louder you speak, the more important the content is considered. You should help the audience to judge the importance of your words by the articulation you make.

5) Questions from the audience

The audience can be activated if you offer chances to answer their questions. One problem with all these questions is that the audience can rarely understand what question has been asked. So if there are no technical tools, the speaker should shortly repeat the question. Then the audience can listen clearly and the person asking the question can correct you in case he meant something else. Furthermore, people in the audience are usually not interested in other people's questions. Therefore, it is common to answer questions at the end of the talk. It is a good habit to also offer to ask questions privately after the talk. Then people also can ask their questions who do not feel comfortable speaking in front of everybody (sometimes these are really interesting questions).

ACADEMIC ENGLISH FOR BUSINESS

Unit 3
Crowdfunding

商务学科英语

1 Search for Background Information

1.1 Search for the meanings of the following terms from texts or about the subject.

1) **crowdfunding:** _____
2) **rewards-based crowdfunding:** _____
3) **equity crowdfunding:** _____
4) **debt-based crowdfunding:** _____
5) **donation-based crowdfunding:** _____
6) **pre-order:** _____
7) **profit sharing:** _____
8) **advance payment:** _____
9) **information asymmetry:** _____
10) **IPO:** _____
11) **P2P lending:** _____
12) **venture capital:** _____
13) **Kickstarter :** _____
14) **JOBS Act:** _____
15) **SEC:** _____

Web Resources

https://en.wikipedia.org/wiki/Crowdfunding
www.fundable.com/learn/resources/guides/crowdfunding-guide/rewards-based-crowdfunding
https://en.wikipedia.org/wiki/Equity_crowdfunding
https://www.investopedia.com/terms/d/donationbased-crowd-funding.asp
https://en.wikipedia.org/wiki/Pre-order
https://en.wikipedia.org/wiki/Profit_sharing
https://en.wikipedia.org/wiki/Advance_payment
https://www.investopedia.com/terms/a/asymmetricinformation.asp
https://en.wikipedia.org/wiki/Initial_public_offering
https://en.wikipedia.org/wiki/Peer-to-peer_lending
https://en.wikipedia.org/wiki/Venture_capital

Unit 3 Crowdfunding

https://www.kickstarter.com/
https://en.wikipedia.org/wiki/Jumpstart_Our_Business_Startups_Act
https://www.sec.gov/

1.2 Present what you've found to the class orally with or without PowerPoint in three minutes.

2 Discuss the Words' Meaning

2.1 Define the following underlined words. An example is given for you.

e.g. Normally, the owners of a healthy company may accept the expense of issuing <u>equity</u> rather than debt.
   equity: shares in a company from which the owner of the shares receives some of the company's profits rather than a fixed regular payment.

1) A supportive house for eight to ten older people, each with his or her own room, provides privacy and a sense of <u>community</u>.
   community: _____

2) These students from Loyola University in Chicago are demonstrating how to <u>transform</u> ordinary cooking oil into fuel for cars.
   transform: _____

3) The government's <u>opaque</u> accounting makes it impossible to know how it has used the money.
   opaque: _____

4) For one party, the Indian economy's amazing growth rates indicate that the country is a <u>nascent</u> superpower—an "American" in the making.
   nascent: _____

5) We revise it, improve it, and <u>refine</u> related plans almost every day.
   refine: _____

6) The thermostat will <u>gauge</u> the temperature and control the heat.
   gauge: _____

7) Note that Voice Chat requires a stereo <u>headset</u> with a microphone; click the Help button for more information.
   headset: _____

8) There was a complimentary bottle of champagne in the hotel room.
   complimentary: _____
9) My kids are six and eight, and I often feel that now is the time to instill my values in them, before they are teens (or preteens) and peer pressure takes over.
   instill: _____
10) The book analyzes the social and political ramifications of AIDS for the gay community.
    ramification: _____
11) The tragedy could have been averted if the crew had followed safety procedures.
    avert: _____
12) The space program has been eclipsed by other pressing needs.
    eclipse: _____
13) Innovators are individuals with the strength of character to bring their dreams to fruition.
    fruition: _____
14) To bolster its overall competitiveness, Nokia has been focused on improving its smartphone offerings.
    bolster: _____
15) New transport links are being built to expand China's burgeoning trade with its ASEAN neighbors.
    burgeoning: _____
16) Because of this legal provision, very often employers think that they must hire men first, and then if anything is left, to hire a woman.
    provision: _____
17) But for most companies, setting up the engineering infrastructure is a huge step full of peril.
    peril: _____
18) A common pitfall that self-organizing teams face is the perception that they do not need any management.
    pitfall: _____
19) Imagine that we have been appointed Guardian of the Gate, and our job is to keep vigilant and watch over who passes through.
    vigilant: _____
20) The income tax is to be reimposed next year after ten years' exemption.
    exemption: _____
21) If you are a savvy shopper, and know pretty well how much what will sell and how much it will sell for, you can do well in the consignment business.
    savvy: _____

22) We recognize them as the <u>legitimate</u> government of Libya.
    legitimate: _____
23) It became easy to <u>dupe</u> him with a fake gold ring or an ivory statuette of a bare-breasted Minoan goddess.
    dupe: _____
24) If you say that something is <u>disconcerting</u>, you mean that it makes you feel anxious, confused, or embarrassed.
    disconcerting: _____
25) People who marry into the royal family will have to be <u>vetted</u> much more carefully in future.
    vet: _____
26) President Lee Myung-bak sacked three of his ministers in an attempt to <u>recoup</u> his lost popularity.
    recoup: _____
27) Shareholders rarely reject company <u>remuneration</u> reports but anger has mounted as share prices have tumbled.
    remuneration: _____
28) Both of the wrestlers tried to tumble the <u>adversary</u> with all their strength.
    adversary: _____
29) Sixteen years ago, Quebec <u>mandated</u> that all immigrants send their children to French schools.
    mandate: _____
30) Commercial property is very sensitive to economic conditions and would suffer if this <u>scenario</u> took place.
    scenario: _____

2.2 Fill in the following blanks with various forms of each word. An example is given for you.

No.	Base form	Variations in the word family
e.g.	entrepreneur	entrepreneurship, entrepreneurial, entrepreneurialism
1)	create	
2)	innovate	
3)	execute	
4)	valid	
5)	diverse	

(Continued)

No.	Base form	Variations in the word family
6)	allocate	
7)	regulate	
8)	participate	
9)	fraud	
10)	enthusiast	
11)	orient	
12)	favor	
13)	consider	
14)	litigate	
15)	decide	

2.3 Explain the meaning of the following roots or affixes. Add at least five similar derivatives with their Chinese definitions. An example is given for you.

No.	Roots/Affixes	Meaning	More derivatives with Chinese translation
e.g.	audi	hear	audience 听众；audient 倾听的，倾听者；auditorium 礼堂；audition 听力；auditory 听觉的
1)	cept		
2)	circ		
3)	dis-		
4)	mis-		
5)	ject		
6)	contra-		
7)	de-		
8)	-ship		

Unit 3 Crowdfunding

3 Watch the Video

Difficult Words and Expressions

★ centralize /'sentrəlaɪz/ v. 使集中；使集权
★ decentralize /ˌdiː'sentrəlaɪz/ v. 使分散；使分权
★ congregate /'kɑːŋɡrɪɡeɪt/ v. 聚集
★ transaction /træn'zækʃən/ n. 交易
★ facilitate /fə'sɪlɪteɪt/ v. 使……容易
★ intersection /ˌɪntə'sekʃən/ n. 交叉点；十字路口

3.1 Watch the first part of the video and answer the following questions.

1) What are the trends in crowdfunding in the past 10 years?
2) Thousands of years ago, who were the only ones to do a major project?
3) What are the reasons for them to do a major project?
4) A hundred years ago, who had the power to do a major project in America and Europe?
5) In the face of change, what we should do according to the speaker?

3.2 Watch the second part of the video and take notes according to the questions in the left column.

No.	Questions	Notes
1)	How many stock exchanges do Australia and England have respectively?	
2)	What are the two trends to make crowdfunding possible?	
3)	Why has crowdfunding risen according to the speaker?	
4)	What are the four common ways to do crowdfunding?	
5)	What are the three circles in the speaker's mind?	

3.3 Watch the whole video again and write a short summary of it according to your answers and notes.

_____

_____

3.4 Share your summary with your partner and present it to the class.

4 Read for Information

TEXT A

The Unique Value of Crowdfunding Is Not Money—It's Community[1]

Ethan Mollick

❶ Crowdfunding has been growing explosively, with over $2 billion raised via **equity** and reward crowdfunding in the United States in 2015 alone. However, crowdfunding is more than another way of raising funds. In connecting **creators** and **entrepreneurs** directly with customers and funders, it **transforms** the **opaque** and **oligarchical** market for early-stage fundraising into a more democratic, open one. Rather than relying on venture capitalists and marketers to try to project **nascent** demand for new innovations, creators can directly reach out to customers and communities to **refine** ideas and **gauge** interest. Crowdfunding acts as a platform, matching innovators with those who need innovation, and thus is reshaping which ideas come to market.

❷ For example, the hot technology of the moment, virtual reality (VR), was largely ignored by traditional funders after the disappointment of VR technology in the 1990s. In 2012, Palmer Luckey, a member of a VR community message board, mentioned that he wanted to launch a Kickstarter project to raise crowdfunding for a new virtual reality **headset** he had been **tinkering with**, the Oculus Rift. He asked for help from his community members to support the campaign, but also to assist in developing logos, creating sales pitches, and refining technology. Based on this **groundwork**, the Kickstarter campaign, launched a couple of months later, was a huge success, raising millions. Suddenly, virtual reality was no longer a forgotten '90s trend but had become a hot area of technology. Not only was Oculus soon bought by Facebook for $2 billion, but the field

---

1　Adapted from Mollick, E. (2016, April 21). *The unique value of crowdfunding is not money—it's community*. Retrieved from http://hbr.org/2016/04/the-unique-value-of-crowdfunding-is-not-money-its-community

of virtual reality has experienced explosive growth, with Microsoft, Sony, Samsung, and others announcing major products.

❸ This would not have happened without crowdfunding.

❹ My surveys of successful crowdfunders show that crowdfunding serves to **validate** demand and build communities of support. In the case of Oculus, crowdfunding acted as a platform that allowed Luckey's enthusiastic community of VR **hobbyists** to directly support one of their own, making Oculus a reality without needing to go through traditional gatekeepers. In a variety of research projects, I and my co-authors have tried to understand what this more democratic world of fundraising looks like, and what it means to use the power of platforms to transform the early-stage funding of ideas.

❺ One result of raising money over a platform is that it establishes a direct connection between the project creator and the funder. The community owning the project often comes to feel a sense of ownership for the projects that they support. This ownership is often quite positive, as it can lead to communities creating **complimentary** products (such as apps that use a new crowdfunded technology) and promotional support.

❻ The pressure of community support also **instills** a sense of obligation in project creators as well. As a result, despite there being limited **ramifications** from project creators failing to deliver on their goals, failure is remarkably rare in crowdfunding. Only around 9% of projects fail to deliver, and creators can go through extraordinary efforts, such as spending their own money, to fulfill promises to backers. In a setting where money is given as an impersonal investment, there is still a substantial cost of failure, but it is much less personal. A founder whose first start-up fails due to factors outside their control may still receive VC funding in the future, but a project creator who does not deliver to their backers is likely to find a less forgiving audience.

❼ The dynamics between project creators and backers go beyond just obligation, however. The fact that there are so many backers (over 9 million on Kickstarter alone), means that crowdfunding platforms can create many more kinds of matches between project creators and backers, increasing the **diversity** of ideas that get funded. Most forms of traditional fundraising rely on personal networks and rules-of-thumb to assess the quality of a founder. Due to (often unconscious) biases in these approaches, fundraising tends to favor certain individuals, such as white males from a few top universities. Women, for example, are much less likely to be funded than men; so much so that less than 8% of all VC backed companies have female cofounders.

❽ In crowdfunding, however, women **outperform** men. My research with Jason Greenberg of NYU shows that, all else being equal, women are 13% more likely to succeed in raising money on Kickstarter than men. Further, we find that this success comes from the support of other women, and especially when the female project creators are operating in a male-dominated space, such as technology or video games. Since crowdfunding operates like a platform, backers can have all sorts of reasons for supporting projects, including the desire to help a community or advance a cause.

⑨ Despite the diversity of backers, the research I have conducted with Ramana Nanda of HBS shows that they are often at least as good at making decisions as experts. Crowdfunding has **eclipsed** the National Endowment of the Arts as a source of funding for the arts, a subject of considerable concern to critics who worried that crowds would favor low culture crowd pleasers over serious theater (more musicals about dancing cats, less experimental work). Together, Ramana and I examined whether the crowd and experts agreed or disagreed on what to fund by asking professional critics to evaluate projects on Kickstarter. We found that the crowd and experts largely agreed, and, when they did not, the crowd was more likely to **take a chance** on projects than experts. Further, the projects the crowd (but not the experts) supported ultimately produced a higher number of critical and commercial hits than the projects that the experts approved of. This suggests that platform-based allocation of resources can **supplement** more traditional expert-based decision making.

⑩ Consumer-oriented platforms are often **associated with** the "gig" economy—connecting customers to suppliers for short-term contracts. Crowdfunding, however, shows that platforms can also serve as the basis for lasting businesses and important innovations. Moving from an expert-centered process to a platform approach increases diversity, leads to high quality results, and generally results in successful outcomes.

(1009 words)

Notes

virtual reality: 虚拟现实。VR is a computer-generated scenario that simulates experience through senses and perception. The immersive environment can be similar to the real world or it can be fantastical, creating an experience not possible in our physical reality. Current VR technology most commonly uses virtual reality headsets or multi-projected environments, sometimes in combination with physical environments or props, to generate realistic images, sounds, and other sensations that simulate a user's physical presence in a virtual or imaginary environment. A person using virtual reality equipment is able to "look around" the artificial world, move around in it, and interact with virtual features or items. The effect is commonly created by VR headsets consisting of a head-mounted display with a small screen in front of the eyes, but can also be created through specially designed rooms with multiple large screens.

sales pitch: 推销商品的言辞。Sales pitch means a planned presentation of a product or service designed to initiate and close a sale of the same product or service. It is essentially designed to be either an introduction of a product or service to an audience who knows nothing about it, or a descriptive expansion of a product or service that an audience has already expressed interest in. Sales professionals prepare and give a sales pitch, which can be either formal or informal, and

Unit 3 Crowdfunding

might be delivered in many number of ways. For a sales pitch to be effective, the presenter must know their product well. Though a good one will leave few questions unanswered, the presenter must be able to answer any questions that arise as a result of piqued interest. Even if the pitch is delivered effectively, the presenter must be prepared to overcome any obstacles that might prevent the close of the sale.

rules of thumb: 经验法则。Rules of thumb refer to a principle with broad application that is not intended to be strictly accurate or reliable for every situation. It refers to an easily learned and easily applied procedure or standard, based on practical experience rather than theory. The origin of the phrase can be traced back to the seventeenth century when under English law, a man may beat his wife with a stick no wider than his thumb. And then in the 1970s, this phrase first became associated with domestic abuse.

HBS: 哈佛商学院。Harvard Business Schools is the graduate business school of Harvard University in Boston, Massachusetts, the United States. The school offers a large full-time MBA program, doctoral programs, HBS, Online and many executive education programs. It owns Harvard Business School Publishing, which publishes business books, leadership articles, online management tools for corporate learning, case studies, and the monthly *Harvard Business Review*.

National Endowment of the Arts: 国家艺术基金会。It is an independent federal agency that funds, promotes, and strengthens the creative capacity of all communities by providing all Americans with diverse opportunities for arts participation. Established by the Congress in 1965, the NEA's funding and support gives Americans the opportunity to participate in the arts, exercise their imaginations, and develop their creative capacities. Through partnerships with state arts agencies, local leaders, other federal agencies, and the philanthropic sector, the NEA supports arts learning, affirms and celebrates America's rich and diverse cultural heritage, and extends its work to promote equal access to the arts in every community across America.

gig economy: 零工经济，临时工经济。It is a labor market characterized by the prevalence of short-term contracts or freelance work, as opposed to permanent jobs. In the gig economy, instead of a regular wage, workers get paid for the "gigs" they do, such as a food delivery or a car journey. Proponents of the gig economy claim that people can benefit from flexible hours, with control over how much time they can work as they juggle other priorities in their lives. In addition, the flexible nature often offers benefits to employers, as they only pay when the work is available, and do not incur staff costs when the demand is not there. Meanwhile, workers in the gig economy are classed as independent contractors. That means they have no protection against unfair dismissal, no right to redundancy payments, and no right to receive the national minimum wage, paid holiday, or sickness pay.

4.1 Read Text A and answer the following questions.

1) What is the most significant function of crowdfunding?
2) What is the purpose for the author to cite Oculus example?
3) What is the relationship between the project creator and the funder in crowdfunding?
4) Why crowdfunding is more likely to succeed compared with other traditional fundraising?
5) Compared with an expert-centered process, what are the advantages of the platform-based crowdfunding?

4.2 Read Text A again and write a summary.

Summary (about 100 words): _____

_____

_____

_____

Crowdfunding: Potential Legal Disaster Waiting to Happen[1]

Bryan Sullivan and Stephen Ma

❶ In theory, **crowdfunding** appears to be a great way for people with good ideas to take advantage of the Internet. Throw your idea online and a slew of like-minded investors will give you money to bring your idea to **fruition**. Artists have been doing it successfully for a few years on Kickstarter to fund creative projects, and teachers on Funding4Learning to fund education projects. To **bolster** this **burgeoning** concept, in April 2012, the United States government passed the Jumpstart Our Business Start-ups (JOBS) Act, which contains crowdfunding **provisions** to help these entrepreneurs raise funds. Taking a closer look at crowdfunding reveals a system **fraught with peril** that will likely lead to an increase in **litigation**.

❷ The JOBS Act allows any Zuckerberg **wannabe** with an idea to **skirt** securities laws to attract equity investors. Anyone, be it an entrepreneur or corporate entity, can raise up to $1

---

1 Adapted from Sullivan, B., & Ma, S. (2012, October 22). *Crowdfunding: Potential legal disaster waiting to happen*. Retrieved from https://www.forbes.com/sites/ericsavitz/2012/10/22/crowdfunding-potential-legal-disaster-waiting-to-happen/#23fe3aa7576c

Unit 3 Crowdfunding

million from investors putting in no more than $10,000 each, or no more than 10% of their income, whichever is less. That amount increases to $2 million if the crowdfunding entity supplies the "crowd" investors with audited financial statements. Under this system, a crowdfunder will not have to **disclose** financial statements until it has more than 1,000 shareholders; traditional, full regulatory SEC disclosure rules kick in at 500 shareholders. Essentially, it allows start-ups to raise up to $50 million in an IPO without having to **comply with** the SEC's full regulatory structure and related fees. Yes, you read that correctly—and we can only guess the disasters and class actions resulting from the future of crowdfunding.

❸ William Galvin, Secretary of the Commonwealth for Massachusetts, was so concerned about crowdfunding risks that in August he sent a letter to the SEC identifying crowdfunding's many **pitfalls**. The letter is **spot on**. Mr. Galvin writes:

"While this picture of the potential benefits of crowdfunding is undeniably attractive, as regulators we must be **vigilant** that the **exemption** will not become a tool for financial **fraud** and abuse...**Unscrupulous** penny stock promoters have used **misrepresentations** to market obscure and low-value stocks to individuals, often through pump and dump schemes. These kinds of fraud operators have not gone away."

❹ The risk for fraud is far more real than crowdfunding participants or the SEC want to admit. By its nature, crowdfunding appeals to less sophisticated investors who will invest in any project they think will be the next Facebook. Typical crowdfunding investors, even with basic disclosure requirements for participation, won't have the investment **savvy** to determine whether an investment is real or a fraud. After all, many fraudsters and scam artists are brilliant at presenting their investments on paper to meet the very basic disclosures of crowdfunding. Just look to Charles Ponzi and Bernie Madoff, both appearing as entirely **legitimate** businessmen, who were able to **dupe** sophisticated investors and, in Madoff's case, the SEC itself. The bottom line is that, while unintentional, crowdfunding is tailor made to assist fraudsters in duping unsophisticated "investors". Indeed, even if the SEC, in an attempt to **avert** fraud, increases the amount of disclosures, the individual investment contributions will still be too small for law enforcement authorities to expend resources to investigate or for attorneys to take on a fraud lawsuit, unless of course a **contingency** business litigator can bring a class action. Galvin would likely agree with this concern since he specifically notes: "The typical crowdfunding offering will be small (many may be far below $1 million), so there is the great risk that these offerings will fly under the radars of many regulators."

❺ Even more **disconcerting** is the impact of social networking and potential fraudulent schemes through crowdfunding. On this issue, Galvin writes:

"We expect that various kinds of social media will be used **in tandem** with crowdfunding. This may involve forums or message sharing through a portal's website; it may involve current social media channels (especially Twitter and Facebook); and it is likely to involve new channels and technologies. There is the great risk that pump and dump operators will use social media to improperly promote these offerings."

❻ Even if the particular crowdfunding investment is legitimate, the entire process will still be fraught with risk since unsophisticated business people will likely use crowdfunding to raise money for their new enterprises. After all, if they were sophisticated, they would probably pursue traditional routes to raise money, such as preparing an **airtight** business plan for the full execution of their ideas displayed in a "deck" for potential investors who **vet** the likelihood of the venture's and its participants' success. Many crowdfunding investors will not be able to provide useful feedback since many of them will be seeking a "get rich quick" scheme; and they will be sadly disappointed when the business they invest in fails since many do within the first five years. For every Facebook, there are ten Friendsters.

❼ Such business failures will inevitably result in litigation as people attempt to **recoup** whatever money they can from a failing crowdfunding entity. When they accept the inability to recover from the judgment-proof (due to a lack of personal funds) individuals behind the crowdfunding entity, crowdfunding losers may target the U.S. government and the JOBS Act for **remuneration** just as some did **in the wake of** the Madoff scandal when, among others, the Litwin Foundation, a charitable foundation, sued the SEC for blowing "countless opportunities" to stop Madoff.

❽ While crowdfunding requires certain minimum disclosures, people seeking funds via crowdfunding portals will not have to **adhere to** the same level of disclosure as normal businesses with a prospectus. Many lawsuits against crowdfunding entities may likely have **merit** since these entities won't have the business experience or savvy to make even the minimum appropriate disclosures or hire an attorney to guide them through disclosure drafting and execution. This concern is raised by Galvin as well: "In this segment of the market, company information may be limited or simply false, and investors typically lack investment sophistication and are often insufficiently cautious."

❾ Entrepreneurs who use crowdfunding are also at risk. Crowdfunding puts the ideas of many early stage entrepreneurs at risk of being stolen by better-funded investors or large corporations. In the traditional investment model, entrepreneurs can use non-disclosure and non-circumvention agreements to protect their ideas and business plans. However, many crowdfunding enthusiasts will lack the expertise and knowledge to properly execute and **implement** such protections. Moreover, if their ideas are stolen, many crowdfunding users will lack resources to fully litigate against a better-funded **adversary** who lifted the ideas.

Unit 3 Crowdfunding

⑩ In order for crowdfunding to work without disastrous results, the government will have to, among other things, **mandate** that entrepreneurs seeking funds provide as much disclosure as possible, clearly define investor rights, and possibly commit to a specific schedule of financial reporting or business updates to ensure proper communication between the crowdfunding entities and investors. Without these, people receiving the capital contributions can "disappear", and investors will be left wondering what is going on and where their money is being spent. The SEC would be wise to **take heed** and carefully read Galvin's letter to avert such disasters, or this could be another instance of the U.S. government attempting to show the public that it is forward thinking while neglecting to think ahead.

⑪ Ultimately, the likely **scenario** is that crowdfunding will lead to, perhaps, one Google and thousands of Friendsters. And plenty of lawsuits.

(1233 words)

Notes

financial fraud: 金融诈骗。Financial fraud is a situation in which the legal and ethical management of financial resources does not take place. In most countries around the world, this type of fraud occurs due to deliberate decisions and actions made by people who handle money and other assets on behalf of employers or clients. However, there are a few places around the world where the unintentional mishandling of funds is also classified as fraud and is subject to the same legal censure as any deliberate action. There are several different ways that financial fraud can take place. The most common approach is to misappropriate funds or other resources. For example, submitting an expense report containing line items for legitimate expenses that never took place could be considered fraudulent activity. In like manner, inventory theft or the deliberate padding of payroll disbursements would also be considered unethical and usually illegal activity.

pump and dump: 哄抬股价，逢高卖出。Pump and dump is a scheme that attempts to boost the price of a stock through recommendations based on false, misleading, or greatly exaggerated statements. The perpetrators of this scheme, who already have an established position in the company's stock, sell their positions after the hype has led to a higher share price. This practice is illegal based on securities law and can lead to heavy fines. It was traditionally done through cold calling. With the advent of the Internet, this illegal practice has become even more prevalent. These schemes usually target micro- and small-cap stocks, as they are the easiest to manipulate. Due to the small float of these types of stocks, it does not take a lot of new buyers to push a stock higher.

class action: 集体诉讼。A class action is a type of lawsuit where one of the parties is a group of people who are represented collectively by a member of that group. The class action originated in the United States and is still predominantly a U.S. phenomenon. In a typical class action, a plaintiff sues a defendant or a number of defendants on behalf of a group, or class, of absent parties. This differs from a traditional lawsuit, where one party sues another party for redress of a wrong, and all of the parties are present in court. Although standards differ between states and countries, class actions are most common where the allegations involve a large number of people (usually 40 or more) who have been injured by the same defendant in the same way. Instead of each damaged person bringing his or her own lawsuit, the class action allows all the claims of all class members—whether they know they have been damaged or not—to be resolved in a single proceeding through the efforts of the representative plaintiff(s) and appointed class counsel.

4.3 Read Text B. Write a summary in the following form and take notes according to the table below.

Subject: _____
Key words: _____
Organization types: _____
Thesis statement (or main ideas): _____
_____

Conclusion (or major findings): _____
_____

No.	Paragraph(s)	Structure	Content
1)		Introduction and thesis statement	
2)		Cause 1	
3)		Cause 2	
4)		Cause 3	
5)		Cause 4	
6)		How to avert the legal disasters	
7)		Conclusion	

4.4 Read Text B again and answer the following questions.

1) In which aspect does Text B differ from Text A?
2) How does Text A illustrate the unique value of crowdfunding?

Unit 3 Crowdfunding

3) How does Text B illustrate the potential legal disasters of crowdfunding?
4) Why the two authors' ideas are so completely different towards the same crowdfunding?
5) What's your attitude towards the crowdfunding?

UNIT PROJECT

Read Text B and Text A again, form two groups, and hold a debate on the topic "For crowdfunding, the risks outweigh the benefits". Give evidence to support your arguments and refute your opponents'.

 Practice for Enhancement

5.1 Read four words in each group and cross the word which is not a synonym for the bold word. An example is given for you.

e.g. **litigation**
   × rebut   ☐ lawsuit   ☐ judicial action   ☐ prosecution
1) **skirt**
   ☐ shun   ☐ dress   ☐ avoid   ☐ circle round
2) **project**
   ☐ design   ☐ frame   ☐ schedule   ☐ reject
3) **launch**
   ☐ release   ☐ lunch   ☐ emission   ☐ send out
4) **gatekeeper**
   ☐ doorman   ☐ ostiary   ☐ janitor   ☐ gate stop
5) **scam**
   ☐ scheme   ☐ fraud   ☐ swindle   ☐ scan
6) **obligation**
   ☐ debt   ☐ duty   ☐ enforcement   ☐ liability
7) **assess**
   ☐ assemble   ☐ evaluate   ☐ rate   ☐ value
8) **supplement**
   ☐ recruit   ☐ complimentary ☐ renew   ☐ replenish

9) **transaction**

☐ trade ☐ relations ☐ transcend ☐ truck

5.2 Match the word in the box with the words in each column that regularly go together. An example is given for you.

| market, community, sale, connection, deliver, fulfill, funding, advantage, statement, disclosure |

e.g. sale
 garage-
 -tax
 -price
 commission-

1) _____
 -ababy
 -pamphlets
 -a speech
 -goods

2) _____
 -health
 -service
 virtual-
 -charge

3) _____
 -oneself
 -acontract
 -obligations
 realize-

4) _____
 -economy
 -efficiency
 -expansion
 -entry

5) _____
 parallel-
 network-
 close-
 direct-

6) _____
 public-
 -research
 seed-
 -liquidity

7) _____
 absolute-
 public-
 cost-
 competitive-

8) _____
 financial-
 income-
 joint-
 final-

9) _____
 full-
 -system
 information-
 voluntary-

5.3 Paraphrase the following sentences. An example is given for you.

e.g. Crowdfunding acts as a platform, matching innovators with those who need innovation, and thus is reshaping which ideas come to market.
 Crowdfunding is done on a platform which is easily to link creators and funders. In this way, the two sides decide together whether their idea can be put into practice.

1) In a setting where money is given as an impersonal investment, there is still a substantial cost of failure, but it is much less personal.

2) Further, the projects the crowd (but not the experts) supported ultimately produced a higher number of critical and commercial hits than the projects that the experts approved of.

Unit 3 Crowdfunding

3) This suggests that platform-based allocation of resources can supplement more traditional expert-based decision making.

4) Moving from an expert-centered process to a platform approach increases diversity, leads to high quality results, and generally results in successful outcomes.

5) Throw your idea online and a slew of like-minded investors will give you money to bring your idea to fruition.

6) While this picture of the potential benefits of crowdfunding is undeniably attractive, as regulators we must be vigilant that the exemption will not become a tool for financial fraud and abuse.

7) The bottom line is that, while unintentional, crowdfunding is tailor made to assist fraudsters in duping unsophisticated "investors".

8) Ultimately, the likely scenario is that crowdfunding will lead to, perhaps, one Google and thousands of Friendsters. And plenty of lawsuits.

5.4 Translate the following sentences into Chinese.

1) In a variety of research projects, I and my co-authors have tried to understand what this more democratic world of fundraising looks like, and what it means to use the power of platforms

to transform the early-stage funding of ideas.

_____

2) Crowdfunding acted as a platform that allowed Luckey's enthusiastic community of VR hobbyists to directly support one of their own, making Oculus a reality without needing to go through traditional gatekeepers.

_____

3) A founder whose first start-up fails due to factors outside their control may still receive VC funding in the future, but a project creator who does not deliver to their backers is likely to find a less forgiving audience.

_____

4) The fact that there are so many backers (over 9 million on Kickstarter alone), means that crowdfunding platforms can create many more kinds of matches between project creators and backers, increasing the diversity of ideas that get funded.

_____

5) Crowdfunding has eclipsed the National Endowment of the Arts as a source of funding for the arts, a subject of considerable concern to critics who worried that crowds would favor low culture crowd pleasers over serious theater (more musicals about dancing cats, less experimental work).

_____

6) Many lawsuits against crowdfunding entities may likely have merit since these entities will not have the business experience or savvy to make even the minimum appropriate disclosures or hire an attorney to guide them through disclosure drafting and execution.

_____

Unit 3   Crowdfunding

6 Movie Exploration: *Inside Job* (2010)

Cast

Directed by: Charles Ferguson
Produced by: Audrey Marrs
                Charles Ferguson
Narrated by: Matt Damon
Music by: Alex Heffes

Plot

- Part I: How We Got Here. At the end of the 1980s, the American financial industry was deregulated after decades of regulation and the financial sector had consolidated into a few giant firms in the late 1990s when derivatives became popular in the industry. Efforts to regulate derivatives were weak under the Commodity Futures Modernization Act of 2000. Investment banks, such as Goldman Sachs, Morgan Stanley, Lehman Brothers, Merrill Lynch, and Bear Stearns, sold CDOs to investors. Rating agencies gave many CDOs AAA ratings. Subprime loans led to predatory lending. As a consequence, many home owners were given loans they could never repay.
- Part II: The Bubble (2001–2007). During the housing boom, as a result of the lack of supervision, speculators could buy CDSs to bet against CDOs they did not own. And they lied to investors, promising them that they were high-quality. The three biggest ratings agencies also were part of the lies, contributing to the problem.
- Part III: The Crisis. The market for CDOs collapsed and investment banks were left in trouble as a result of their greed. The time of the Great Recession came when most of the giant firms were dragged into this crisis. Some of them were on the edge of collapse and some of them went bankrupt. Even after the government intervened, global stock markets continued to fall.
- Part IV: Accountability. When those firms struggled in the crisis, their top executives could got away with their personal fortunes intact. Both the major banks and academic economists still advocated for deregulation and opposed reform. It was disclosed that many of these economists had conflicts of interest, with the companies and other groups involved in the financial crisis.
- Part V: Where We Are Now. The average Americans suffered the most. Many workers were laid off. The policy of the Bush Administration worsened the situation. Despite his claim to

reform the industry, Obama's financial policies were weak, unable to make a change.

6.1 Search for the meanings of the following terms from the movie.

1) infrastructure: _____
2) AIG: _____
3) CDS: _____
4) executive compensation: _____
5) Commodity Future Modernization Act of 2000: _____
6) Emergency Economic Stablization Act of 2008: _____
7) Fannie Mae & Freddie Mac: _____
8) Merrill Lynch: _____

> **Web Resources**
>
> https://en.wikipedia.org/wiki/Infrastructure
> https://en.wikipedia.org/wiki/American_International_Group
> https://www.investopedia.com/terms/c/creditdefaultswap.asp
> https://en.wikipedia.org/wiki/Executive_compensation
> https://en.wikipedia.org/wiki/Commodity_Futures_Modernization_Act_of_2000
> https://en.wikisource.org/wiki/Emergency_Economic_Stabilization_Act_of_2008
> https://en.wikipedia.org/wiki/Fannie_Mae
> https://en.wikipedia.org/wiki/Freddie_Mac
> https://en.wikipedia.org/wiki/Merrill_Lynch

6.2 While watching, listen to the fourth part of the documentary and complete it by filling in the blanks.

> In this part, the narrator (N for narrator) discloses what the government has done, including the Bush Administration (B for Bush) and the Obama Administration (O for Obama) after the 2008 crisis.

N: Meanwhile, American tax policy 1)_____ the wealthy.
B: When I first came to office, I thought taxes were too high and they were.
N: The most 2)_____ change was a series of tax cuts designed by Glenn Hubbard, who was serving as President Bush's chief economic advisor. The Bush Administration 3)_____ taxes on investment gains, stock dividends, and 4)_____ the estate

Unit 3 Crowdfunding

tax.

B: We had a 5)_____ plan that when acted, has left nearly $1.1 trillion in the hands of American workers, families, investors, and small business owners.

N: Most benefits of these cuts went to the wealthiest 1% of Americans.

B: By the way, it was the 6)_____, in many ways, of our economic recovery policy.

N: 7)_____ in the United States is now higher than in any other developed country. American families responded to these changes in two way, by working longer hours and by going into debt…American families borrowed to finance their homes, their cars, their health care, and their children's educations…For the first time in history, average Americans have less education and are less prosperous than their parents.

O: The era of greed and irresponsibility on Wall Street and in Washington has led us to a financial crisis as serious as any that we've faced since the 8)_____.

N: When the financial crisis struck before the 2008 election, Barack Obama pointed to Wall Street's greed and regulatory failures as examples of the need for change in America.

O: 9)_____ in Washington and on Wall Street is exactly what got us into this mess.

N: After taking office, Obama spoke of the need to reform the industry.

O: We want a risk regulator, increased capital requirements. We need a 10)_____. We need to change Wall Street's culture.

N: But when finally enacted in mid-2010, the Administration's financial reforms were weak. And in some critical areas, including the rating agencies, lobbying, and compensation, nothing significant was even proposed.

6.3 After watching, cross the word or phrase that is closest in meaning to the bold one in each of the following sentences from the movie. An example is given for you.

e.g. We had the complete infrastructure of a modern society, almost **end-of-history** status.

　　□ unrivaled　　　　　　× modest　　　　　　□ inferior

1) The fears generated by the global crisis **gripped** the market overnight.

　　□ worried　　　　　　□ seized　　　　　　□ destroyed

2) The financial deregulation started in the Reagan Administration seemed to become the biggest **heist** in the U.S. history.

　　□ disaster　　　　　　□ robbery　　　　　　□ success

3) Greenspan praised Keating's **sound** business plans and expertise and said he saw no risk in allowing Keating to invest customers' money.

　　□ promising　　　　　　□ defective　　　　　　□ reasonable

4) Markets are **inherently** unstable.

    ☐ intrinsically   ☐ completely   ☐ potentially

5) There's just a **blatant** disregard for the impact that their actions might have on society, on family.

    ☐ huge   ☐ general   ☐ obvious

6) Triple-A-rated instruments **mushroomed** from just a handful to thousands and thousands.

    ☐ upgraded   ☐ proliferated   ☐ devastated

7) In early 2008, Charles Morris published his book about the **impending** crisis.

    ☐ major   ☐ unbelievable   ☐ forthcoming

8) Martin Feldstein is a professor at Harvard and one of the world's most **prominent** economists.

    ☐ outstanding   ☐ reliable   ☐ knowledgeable

9) There would be significant professional **sanction** for failure to disclose financial conflict of interest.

    ☐ encouragement   ☐ restriction   ☐ punishment

6.4 Work in groups and discuss the following questions.

1) In the 2008 crisis, who become the biggest losers, the broker companies or the general bondholders? Why and how?
2) Should economists who do research on a topic disclose if they have any financial conflict with that research?

7 Listening Skills

How to Listen to a Lecture[1]

Lectures are a major source of your academic studies and research. You will get information no less than reading essays and articles. To listen to an academic lecture effectively, however, you may do some homework beforehand. The following are some tips:

- Find out the topic of the lecture to be delivered.
- Research and read the topic-related sources or the assigned material.
- Familiarize yourselves with the subject and list out questions if possible.
- Sort out subject-specific words and terms the lecture may use.

---

1 Adapted from Cai, Z. J. (2014). Listening skills: How to listen to lectures. Li, L., & Zhang, Q. (Eds.). *Legal English* (I) (2nd ed.). Shanghai: Fudan University Press.

Unit 3 Crowdfunding

- Check the meaning and pronunciation of the terms and words.

How to gain main points through the introduction

To understand a lecture, focusing your attention on the introduction part is very important because it helps you to predict the content or the main ideas. Slightly different from an academic essay, a lecture often begins with two ways. Speakers will either tell an interesting story, or introduce the points to be covered in the talk directly. When listening to the story, you should think of its theme, guessing the topic and the attitude of the speaker towards it. Similarly, being informed of the outline of the lecture, you may pay attention to the following patterns the speaker tend to use when introducing their ideas:

- To start with, I'll talk about…Then I'll discuss…After that, we'll look at…I'll finish by giving a summary of…
- In the first part, I'll explain/talk…Then in the second part, I will present/examine/analyze…

In short, listening to the introduction carefully, you will have a good understanding of the main ideas of the lecture as well as the structure of the lecture—cause and effect, comparison and contrast, advantages and disadvantages, or problems and solution. The initial understanding will help you to follow the lecture easily.

How to understand the ideas through examples

Unlike an academic essay in which a speaker tends to fill his lecture with examples, personal experience, and anecdotes, the purpose of a lecture is to illustrate a difficult idea or an abstract theory and to make his talk more vivid, attractive, and easier to follow. Hence, it is important to take an example or anecdote seriously and ask what the point of the example is when you hear it. You may especially pay attention to the signal words like "for example", "for instance", "the following example (story/incident) illustrates/demonstrates", "such as", "as in the case of", "a good case in point", because before or after the speaker tell a story or an example, there is always a key sentence which sums up the theme of the story or the example.

How to use signal words to follow the lecture

There are two kinds of signal language the speaker of a lecture tend to use. One is signpost language, and the other is transitional language.

Signpost language refers to words and phrases which serve a signpost pointing towards the moving of a lecture. To be alert to them will help you follow the lecture easily. The following are some of them:

1) Topic
- Today I'm going to take up the subject of…
- The topic I'd like to develop…

2) Structure
- Now let me look at this from a different point of view…

- Now let us consider…
- Now let me put it another way…
- We may here review the factors that…
- There are many factors/causes that…

3) Shift
- Now, let's move on to…
- Another special feature is that…
- Another reason is that…
- Another problem is…
- Let's turn now to the causes…
- Other factors that could be contributing to…include…

4) Explanation
- What I mean is, …
- That is to say…
- To put it another way, …
- I may use an example to illustrate…

Transitional language refers to words and phrases which contribute to the understanding of the ideas as well as to the coherence of the lecture. There are several categories according to their semantic meaning.

1) Illustration
- For example, for instance, a good case in point is…, in particular, etc.

2) Cause
- Because, owing to, due to, on account of, since, as, etc.

3) Effect
- Therefore, as a result, consequently, so, etc.

4) Comparison
- In comparison, similarly, one advantage is, likewise, etc.

5) Condition
- If, unless, assuming that, etc.

6) Contrast
- However, nevertheless, on the other hand, by contrast, etc.

7) Listing
- First, in the first place, second, then, additionally, finally, moreover, furthermore, etc.

8) Classification
- Can be divided/classified into, one category/one feature is…, etc.

9) Summary
- To sum up, to conclude, in brief, etc.

ACADEMIC ENGLISH FOR BUSINESS

Unit 4
Brexit

商务学科英语

1 Search for Background Information

1.1 Search for the meanings of the following terms from texts or about the subject.

1) EU: _____
2) Brexit: _____
3) hard and soft Brexit: _____
4) divorce bill: _____
5) referendum: _____
6) Keynesian economics: _____
7) customs union: _____
8) non-tariff barriers to trade: _____
9) civic nationalism: _____
10) immigrants from the EU: _____
11) single market: _____
12) Euroscepticism: _____
13) income distribution: _____
14) median income: _____
15) populism: _____

Web Resources

https://en.wikipedia.org/wiki/European_Union
https://en.wikipedia.org/wiki/Brexit
https://en.wikipedia.org/wiki/Referendum
https://en.wikipedia.org/wiki/Keynesian_economics
https://en.wikipedia.org/wiki/Customs_union
https://en.wikipedia.org/wiki/Non-tariff_barriers_to_trade
https://en.wikipedia.org/wiki/Civic_nationalism
https://en.wikipedia.org/wiki/Modern_immigration_to_the_United_Kingdom
https://en.wikipedia.org/wiki/Single_market
https://en.wikipedia.org/wiki/Euroscepticism
https://en.wikipedia.org/wiki/Income_distribution
https://en.wikipedia.org/wiki/Median_income
https://en.wikipedia.org/wiki/Populism

Unit 4　Brexit

1.2 Present what you've found to the class orally with or without PowerPoint in three minutes.

2 Discuss the Words' Meaning

2.1 Define the following underlined words. An example is given for you.

e.g. At least a <u>semblance</u> of normality has been restored to parts of the country.
   semblance: <u>a situation, condition, etc., that is close to or similar to a particular one.</u>

1) He has a hard core of support among white <u>racists</u>.
   racist: _____

2) In a recent survey, questionnaires were sent to reporters in five middle-size cities around the country, plus one large <u>metropolitan</u> area.
   metropolitan: _____

3) China is more prosperous and <u>cosmopolitan</u> than at any time in history.
   cosmopolitan: _____

4) During his election <u>campaign</u>, he promised to put the economy back on its feet.
   campaign: _____

5) Our strong sense of national <u>identity</u> has been shaped by our history.
   identity: _____

6) Whether in California or Calcutta, it boils down to the existential question: Does business credit <u>matter</u>?
   matter: _____

7) Business interests are <u>incompatible</u> with public office.
   incompatible: _____

8) Memories can sometimes be pure <u>fantasy</u>, rather than actual recollections.
   fantasy: _____

9) In the <u>pursuit</u> of profits, the company traded commodities, such as spices, sugar, fur, and slaves.
   pursuit: _____

10) The <u>decline</u> in sales embarrassed our company.
    decline: _____

11) But a U.N. spokeswoman said it was because of rules—<u>procedural</u> reasons.
    procedural: _____

12) They have made it clear that they will not reverse the decision to increase prices.
    reverse: _____
13) That would take the risk of further deflation, and it wouldn't destabilize neighboring economies.
    destabilize: _____
14) When you go to a new country, you must adapt yourself to new manners and custom.
    adapt: _____
15) The rich were the main beneficiaries of the tax cuts.
    beneficiary: _____
16) The safety and security of Americans takes, and should take, precedence over economic interests.
    precedence: _____
17) Businesses that overlook this fact run the risk of seeing their market share shrink.
    overlook: _____
18) They're a world-class team and it was no surprise that they won by such a wide margin.
    margin: _____
19) His business empire collapsed under a massive burden of debt.
    collapse: _____
20) As you can see from this overview, developing an effective transaction strategy is not always a straightforward task.
    straightforward: _____
21) We persuaded him out of lending his money to that untrustworthy man.
    untrustworthy: _____
22) By static, I mean that the resources allocated to each partition do not change over time.
    static: _____
23) At least that's what the data reveal.
    reveal: _____
24) Four quarts constitute a gallon.
    constitute: _____
25) But immigration should not be the only pathway for those seeking opportunity.
    immigration: _____
26) That's why you see governments trying to subsidize manufacturers or the consumer.
    subsidize: _____
27) But the distribution of these gains is extraordinarily unequal.
    distribution: _____
28) Our forecasts are coming out next week, so I will confine myself today to broad trends.
    confine: _____

29) We believe the reduction should be easily offset by the unexpected increase in investment growth.
   offset: _____

30) The best antidote to a growing deficit, by the way, is a growing economy.
   antidote: _____

2.2 Fill in the following blanks with various forms of each word. An example is given for you.

No.	Base form	Variations in the word family
e.g.	identify	identification, identity, identical, identifiable, identifying
1)	compatible	
2)	pursue	
3)	process	
4)	substitute	
5)	adapt	
6)	race	
7)	precede	
8)	account	
9)	margin	
10)	constitute	
11)	immigrate	
12)	distribute	
13)	confine	
14)	subsidy	

2.3 Explain the meaning of the following roots or affixes. Add at least five similar derivatives with their Chinese definitions. An example is given for you.

No.	Roots/Affixes	Meaning	More derivatives with Chinese translation
e.g.	in-	opposite	incompatible不相容的；incapable无能力的；incorrect不正确的；incomplete不完全的；in human不人道的
1)	sub-		
2)	bene-		
3)	pro-		
4)	di-		
5)	pre-		
6)	out-		
7)	trans-		
8)	macro-		

3 Watch the Video

Difficult Words and Expressions

★ spearhead /'spɪəhed/ v. 带头做某事
★ uncertainty /ˌʌn'sɜːtənti/ n. 不确定
★ prominent /'prɒmɪnənt/ adj. 突出的
★ Mafia /'mæfiə/ n. 黑手党
★ burdensome /'bɜːdns(ə)m/ adj. 累赘的
★ curb /kɜːb/ v. 抑制

3.1 Watch the first part of the video and answer the following questions.

1) When will Britain vote to remain in or leave the EU?
2) Why do British people decide to vote?
3) How many members does the EU have up to now?
4) What is the possible impact of Britain's exit from the EU?
5) What is Mr. Cameron doing before the vote?

Unit 4 Brexit

3.2 Watch the second part of the video and take notes according to the questions in the left column.

No.	Questions	Notes
1)	According to Mr. Cameron, in what aspects will the Brexit do harm to the U.K.?	
2)	Why is the EU membership so important to the U.K.?	
3)	Who are the major supporters of the remain campaign?	
4)	Who are campaigning for Britain's departure?	
5)	What does the leave campaign argue?	

3.3 Watch the whole video again and write a short summary of it according to your answers and notes.

_____
_____
_____
_____

3.4 Share your summary with your partner and present it to the class.

4 Read for Information

Meaning over Money[1]

Charles Leadbeater

❶ The liberal left has gone through various forms of disbelief since the Brexit vote. People

---

1 Adapted from Leadbeater, C. (2016). Meaning over money: How the left can win back the leavers. *New Statesman*, *145*(5322), 18–19.

voted Leave for many different reasons. At one end were people who are clearly **racists**; at the other were **utopian** liberal internationalists. For much of the working class, however, I think that it came down to five things. These are made for the left to respond to—if only we could work out how to bridge the gap between **metropolitan**, **cosmopolitan** progressives and working class voters who believe in **solidarity** and **community**.

This was a vote for meaning rather than money.

❷ The Remain **campaign** was all about money and how much people would lose if Britain exited the EU. The Leave campaign was all about **restoring** a **semblance** of meaning to people's lives, despite not having much money. As a vote for something more than money—for pride, belonging, community, **identity**, a sense of "home"—it was a rejection of the market. We might not much like some elements of this "vote for meaning", but it was a vote with the heart, rather than the wallet. The result was a reminder that people need something in their lives that feels more important than money—especially, perhaps, when they have little prospect of having much. Above all, they need a sense of narrative.

It was a vote for democratic decision-making over opaque and distant power.

❸ The European Union has a distant, opaque, and ineffective decision-making process. Understandably, people want decisions made closer to home. Read Martin Wolf in the *Financial Times* or the Harvard-based economist Dani Rodrik: Globalization, democracy, and the nation state are **incompatible**.

❹ Nationalism may be the price that we have to pay for a sense of democratic control over our lives. This was a vote to **reassert** nation state democracy in a time of global markets. That may be romantic and **naive** but it was a vote for democracy over global forces. There is nothing wrong with people wanting control over their lives: That is what social democracy was supposed to provide. Jacqueline Rose explored this subject in her book *States of Fantasy*, which examines how politics is driven by a shared public **fantasy**. The U.S. political life is devoted to the **pursuit** of the "American Dream", not the "American Reality". The vote on June 23 was for a kind of "British Dream"—though it may yet turn out to be a nightmare.

This is high-energy politics.

❺ People have become more engaged in political debate, and it truly **matters** to them for the first time in years. **Impassioned** conversations are everywhere, between all sorts of people, about what kind of society we should be and what a good society is. The long-established political systems are in **decline**. Politics is seen as **procedural**, distant, and **untrustworthy**. Yet all voters feel that they have something at stake in the outcome, something they want to defend or stand up for.

❻ The left-wing philosopher Roberto Mangabeira Unger called for a "high-energy" politics to take over from the exhausted forms of representative democracy in his book *What Should the Left*

Unit 4 Brexit

Propose?—and this is it. Having more people politically engaged should be good for progressives, because they believe in the power of democratic politics to shape markets.

Objects of public love

⑦ National symbols are still the most **potent** objects of public love. North of the border, the Scottish National Party seems to have fashioned a forward-looking **civic** nationalism. If only England, led by the left, could do something similar through localism—real devolution of power to cities, towns, wards, and neighborhoods—and a new civic activism.

⑧ Most leaders of social-democratic politics are schooled in the tradition of John Rawls, which reduces the search for a fair society to a set of **equations**. A cheque in the post has become a **substitute** for human solidarity. The U.S. legal theorist Bonnie Honig argues that as a result proceduralism—politics as a process of allocating rights and responsibilities, rather than a forum for **substantive** discussions about what makes for a good life or society—has replaced real engagement.

⑨ Honig's **antidote** to proceduralism is a politics that is **tumultuous**, unpredictable, **contingent**, and fragile, driven by passions and fantasies. She is more interested in a politics that **destabilizes** existing procedures and leads to new forms of political power.

⑩ Welcome to the Brexit world. Suck it up. Learn to **adapt to** it. According to Honig, part of the answer is the creation and defense of "objects of public love", which are the icons of our common life. These help make us a society, because we see ourselves reflected in them. In 2012, a public campaign prevented the privatization of British forests, which became objects of public love. The 2012 London Olympics were and remain an object of public love for people in the U.K., although they now feel more like a long-lost holiday romance (one involving Boris Johnson). The NHS is an object of public affection and loyalty, if not love.

This was a vote for a version of equality.

⑪ People who think that they have little to gain from globalization voted for a new Brexit settlement in which those who already gained would find it harder to do so. The **beneficiaries** of a globalized, network economy will struggle now to do as well as they once did. That they will find life harder and the economy may grow less quickly matters little to people in industrial towns left **stranded** and with no growth in their incomes for two decades. House prices in London will fall. High earners may flee. The creative industries will suffer.

⑫ The truth is that, for a while now, growth has failed to deliver its moral **dividend** alongside its economic one because the increased prosperity has not been shared fairly. It should be no surprise that those who have spent years feeling **overlooked** and neglected by both the market and politics should now feel such **resentment** and so little **sympathy** for people with wealth, who might feel, for the first time, that the world is slipping away from them. On the contrary, it might be the cause for celebration and satisfaction.

⑬ In recent times, economic growth has not delivered many dividends at the bottom of the income pile. Will slower growth after Brexit make much difference? The country may be poorer but it could become less unequal. It will almost certainly become uglier.

⑭ The post-war settlement was founded on Keynesian principles, a welfare state and an industrial, fully-employed economy. The Thatcherite settlement was about the individual, the private, and the market taking **precedence** over the collective, the public, and the state. It was complex because it combined a belief in the strong state and the open market, and yet also a national purpose. We now stand on the verge of a Brexit settlement that will **redress** the relationships between Britain and Europe, between the white working class and immigrants, and between the cosmopolitan and urban and the communal and provincial.

⑮ Seen from this perspective, there should be a lot for the left to work with in the aftermath of the Brexit vote. People want more meaning in their lives. They want more democracy. They want an engaged, high-energy politics. They will rally around objects of public love if they are attractive and meaningful. They want greater equality and more of a sense of community. They want lives that have a narrative, and they want national pride to be a part of that. They want a sense that they can **exert** some control over what is going on around them.

⑯ This is everything that the left should stand for. We just need to show how all of this is made more possible in the U.K. that is a part of Europe and, like countries such as Norway and Canada, unafraid of the free flows of people, trade, and ideas that also make us rich, **diverse**, and exciting.

(1299 words)

Notes

utopia: 乌托邦。A utopia is an imagined community or society that possesses highly desirable or nearly perfect qualities for its citizens. One could also say that utopia is a perfect "place" that has been designed so there are no problems. Utopian ideals often place emphasis on egalitarian principles of equality in economics, government, and justice, though by no means exclusively, with the method and structure of proposed implementation varying based on ideology.

American Dream: 美国梦。The American Dream is a national ethos of the United States, the set of ideals (democracy, rights, liberty, opportunity, and equality) in which freedom includes the opportunity for prosperity and success, as well as an upward social mobility for the family and children, achieved through hard work in a society with few barriers. The American Dream is rooted in the Declaration of Independence, which proclaims that "all men are created equal" with the right to "life, liberty, and the pursuit of happiness".

Scottish National Party (SNP): 苏格兰民主党。It is a Scottish nationalist and social-democratic political party in Scotland. The SNP supports and campaigns for Scottish independence. It is the

Unit 4 Brexit

second-largest political party by membership in the United Kingdom, behind the Labor Party; it is the third-largest by overall representation in the House of Commons, behind the Labor Party and the Conservative Party: and it is the largest political party in Scotland, where it has the most seats in the Scottish Parliament and 35 out of the 59 Scottish seats in the House of Commons of the Parliament of the United Kingdom.

NHS: 英国国民健康保险服务体系。It is the abbreviation for Britain National Health Service. NHS is the name used for each constituent country's public health services in the United Kingdom—NHS England, NHS Scotland, NHS Wales, and Health and Social Care in Northern Ireland—as well as a term to describe them collectively. They were established together in 1948 as one of the major social reforms following the Second World War. The founding principles were that services should be comprehensive, universal, and free at the point of delivery. Each service provides a comprehensive range of health services, free for people ordinarily resident in the United Kingdom, apart from dental treatment and optical care. The English NHS also requires patients to pay prescription charges with a range of exemptions from these charges.

4.1 Read Text A and answer the following questions.

1) What is the author's purpose of writing the article?
2) As the author points out, "This was a vote for meaning", what does the "meaning" here exactly refer to?
3) Why does the author say the vote on June 23 was for a kind of "British Dream"?
4) According to Honig, why does the creation and defense of "objects of public love" become the antidote to proceduralism?
5) In the context of Brexit, what does the author advocate the politicians to do?

4.2 Read Text A again and write a summary.

Summary (about 100 words): _____

_____

_____

_____

_____

TEXT B

Brexit's Long-Run Effects on the U.K. Economy[1]

John Van Reenen

❶ In the referendum held on June 23, 2016, the United Kingdom voted to leave the European Union by a **margin** of 51.9% to 48.1%. Although opinion polls had been close, the betting markets had predicted a victory for the campaign to remain, so markets were caught by surprise. Sterling **collapsed**, from $1.50 to $1.33, within hours after the early results were announced. What are likely to be Brexit's medium to long-run effects on the U.K. economy?

❷ The bottom line is **straightforward**: Under all plausible scenarios, Brexit will make Britain poorer compared with remaining in the European Union. This is because the United Kingdom will have higher trade costs with its closest neighbors in Europe (which account for about half of all U.K. trade), and this will reduce its trade and therefore welfare. The **magnitude** of these losses will **outweigh** the modest benefits of lower net **fiscal** transfers to the EU budget.

Trade

❸ Membership in the European Union has reduced trade costs between the United Kingdom and the rest of Europe. Most obviously, there is a customs union between EU members, which means that all tariff barriers have been removed within the EU, allowing for free trade in goods and services.

❹ But equally important in reducing trade costs has been the reduction of non-tariff barriers resulting from the European Union's continuing efforts to create a Single Market within Europe. Non-tariff barriers include a wide range of measures that raise the costs of trade—such as border controls, rules-of-origin checks, cross-country differences in regulations over things like product standards and safety, and threats of anti-dumping. These reductions in trade barriers have increased trade between the United Kingdom and the other members of the European Union. Before the United Kingdom joined the European Economic Community (EEC) in 1973, about one third of the U.K. trade was with the EEC. In 2014, the other 27 EU members **accounted for** 45% of the U.K. exports, and 53% of imports.

❺ This higher trade benefits the U.K. consumers through lower prices and access to better goods and services. At the same time, workers and businesses benefit from new export opportunities that lead to higher sales and profits, and allow the United Kingdom to specialize in those industries where it has a comparative advantage. Through these channels, increased trade raises output, incomes, and living standards in the United Kingdom. These standard "**static**" effects of trade have

---

1 Adapted from Reenen, J. V. (2016). Brexit's long-run effects on the U.K. economy. *Brookings Papers on Economic Activity*, (Fall), 367–383.

been understood for many centuries, but in recent decades, studies of trade have also **revealed** trade's positive effects on well-being via other routes, such as higher productivity and innovation.

Foreign direct investment

❻ An important reason for inward FDI to Britain is unfettered access to the EU Single Market, so reduced access will make the United Kingdom a less attractive destination. Studies have usually found that FDI benefits productivity. Randolph Bruno and others estimate a gravity model of FDI between 34 OECD countries and find that Brexit would likely lead to a fall in FDI to the United Kingdom by over a fifth. Dhingra and others calculate that such a fall would reduce GDP by about 3.4%.

❼ Financial services **constitute** about 45% of the stock of FDI, and are particularly vulnerable to Brexit. This is because EU membership allows foreign banks to sell ("passport") their services anywhere in the European Union. For example, Switzerland has a comprehensive set of free trade deals with the EU in goods but not in services, which is one reason why Swiss banks set up **subsidiaries** in the City of London.

Immigration

❽ A major factor in the Brexit referendum was the desire to reduce immigration. Between 1995 and 2015, the number of EU nationals living in the United Kingdom tripled, mainly after the accession of Poland and other former communist countries in 2004. Freedom of movement is a central **tenet** of the European Union and a *quid pro quo* of full access to the Single Market.

❾ EU migrants are on average better educated, more likely to work, and less likely to claim welfare benefits than the British-born workers. Hence, they have effectively **subsidized** the public services of the U.K. nationals. Further, a detailed analysis of the local labor market impact of these large immigrant flows since 2004 shows no significant fall in jobs or wages for British-born workers, for either the average or less-skilled **segments** of the **distribution**. Any negative effects of new waves of immigrants appear to be **confined** to their closest **substitutes**—older waves of immigrants.

❿ Indeed, most macroeconomic assessments suggest that immigration, like free trade and FDI, has been a net benefit for the U.K. economy. Hence, reducing immigration after Brexit will do nothing to **offset** the negative trade and FDI effects of Brexit.

Regulations

⓫ Eurosceptics often point to the promise of better regulations after Brexit. It is important to realize that regulations will not be much affected under the soft Brexit scenario. This is because to access the Single Market, countries like Norway or Switzerland had to adopt the same regulations as the rest of the European Union—but without having a vote on what these regulations are.

⓬ Post-Brexit, the United Kingdom could weaken its social, employment, and environmental regulations to some degree. But even if this were politically possible, the country already has some of the most flexible employment and product market regulations in the developed world, according to the OECD. It is unlikely that further weakening its protections (say, to the U.S. levels) would make a material difference to its GDP.

⑬ Even if the regulatory costs of EU membership were as high as 0.9% of GDP, this is still less than half as large as our estimates of the net cost of a hard Brexit, even in the purely static case, and much lower than the 6%–9% costs under the dynamic case. In the United Kingdom, there are many costs of regulation, such as the planning system, but these problems are primarily homegrown.

Distributional effects: Did only the elite benefit from EU membership?

⑭ One view is that the benefits of EU membership **accrue** overwhelmingly **to** those with high incomes (the "elite"), whereas those below the lower part of the income distribution lose out. However, when we **disaggregate** the expected costs of Brexit, the economic pain appears to be evenly distributed across income groups. This is unsurprising because the EU consists of richer, highly skilled countries that are more similar to the United Kingdom than the emerging economies of China and India (whose imports could potentially have put downward wage pressure on less-skilled British workers).

⑮ Being a member of the European Union helped the United Kingdom **reverse** a century of relative economic decline. The gap in GDP per capita was reduced significantly with that in the United States, France, and Germany between the last referendum in 1975 and the global financial crisis in 2008. Although inequality increased, a difference with the United States is that the U.K. median real wages also increased substantially during this period, and since the early 1990s, even those in the bottom 10th percentile have seen improvements. Things changed dramatically after 2007, of course; there were median real wage declines of more than 8% through 2014. This certainly fueled anger against the elite, but the banking crisis and subsequent **austerity** can hardly be blamed on the European Union.

⑯ At the time of writing, it appears that the United Kingdom is moving toward the most economically damaging form of a hard Brexit. It is **imperative** for an informed debate to continue about the likely impact of a hard Brexit on the United Kingdom compared with alternative policies. The **populist** uprising against globalization risks inflicting the most harm on the very people who are **railing** most strongly against it.

(1290 words)

> Notes

European Economic Community (EEC): 欧洲经济共同体。It was a regional organization which aimed to bring about economic integration among its member states. It was created by the Treaty of Rome of 1957. Upon the formation of the European Union (EU) in 1993, the EEC was incorporated and renamed as the European Community (EC). In 2009, the EC's institutions were absorbed into the EU's wider framework and the community ceased to exist.

OECD: 经济与合作发展组织。It is the abbreviation for the Organization for Economic Co-operation and Development. OECD is an intergovernmental economic organization with 35 member countries, founded in 1961 to stimulate economic progress and the world trade. It is a forum of countries describing themselves as committed to democracy and the market economy, providing a platform to compare policy experiences, seeking answers to common problems, identify good practices, and coordinate domestic and international policies of its members. Most OECD members are high-income economies with a very high Human Development Index (HDI) and are regarded as developed countries. OECD is an official United Nations observer.

4.3 Read Text B. Write a summary in the following form and take notes according to the table below.

Subject: _____

Key words: _____

Organization types: _____

Thesis statement (or main ideas): _____

_____

Conclusion (or major findings): _____

_____

_____

No.	Paragraph(s)	Structure	Content
1)		Argument	
2)		Argumentation 1	
3)		Argumentation 2	
4)		Argumentation 3	
5)		Argumentation 4	
6)		Argumentation 5	
7)		Conclusion	

4.4 Read Text B again and answer the following questions.

1) According to the author, in what ways will the U.K. customers suffer from Brexit?
2) Why does the author believe that Brexit will make the U.K. a less attractive investment destination?
3) Will the reduced immigration benefit the U.K. in the long run?
4) According to the author, why will the economic pain coming from the costs of Brexit be evenly distributed across all income groups?
5) What's your attitude towards Brexit on the basis of the comparison of the two texts?

UNIT PROJECT

Read Text B and Text A again, form two groups, and hold a debate on the topic "Britain will be better off without Europe". Give evidence to support your arguments and refute your opponents'.

5 Practice for Enhancement

5.1 Read four words in each group and cross the word which is not a synonym for the bold word. An example is given for you.

e.g. **community**

☐ village ☐ group ☐ organization ✗ service

1) **fantasy**

☐ fancy ☐ illusion ☐ beauty ☐ imagination

2) **incompatible**

☐ indifferent ☐ unsuitable ☐ contradictory ☐ antipathic

3) **allocate**

☐ assign ☐ distribute ☐ contribute ☐ allot

4) **diverse**

☐ different ☐ similar ☐ varying ☐ unlike

5) **reveal**

☐ prove ☐ disclose ☐ refute ☐ expose

6) **constitute**

☐ attribute ☐ found ☐ build ☐ establish

7) **subsidize**
   ☐ fund   ☐ aid   ☐ endow   ☐ counter
8) **offset**
   ☐ generate   ☐ counteract   ☐ neutralize   ☐ compensate
9) **confine**
   ☐ restrict   ☐ conceive   ☐ limit   ☐ block

5.2 Decide what words can go with the following verbs. An example is given for you.

e.g. reassert: one's control, one's authority, core values, basic principles, one's superiority, etc.
1) pursue:
2) allocate:
3) overlook:
4) redress:
5) exert:
6) outweigh:
7) reveal:
8) subsidize:
9) offset:

5.3 Paraphrase the following sentences. An example is given for you.

e.g. We might not much like some elements of this "vote for meaning", but it was a vote with the heart, rather than the wallet.
<u>Although to a certain extent, we might dislike some parts of wordings like "vote for meaning", we have to admit that people voted out of their true emotions instead of money.</u>

1) Globalization, democracy, and the nation state are incompatible.

2) Most leaders of social-democratic politics are schooled in the tradition of John Rawls, which reduces the search for a fair society to a set of equations.

3) The truth is that, for a while now, growth has failed to deliver its moral dividend alongside its economic one because the increased prosperity has not been shared fairly.

4) The Thatcherite settlement was about the individual, the private, and the market taking precedence over the collective, the public, and the state.

5) The bottom line is straightforward: Under all plausible scenarios, Brexit will make Britain poorer compared with remaining in the European Union.

6) Freedom of movement is a central tenet of the European Union and a *quid pro quo* of full access to the Single Market.

7) Hence, reducing immigration after Brexit will do nothing to offset the negative trade and FDI effects of Brexit.

8) This certainly fueled anger against the elite, but the banking crisis and subsequent austerity can hardly be blamed on the European Union.

5.4 Translate the following sentences into Chinese.

1) These are made for the left to respond to—if only we could work out how to bridge the gap between metropolitan, cosmopolitan progressives and working class voters who believe in solidarity and community.

2) The result was a reminder that people need something in their lives that feels more important than money—especially, perhaps, when they have little prospect of having much.

3) Honig's antidote to proceduralism is a politics that is tumultuous, unpredictable, contingent, and fragile, driven by passions and fantasies. She is more interested in a politics that destabilizes existing procedures and leads to new forms of political power.

4) The beneficiaries of a globalized, network economy will struggle now to do as well as they once did. That they will find life harder and the economy may grow less quickly matters little to people in industrial towns left stranded and with no growth in their incomes for two decades.

5) It should be no surprise that those who have spent years feeling overlooked and neglected by both the market and politics should now feel such resentment and so little sympathy for people with wealth, who might feel, for the first time, that the world is slipping away from them.

6) It is imperative for an informed debate to continue about the likely impact of a hard Brexit on the United Kingdom compared with alternative policies. The populist uprising against globalization risks inflict the most harm on the very people who are railing most strongly against it.

Movie Exploration: *Margin Call* (2011)

Cast

Directed by: J. C. Chandor
Starring: Kevin Spacey as Sam Rogers
               Jeremy Irons as John Tuld

商务学科英语

Stanley Tucci as Eric Dale
Zachary Quinto as Peter Sullivan
Simon Baker as Jared Cohen

Plot

- Eric Dale, head of risk management, is fired by his company, leaving part of his work unfinished. He gives a disk to Peter Sullivan, a senior risk analyst and tells him to be careful.
- Sullivan works late that night to finish Dale's project, and discovers that something goes wrong. Immediately, he calls his head back to the office and then everyone is being alert to what is going to happen.
- Through out the night, members of the executive committee have a meeting and decide to dump all of the toxic assets in a fire sale before the market learns of their worthlessness.
- Before in a morning speech to his traders in preparation to carry out Jared Cohen's plan, Sam Rogers warns them that they are going to ruin their reputations and ending their careers in the industry by doing all of these.
- John Tuld persuades Rogers to stay at the firm for another two years, promising that there will be a lot of money to be made from the coming crisis.
- Rogers buries his dog that has passed away in the front yard of his ex-wife's house in the middle of the night and is relieved when hearing that his son's company is okay.

6.1 Search for the meanings of the following terms from the movie.

1) **risk management:** _____
2) **severance pay:** _____
3) **VAR model:** _____
4) **volatility:** _____
5) **liquidation:** _____
6) **current market value:** _____
7) **OTB:** _____
8) **asset classes:** _____

Web Resources

https://en.wikipedia.org/wiki/Risk_management
https://www.investopedia.com/terms/s/severancepay.asp

Unit 4   Brexit

> https://en.wikipedia.org/wiki/Vector_autoregression
> https://en.wikipedia.org/wiki/Volatility_(finance)
> https://en.wikipedia.org/wiki/Liquidation
> http://www.investorwords.com/1255/current-market-value.html
> https://en.wikipedia.org/wiki/Overseas_Trust_Bank
> https://en.wikipedia.org/wiki/Asset_classes

6.2 While watching, listen to the conversation among the members of the executive committee and complete it by filling in the blanks.

> In this meeting, John Tuld, CEO of the company (T for Tuld), is caught up with what has happened by Jared Cohen (C for Cohen) and decides to take countermeasures. But Sam Rogers (R for Rogers) opposes it.

T: Welcome everyone. I must apologize for 1)_____ you all here at such an uncommon hour, but from what I've been told, this matter needs to be handled urgently! So urgently, in fact, it probably should have been 2)_____ weeks ago, but that is 3)_____. So, why doesn't somebody tell me what they think is going on here.

C: Well, Mr. Tuld, as I mentioned earlier, if you compare the figure at the top page 13…

T: Jared, it's a…? Just speak to me in 4)_____ English. But I'd like to speak to the guy who put this together…Mr. Sullivan, is it…?

C: Certainly, that would be Peter Sullivan. Right here.

T: Oh Mr. Sullivan. You are here! Good morning. Maybe you could tell me what you think is going on here. And please speak as you might to a young child or a golden retriever. It wasn't brains that got me here. I can assure you of that.

(Peter Sullivan explains what he has found out…)

T: So, what you're telling me is that the music is about to stop. And we are gonna be left holding "the biggest bag of odorous excrement" ever 5)_____ in the history of 6)_____…Let me tell you something, Mr. Sullivan. Do you care to know why I'm in this chair with you all? I mean why I earn the 7)_____. I'm here for one reason and one reason alone. I'm here to guess what the music might do, a week, a month, a year from now. I'm afraid that I don't hear…a…thing, just…silence!…Mr. Cohen, what do you have for us?

(Tuld asks Cohen what he is going to do…)

T: What have I told you since the first day you stepped into my office. There are three ways to make a living in this business. 8)_____. And although I like to think we've some pretty smart people in this building. It sure is a hell of a lot easier to just be first.

(Cohen suggests selling the company. Tuld asks Sam whether it is possible…)

R: The real question is who we are selling this to?
T: The same people we've been selling to for the last two years and whoever else will buy it.
R: But John, if you do this, you would've 9)_____ that market for years. It's over. And you are selling something that you know has no value.
T: We are selling willing buyers at a 10)_____, so that we may survive!
R: You will never sell anything to any of those people ever again.

6.3 After watching, cross the word or phrase that is closest in meaning to the bold one in each of the following sentences from the movie. An example is given for you.

e.g. This is what the firm can offer you. You can either take the offer or it will be **revoked**.

  ☐ retreated   ☐ rescinded   ✗ invalidated

1) Due to the highly sensitive nature of your work, the firm has to take precautions for security purposes that may seem **punitive**.

  ☐ necessary   ☐ punishing   ☐ important

2) The **projected** losses are greater than the current value of the company.

  ☐ anticipated   ☐ approximate   ☐ actual

3) As I was saying **off the record**, it's only a matter of time before someone else starts putting these in.

  ☐ unofficially   ☐ unconfidently   ☐ doubtfully

4) I'd like to speak to the analyst who seems to have **stumbled across** this mess.

  ☐ got across   ☐ put across   ☐ come across

5) In any other circumstance, thereby push the risk profile without raising any **red flags**.

  ☐ warning signals   ☐ general awareness   ☐ necessary preventions

6) Sometimes in an **acute** situation such as this, often what is right can take on multiple interpretations.

  ☐ critical   ☐ competitive   ☐ private

7) The **crux** of it is that the firm went bankrupt this morning.

  ☐ answer   ☐ core   ☐ rationale

8) There is going to be considerable **turmoil** in the markets for the foreseeable future.

  ☐ chaos   ☐ concern   ☐ discontent

9) They **got hammered**, but were able to get out alive of the pub.

  ☐ got beaten   ☐ got arrested   ☐ got drunk

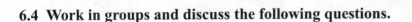

Unit 4　Brexit

6.4 Work in groups and discuss the following questions.

1) To what extent do you agree with the saying "no businessman trades without fraud"?
2) If you were Sam Rogers, would you resign or keep your job?

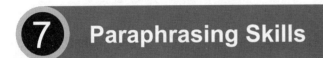 **Paraphrasing Skills**

How to Paraphrase Sources[1]

When you paraphrase, you state someone else's idea in your own words. Paraphrasing is the most important tool for sharing the research of others as relevant to your own study.

What is paraphrasing?

The definition of paraphrasing is when you state someone else's idea in your own words. The goal is to keep the same meaning as the original text without copying it word-for-word (quoting).

In general, you will paraphrase more than you quote throughout your paper. This is due to three main reasons:

- Paraphrasing shows that you clearly understand the meaning.
- You do not copy the research of others and plagiarize their work.
- Your own voice will remain dominant throughout your paper.

The following is an example of paraphrasing:

- Original passage: The number of foreign and domestic tourists in the Netherlands rose above 42 million in 2017, an increase of 9% and the sharpest growth rate since 2006, the national statistics office CBS reported on Wednesday.
- Paraphrased version: The national statistics office, CBS, stated that the Netherlands experienced dramatic growth in the number of tourists visiting in 2017. More than 42 million tourists travelled to the Netherlands that year, representing a 9% increase—the sharpest growth in 12 years.

The paraphrased passage meets all the paraphrasing criteria:

- The text is stated in your own words.
- The meaning of the text did not change.
- The source is cited correctly (see below for details of citing paraphrase).

1　Adapted from Gahan, C. (2018). *How to paraphrase sources*. Retrieved from https://www.scribbr.com/citing-sources/how-to-paraphrase/ & Lund University. (2016). *How to give references*. Retrieved from https://awelu.srv.lu.se/sources-and-referencing/how-to-give-reference

How to paraphrase

There are six steps in paraphrasing:

- Read the passage several times so you fully understand the idea.
- Note the key concepts if you need to.
- Write your version of the text without looking at the original (see the tips listed below if you're stuck at this stage).
- Read your own version of the paraphrased text against the original version, and note any phrases that remain too similar.
- Make minor adjustments as needed. You may not be able to change all phrases.
- Note the source from where you took the idea, with all the information you will need to properly write the citation.

Paraphrasing tips

These steps may seem straightforward enough to follow, but it can be hard to see where to begin when it comes to actually writing an idea in a different way than the published version. There are a few tricks you can apply to help you do so.

Let's start with a new example.

- Original passage: But the hearing was about more than Facebook; it exposed a critical turning point as the power, sophistication, and potential exploitation of technology outpaces what users, regulators, or even its creators expected or seem prepared to handle.

- Paraphrased version: The hearing made it apparent that the expectations of creators, regulators, and users have been rapidly eclipsed by technology in general, not only Facebook. Such technologies now extend beyond what these parties are able to manage, due to their immense influence, potential for exploitation and sophistication.

Then look at the following tips:

- Tip 1: Start your first sentence at a different point from that of the original source.

In the example above, you can see that we started by introducing the context (the hearing) followed by the last part of the original sentence: the expectations of creators, regulators, and users. In fact, the key pieces of information are mentioned in a completely different order.

- Tip 2: Use as many synonyms as possible.

While there are certain parts of the original quote that cannot be changed because there is no ideal synonym (e.g. the hearing; creators, regulators, and users; technology), other words or phrases have been replaced with synonyms (e.g. exposed a critical turning point→made it apparent, outpaces→rapidly eclipsed, power→immense influence).

- Tip 3: Change the sentence structure.

For example, if the sentence is originally in the active voice, change it to passive. In this example, *technology* is the subject; *the expectations of creators, regulators, and users* are the

object. Therefore, the original quote is written in the active voice, while the paraphrased example favours the passive voice.
- Tip 4: Break the information into separate sentences.

Although paraphrasing will usually result in a word count roughly the same as an original quote, you may be able to play with the number of sentences to make the text different. In this example, one long sentence is broken into two. The opposite could also be the case, i.e. if the original quote is comprised of two sentences, you may be able to combine the information into one.

When to quote and when to paraphrase

If you complete thorough research and note-taking of the extant literature, you will naturally end up paraphrasing most of the important information you find, rather than using direct quotes. It is wise to limit the number of direct quotes in your paper, as heavy use can make it appear as though you do not properly understand the sources or are too lazy to write in your own words. Quotes also reduce the readability of your thesis. In general, you should prefer to paraphrase or summarize sources and studies you find. Quotes should be limited to only when:
- You wish to use an exact definition.
- The original wording is so perfect you cannot hope to write it better.
- You need to provide evidence or support an argument.

How to cite paraphrases

There are two ways of incorporating paraphrases into your work: non-integral citation and integral citation.

Non-integral citation, also known as information-prominent, is where you paraphrase or quote information from another source and only mention the author in your reference. This gives greater emphasis to the information you're providing rather than its origin. The following is an example of non-integral citation:
- Despite the goals of and expectations placed on social work practice, very little is known about the outcomes of social service interventions. This is true for both their effectiveness (Cederblad, 2005) and efficiency (Mossler, 2008). This has led some to advocate for evidence-based practice (EBP) within the social services, spurring a wave of debate (Hansson, 2005; Jergeby & Tengvald, 2005; Månsson, 2000, 2001, 2007; Pettersson & Johansson, 2001; Sandell, 2005; Tengvald, 2001a, 2001b; Gundersen et al., 2006).

Integral citation, also known as author-prominent, is where you include the author's name as part of your sentence. This draws attention to the author's important role in developing the information you're using. In integral citations, the name of the author appears in the sentence itself. However, in non-integral citations, the name of the author normally appears in parenthesis after the sentence, usually by using the author's last name and the year of publication. The following are

examples of integral citation:
- Smith (1983) argues that…
- Several studies show that…(Smith 1983)
- According to Smith (1983), …
- Smith's theory (1983) is that…
- An opposing viewpoint is expressed by Smith (1983) that…

In the examples above, a linguistic device known as a reporting verb or reporting phrase can be used to identify the author of the source in the text. As the term suggests, these verbs report what the source states. Depending on the effect desired, writers need to choose a suitable reporting verb. Common reporting verbs are: show, present, argue, suggest, report, address, identify, describe, analyze, note, demonstrate, criticize, compare, observe, etc.

ACADEMIC ENGLISH FOR BUSINESS

Unit 5
Outsourcing

商务学科英语

1 Search for Background Information

1.1 Search for the meanings of the following terms from texts or about the subject.

1) offshoring: _____
2) outsourcing: _____
3) economic nationalism: _____
4) Wall Street: _____
5) Jazzercise: _____
6) high-tech manufacturing: _____
7) partisan divisions: _____
8) business gurus: _____
9) labor productivity: _____
10) core competency: _____
11) know-how: _____
12) supply chain efficiencies: _____
13) host governments: _____
14) Human Genome Project: _____
15) revenues and margins: _____

Web Resources

https://marketbusinessnews.com/financial-glossary/offshoring/
https://www.thebalancesmb.com/what-is-outsourcing-2533662
https://nationaleconomicseditorial.com/2017/03/21/economic-nationalism/
https://www.investopedia.com/terms/w/wallstreet.asp
https://www.jazzercise.com/
https://www.wisegeek.com/what-is-high-tech-manufacturing.htm
https://www.icpsr.umich.edu/icpsrweb/ICPSR/series/132
https://www.forbes.com/2009/10/13/influential-business-thinkers-leadership-thought-leaders-guru_slide.html#6db11b1064af
https://www.bls.gov/lpc/
https://www.thebalancesmb.com/core-competency-in-business-2948314
https://definitions.uslegal.com/k/know-how-intellectual-property-rights/

Unit 5 Outsourcing

https://www.plslogistics.com/blog/supply-chain-management-best-practices-efficiency-effectiveness/
http://www.teachmefinance.com/Scientific_Terms/Host_government.html
https://www.genome.gov/human-genome-project
https://www.businessinsider.com/revenue-vs-margin-2014-3

1.2 Present what you've found to the class orally with or without PowerPoint in three minutes.

2 Discuss the Words' Meaning

2.1 Define the following underlined words. An example is given for you.

e.g. In the State of the Union address, President Obama declaimed: "No, we will not go back to an economy weakened by out sourcing…"
address: a formal speech delivered to an audience.

1) For much of the past two decades, the stunning growth of the U.S. economy was widely hailed in academic, business, and government circles.
hail: _____

2) Yet, the imperatives of offshore facilities and employees are—and will remain—central to American companies' international competitiveness.
imperative: _____

3) A company's foreign sales can approach or exceed 50%; its non-U.S. employees can be 25% or greater of total workforce; its supply chain of third parties is vital.
approach: _____

4) Yes, everyone would agree that we have serious economic policy issues at home…about reconciling the cost of any governmental initiatives with significant debt reduction.
reconcile: _____

5) However, …, these issues will stay in flux—and will be distorted or obfuscated as the campaigns jockey for position—until after the election.
obfuscate: _____

6) American companies will, …, continue to participate in this transformative era of global economic change by increasing activities and hiring workers outside the U.S., …
   transformative: _____

7) Yet, politicians oppose—or at least do not defend, and certainly do not fairly explain—this most fundamental international dimension of global business reality.
   dimension: _____

8) The Republican candidates largely stand mute on offshoring because of jobless pain at home and the difficulty of explaining that trade is only one factor causing unemployment.
   mute: _____

9) It is therefore vital for global businesses, which may be subject to exacting scrutiny, to defend offshoring with clear positions and clear actions.
   exact: _____

10) So here, in brief compass, are my views on the responsible, competitive basics of offshoring and outsourcing which global companies must be prepared to embrace forcefully—and to articulate clearly in their communities, with their stakeholders and, as necessary, in the political maelstrom.
    articulate: _____

11) The need to manufacture, assemble, provide services, and do R & D in order to understand and sell in a local market, and to attract great local talent for jobs that would not ever be offered in the U.S.
    assemble: _____

12) Similarly, companies must be more forceful in explaining the uses of revenues and margins derived from offshoring or outsourcing's competitive cost structures and local appeal.
    revenue: _____

13) In a well-run, responsible company, only a tiny percentage of cash from global "profits" is used for executive compensation.
    compensation: _____

14) One of the traditional arguments against globalization is that multinationals offshore to emerging markets to avoid environmental, health, and safety regulations in the developed world.
    emerge: _____

15) In response to that criticism, international corporations have set—or should set—policies to assure decent working conditions overseas, both in their own facilities and in facilities of third party suppliers.
    facility: _____

Unit 5 Outsourcing

16) For example, multinationals might adopt a minimum age of 16 for child labor in all nations both for the welfare of child and for administrative convenience.
    minimum: _____

17) These policies must be made real by implementing systems and processes in education and training, in leadership development, in protocols for qualifying and requalifying suppliers as well as for assessing second and third tier suppliers, and by imposing real sanctions when suppliers violate standards.
    assess: _____

18) Critically, the policies and their implementation must be subject to verification for credibility.
    implementation: _____

19) It is imperative that global companies ensure quality in their offerings with overseas input—whether complying with legal requirements or following self-imposed quality standards.
    input: _____

20) A similar trend is undermining the U.S. software industry.
    undermine: _____

21) Worker Transition at Home.
    transition: _____

22) Whether due to ethical concerns, to sound policy, or to good politics, American multinational companies would be wise to use their balance sheets, when possible, to provide decent severance, job training, and outplacement services to workers displaced in the U.S.
    displace: _____

23) Such company-specific efforts can be coordinated with governmental safety net programs, including Trade Adjustment Assistance.
    adjustment: _____

24) Similarly, capabilities related to thin-film deposition processes are crucial to sophisticated optics.
    crucial: _____

25) Focus on your core competencies, off-load your low-value-added activities, and redeploy the savings to innovation, the true source of your competitive advantage.
    source: _____

26) Such resources may be embedded in a large number of companies and universities.
    resource: _____

27) The geographic character of industrial commons helps to explain why companies in certain industries tend to cluster in particular regions—a phenomenon noted by Michael Porter and other scholars.
    phenomenon: _____

28) What about the popular notion that distance and location no longer matter, or, as Thomas Friedman put it, "The world is flat"?
notion: _____

29) Detailed empirical work on knowledge flows among inventors by our HBS colleague Lee Fleming shows that proximity is crucial.
empirical: _____

30) These dynamics make it difficult for other regions that do not yet have a vibrant biotechnology commons to attract biotech companies, even with generous incentives.
incentive: _____

2.2 Fill in the following blanks with various forms of each word. An example is given for you.

No.	Base form	Variations in the word family
e.g.	phenomenon	phenomena, phenomenal, phenomenally
1)	compete	
2)	economy	
3)	history	
4)	illuminate	
5)	approach	
6)	assess	
7)	appropriate	
8)	resource	
9)	access	
10)	emerge	
11)	implement	
12)	facilitate	
13)	rationalize	
14)	transformative	
15)	empirical	

Unit 5 Outsourcing

2.3 Explain the meaning of the following roots or affixes. Add at least five similar derivatives with their Chinese definitions. An example is given for you.

No.	Roots/Affixes	Meaning	More derivatives with Chinese translation
e.g.	pharmac-	medicine	pharmacy 药店；pharmacist 药剂医师；pharmacodiagnosis 药物诊断；pharmacoangiography 药物血管造影；pharmacochemistry 药物化学
1)	-some		
2)	sym-/syn-		
3)	under-		
4)	infra-		
5)	geo		
6)	aero		
7)	bi/bio		
8)	-ward/-wars		

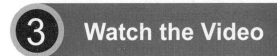

3 Watch the Video

Difficult Words and Expressions

★ currency /ˈkʌr(ə)nsɪ/ n. 货币
★ flip /flɪp/ v. 轻弹；浏览
★ hostage /ˈhɒstɪdʒ/ n. 人质；抵押品
★ level /ˈlev(ə)l/ v. 拉平；变得平坦
★ manual /ˈmænjʊ(ə)l/ adj. 手制的，手工的
★ monitor /ˈmɒnɪtə(r)/ v. 监听，搜集，记录
★ perspective /pəˈspektɪv/ n. 观点；远景
★ rod /rɒd/ n. 杆；棍棒；竿
★ shutdown /ˈʃʌtˌdaʊn/ n. 停止营业；停止运行

3.1 Watch the first part of the video and answer the following questions.

1) What is the main topic of this discussion in the TV program?
2) What exactly is offshoring?

3) What is outsourcing?
4) What are the advantages of offshoring?
5) What are the advantages of outsourcing?

3.2 Watch the second part of the video and take notes according to the questions in the left column.

No.	Questions	Notes
1)	What are the risks of outsourcing?	
2)	What are the risks of offshoring?	
3)	Who is particularly influenced by the risk of offshoring?	
4)	What is the trend in the 90s?	
5)	Why is offshoring slowing down a little bit?	

3.3 Watch the whole video again and write a short summary of it according to your answers and notes.

_____
_____
_____
_____

3.4 Work in groups and give a report to the class on "Offshoring and outsourcing" according to the following clues in five minutes.

1) What views do supporters and opponents have on offshoring and outsourcing?
2) What should be done to ensure a bright future for the United States (or China)?

Unit 5 Outsourcing

4 Read for Information

In Defense of Responsible Offshoring and Outsourcing[1]

Ben W. Heineman

❶ Let's get real—and back to basics.

❷ In an era of high unemployment, and especially in this political season of economic nationalism, both parties outdo themselves with promises to "rebuild America". Yet, the imperatives of offshore **facilities** and employees are—and will remain—central to American companies' international competitiveness. A company's foreign sales can **approach** or exceed 50%; its non-U.S. employees can be 25% or greater of total workforce; its supply chain of third parties is vital.

❸ Yes, everyone would agree that we have serious economic policy issues at home about creating jobs, stimulating growth, increasing exports, improving education, investing in R & D, encouraging high-tech manufacturing—and about **reconciling** the cost of any governmental initiatives with significant debt reduction. However, given **partisan** divisions about proper public or private roles, these issues will stay in **flux**—and will be distorted or **obfuscated** as the campaigns jockey for position—until after the election.

❹ What is not in flux is this fundamental reality: American companies will, for a wide variety of reasons relating to global dynamism, continue to participate in this **transformative** era of global economic change by increasing activities and hiring workers outside the U.S., especially in fast-growing foreign markets. (They may also, on a limited basis, move some jobs back to the U.S. for certain domestic markets due to rising costs abroad and labor productivity at home.) Yet, politicians oppose—or at least do not defend, and certainly do not fairly explain—this most fundamental international **dimension** of global business reality. In the State of the Union address, President Obama **declaimed**: "No, we will not go back to an economy weakened by outsourcing…" The Republican candidates largely stand **mute** on offshoring because of jobless pain at home and the difficulty of explaining that trade is only one factor causing unemployment. Offshoring and outsourcing today are like sex in the Victorian era: repressed or criticized in public discussion, much practiced in private behavior.

---

1 Adapted from Heineman, B. W. (2012). *In defense of responsible offshoring and outsourcing*. Retrieved from https://hbr.org/2012/02/in-defense-of-responsible-offs?autocomplete=true

❺ It is therefore vital for global businesses, which may be subject to **exacting** scrutiny, to defend offshoring with clear positions and clear actions regarding purpose, global standards, and assistance for **displaced** workers. These have always been "must do's" in the long debate about labor markets in globalization, but clarity on these issues is especially necessary this year. So here, in brief compass, are my views on the responsible, competitive basics of offshoring and outsourcing which global companies must be prepared to embrace forcefully—and to **articulate** clearly in their communities, with their stakeholders and, as necessary, in the political maelstrom.

Business purpose

❻ Companies must step up and honestly explain why they offshore business functions and employment in a broad array of product and service activities to compete in a truly global economy. Among the strong (and standard) reasons that non-business people could understand, if properly explained (and if supported by the facts), are:

- The need to stay cost-competitive with companies headquartered elsewhere, either through reduced finished product or service cost or through supply chain efficiencies;
- The need to manufacture, **assemble**, provide services, and do R & D in order to understand and sell in a local market, and to attract great local talent for jobs that would not ever be offered in the U.S.;
- The need to have a significant employment or plant or equipment presence in a local market because host governments demand it;
- Because such a presence can also pull a company's high-end exports from the U.S.;
- Because a presence can strengthen that market's economy and thus increase U.S. exports over time;
- Because any products imported back to the U.S. can benefit consumers and the economy with lower cost (although foreign operations often sell in foreign markets).

Use of revenues and margins

❼ Similarly, companies must be more forceful in explaining the uses of **revenues** and margins derived from offshoring or outsourcing's competitive cost structures and local appeal. They are key both to cash flow which finances dividends, and to "net income" that drives stock price which, in turn, benefits shareholders (heavily American)—especially older individuals who are either direct investors or who rely on pension funds. The cash from high revenues and margins is also often used to **enhance** the corporation: for improving its operations, productivity, technology, and products, or for increasing reach and scale efficiencies through acquisitions. In a well-run, responsible company, only a tiny percentage of cash from global "profits" is used for executive **compensation** (an exception being some financial service companies where a high percentage of revenue goes to compensation).

Unit 5 Outsourcing

Working conditions

❽ One of the traditional arguments against globalization is that multinationals offshore to **emerging** markets to avoid environmental, health, and safety regulations in the developed world. In response to that criticism, international corporations have set—or should set—policies to assure decent working conditions overseas, both in their own facilities and in facilities of third party suppliers.

❾ These policies cover such issues as: prohibitions on child and prison labor, wages and hours, living conditions, worker safety, **adherence** to environmental standards, non-discrimination and non-harassment. Importantly, the policies can be based either on local law or on standards beyond local law corporations voluntarily adopt. For example, multinationals might adopt a **minimum** age of 16 for child labor in all nations both for the welfare of children and for administrative convenience (child labor laws vary across nations).

❿ These policies must be made real by implementing systems and processes in education and training, in leadership development, in protocols for qualifying and requalifying suppliers as well as for **assessing** second and third tier suppliers, and by imposing real sanctions when suppliers violate standards. Critically, the policies and their **implementation** must **be subject to** verification for **credibility**—either by inside or outside **auditors**, or in public reports from independent third party auditors (such as those were established in the late 1990's under the Apparel Agreement between retailers and recently forced on Apple after working conditions in Chinese factories made the front-pages and led to global protests at Apple stores).

Quality

⓫ It is imperative that global companies ensure quality in their offerings with overseas **input**—whether complying with legal requirements or following self-**imposed** quality standards. Serious safety and quality concerns in offshored or outsourced components, ingredients, and products are now a key part of the globalization debate. Lead paint in toys, **antifreeze** in toothpaste, tainted ingredients in blood-thinner medicine, and unsafe food (for people and even pets)—these events have led consumers, parents, patients, and regulators to question whether products using global suppliers are of sufficient quality and safety to protect American end-users—and end-users elsewhere in the world—from grievous harm. Companies must proactively **address** these concerns as a matter of course.

⓬ "Deverticalization" in creation of goods and services through use of third party suppliers does not relieve the **ultimate** seller from ultimate responsibility. The seller must assure tight contracting and a vigilant oversight "system" quality for items sold in the global marketplace to avoid defects that threaten functionality or, more importantly, that risk impairing health and safety.

Worker transition at home

⓭ Whether due to ethical concerns, to sound policy, or to good politics, American multinational companies would be wise to use their balance sheets, when possible, to provide decent severance, job training, and outplacement services to workers displaced in the U.S. Such company-specific efforts can be coordinated with governmental safety net programs, including Trade **Adjustment** Assistance. Aimed specifically at training, job placement, income support, and health care for workers laid off due to international trade, this 50-year-old program was reauthorized last fall by bipartisan majorities in both the House and the Senate. Its funding is not robust; it needs to be coordinated or consolidated with other programs for displaced workers (like unemployment insurance); its effectiveness in placing workers can be improved. But it is a program—and a broader safety net concept—which multinationals should support and improve, in addition to programs for their own displaced workers, to assist those American workers adversely affected by accelerating global technology change and competition.

⑭ After the election, the American people and American companies face many difficult public policy issues on labor markets and competitiveness in the deeply interconnected national and international economies. But for now, one thing is sure: Corporations involved in international competition across the globe must practice and, when challenged, defend, responsible offshoring and outsourcing in fast-growing international markets—and it is especially important for them to do so in this election year when the issue may be distorted, misunderstood, or unpopular.

⑮ Such overseas activity is a fundamental piece of the great puzzle for the future: What is the proper mix of public policies and private actions that will allow the U.S. corporations to compete globally—against corporations benefited by "industrial policy" in other "market capitalism" countries; and against the new class of corporate powerhouses from autocratic nations practicing "state capitalism", who benefit from their governments' blatant favoritism?

(1465 words)

Notes

rebuild America: 重建美国。The U.S. Chamber of Commerce expressed on its website, "Let's rebuild America. Economic productivity and global competitiveness depend on thriving and reliable transportation infrastructure. The U.S. Chamber of Commerce, as the leading voice of America's business community, believes that strong transportation infrastructure will lower operating costs, increase profitability, mitigate logistical challenges, and provide a catalyst for investment. It's time to get America moving again." Once in a speech, President Obama said, "As we rebuild our economy, we're going to rebuild America as well."

R & D: 研发。Research and development (R & D, R+D, or R'n'D), also known in Europe as research and technological development (RTD), refers to innovative activities undertaken by corporations or governments in developing new services or products, or improving existing services or products. Research and development constitutes the first stage of development of a

Unit 5　Outsourcing

potential new service or the production process.

State of the Union address: 国情咨文。The annual State of the Union address is the keynote speech by the president to Congress in which he sets out his agenda for the next year, highlights his accomplishments to the American people, and shapes a political message. It is a requirement of the U.S. Constitution that the president "shall from time to time give to Congress information of the State of the Union, and recommend to their consideration such measures as he shall judge necessary and expedient."

net income: 净收入，收益净额。Net income represents the amount of money remaining after all operating expenses, interest, taxes, and preferred stock dividends (but not common stock dividends) have been deducted from a company's total revenue. Net income is also referred to as the bottom line, net profit or net earnings. The formula for net income is as follows: Total Revenue – Total Expenses = Net Income.

child labor: 童工。Child labor refers to any work or activity that deprives children of their childhood. In effect, these are activities that are detrimental to the physical and mental health of children and that hinder their proper development.

prison labor: 狱中劳役。Many incarcerated men and women work within jails and prisons—often for wages as low as 10 cents per hour, and in some states for no remuneration at all. The jobs typically involve providing janitorial or food preparation services that contribute to the general running of the facility, or participating in a range of production industries that allow states or companies to sell goods and merchandise for a significant profit.

Trade Adjustment Assistance (TAA): 贸易调整援助。TAA is a federal program of the United States government to act as a way to reduce the damaging impact of imports felt by certain sectors of the U.S. economy. The current structure features four components of Trade Adjustment Assistance: for workers, firms, farmers, and communities.

balance sheet: 财务状况表，也叫作资产负债表。A balance sheet reports a company's assets, liabilities, and shareholders' equity at a specific point in time, and provides a basis for computing rates of return and evaluating its capital structure. It is a financial statement that provides a snapshot of what a company owns and owes, as well as the amount invested by shareholders.

4.1 Read Text A and answer the following questions.

1) What factors are essential to the international competitiveness of American companies?
2) What are the basics of offshoring and outsourcing?
3) Which aspects of offshoring are used against globalization?
4) How do the revenues and margins of an offshoring corporation benefit American people?
5) According to this passage, what are the author's views on offshoring and outsourcing?

4.2 Read Text A again and write a summary.

Summary (about 100 words): _____
_____
_____
_____
_____

TEXT B

Restoring American Competitiveness[1]

Gary P. Pisano and Willy C. Shih

The competitiveness problem

❶ For much of the past two decades, the stunning growth of the U.S. economy was widely **hailed** in academic, business, and government circles as evidence that America's competitiveness problem was as obsolete as leg warmers and Jazzercise. The data suggest otherwise. Beginning in 2000, the country's trade balance in high technology products—historically a bastion of U.S. strength—began to decrease. By 2002, it turned negative for the first time and continued to decline through 2007.

❷ Even more worrisome, average real weekly wages have essentially remained flat since 1980, meaning that the U.S. economy has been unable to provide a rising standard of living for the majority of its people. This undoubtedly is one reason that Americans have attempted to borrow their way to prosperity, a strategy that clearly is no longer tenable.

❸ What, then, was actually happening when it seemed things were going so well? Companies operating in the U.S. were steadily outsourcing development and manufacturing work to specialists abroad and cutting their spending on basic research. In making their decisions to outsource, executives were heeding the advice **du jour** of business **gurus** and Wall Street: Focus on your core competencies, off-load your low-value-added activities, and redeploy the savings to innovation, the true **source** of your competitive advantage. But in reality, the outsourcing has not stopped with low value tasks like simple assembly or circuit-board stuffing. Sophisticated engineering and manufacturing capabilities that underpin innovation in a wide range of products have been rapidly leaving, too. As a result, the U.S. has lost or is in the process of losing the knowledge,

---

1 Adapted from Pisano, G. P., & Shih, W. C. (2009, July/August). Restoring american competitiveness. *Harvard Business Review, 87*(7–8),114–125.

Unit 5 Outsourcing

skilled people, and supplier infrastructure needed to manufacture many of the cutting-edge products it invented. Among these are such critical components as light-emitting diodes for the next generation of energy-efficient illumination; advanced displays for mobile phones and new consumer electronics products like Amazon's Kindle e-reader; the batteries that power electric and **hybrid** cars; flat-**panel** displays for TVs, computers, and handheld devices; and many of the carbon fiber components for Boeing's new 787 Dreamliner.

❹ A similar trend is **undermining** the U.S. software industry. Initially, companies outsourced only relatively mundane code-writing projects to Indian firms to lower software-development costs. Over time, as Indian companies have developed their own software-engineering capabilities, they have been able to win more complex work, like developing architectural specifications and writing sophisticated **firmware** and device drivers.

❺ Equally alarming is the U.S.'s diminished capacity to create new high-tech products. For example, nearly every U.S. brand of notebook computer, except Apple, is now designed in Asia, and the same is true for most cell phones and many other handheld electronic devices.

❻ We have heard managers **rationalize** outsourcing decisions by saying that they can always reverse course if the quality of the work isn't good enough, if the **anticipated** cost savings prove **ephemeral**, if supply-chain complexities or risks are too great, or if the work turns out to be more strategic than they originally thought. But this logic overlooks the lasting damage that outsourcing inflicts not only on a firm's own capabilities but also on those of other companies that serve its industry, including suppliers of advanced materials, tools, production equipment, and components. We call these collective capabilities the industrial commons.

The world is not flat.

❼ Centuries ago, "the commons" referred to the land where animals belonging to people in the community would graze. As the name implies, the commons did not belong to any one farmer. All were better off for having access to it. Industries also have commons. A foundation for innovation and competitiveness, a commons can include R & D know-how, advanced process development and engineering skills, and manufacturing competencies related to a specific technology.

❽ Such **resources** may be embedded in a large number of companies and universities. Software knowledge and skills, for instance, are vital to an extremely wide range of industries (machine tools, medical devices, earth-moving equipment, automobiles, aircraft, computers, consumer electronics, defense). Similarly, capabilities related to thin-film deposition processes are **crucial** to sophisticated optics; to such electronic products as semiconductors and disk drives; and to industrial tools, packaging, solar panels, and advanced displays. The knowledge, skills, and equipment related to the development and production of advanced materials are a commons for such diverse industries as aerospace, automobiles, medical devices, and consumer products. Biotechnology is a commons not just for drugs but also for agriculture and the emerging alternative fuels industry.

⑨ More often than not, a particular industrial commons will be **geographically** rooted. For instance, northern Italy is home to a design commons that feeds, and is fed by, several design-intensive businesses, including automobiles, furniture, **apparel**, and household products. The mechanical engineering commons in Germany is tightly coupled to the country's automobile and machine tool industries. The geographic character of industrial commons helps to explain why companies in certain industries tend to cluster in particular regions—a **phenomenon** noted by Michael Porter and other scholars. Being geographically close to the commons is a source of competitive advantage.

⑩ What about the popular **notion** that distance and location no longer matter, or, as Thomas Friedman put it, "The world is flat"? While we agree with the general idea that geographic boundaries to trade are falling and that the global economy is more **intertwined** than ever, the evidence suggests that when it comes to knowledge, distance does matter. Detailed **empirical** work on knowledge flows among inventors by our HBS colleague Lee Fleming shows that proximity is crucial. An engineer in Silicon Valley, for instance, is more likely to exchange ideas with other engineers in Silicon Valley than with engineers in Boston. When you think about it, this is not surprising, given that much technical knowledge, even in hard sciences, is highly tacit and therefore, far more effectively **transmitted** face-to-face. Other studies show that the main way knowledge spreads from company to company is when people switch jobs. And even in America's relatively mobile society, it turns out that the vast majority of job hopping is local.

⑪ This helps to explain why commons **persist** in specific locations in an era when huge amounts of scientific data can be accessed easily from anywhere. For example, even though virtually all the raw data from the Human Genome Project, the decade-plus effort to map the human **genome**, is available electronically all over the world; the drug research it has generated is heavily concentrated in the Boston, San Diego, and San Francisco areas.

⑫ Once an industrial commons has taken root in a region, a powerful virtuous cycle feeds its growth. Experts flock there because that's where the jobs and knowledge networks are. Firms do the same to tap the talent pool, stay **abreast** of advances, and be near suppliers and potential partners. The Swiss pharmaceutical giant Novartis, for instance, chose to move its research headquarters from Basel, Switzerland, to Cambridge, Massachusetts, to be close to universities and research institutes for global leaders in biosciences and the hundreds of biotech firms are already in the area. And its presence, in turn, has increased the Boston area's pull on yet more firms and individuals. These dynamics make it difficult for other regions that do not yet have a vibrant biotechnology commons to attract biotech companies, even with generous **incentives**.

⑬ Our research on the semiconductor, electronics, pharmaceutical, and biotech industries has found that commons are even more important to countries' and companies' prosperity than what is generally believed. That's because innovation in one business can spawn whole new industries.

Unit 5　Outsourcing

⑭ A historical example is the birth of the modern pharmaceutical industry. It began in the late 1800s in Switzerland and Germany because the earliest drugs were based on synthetic dye chemistry and the two countries were home to large chemical companies with strong research labs and deep technical expertise in **synthetic** dye production.

⑮ A current example is the solar panel industry, which is booming in Asian countries such as India, Japan, Korea, and especially China. India owes its position to Moser Baer, a leading manufacturer of optical storage media, which used its capabilities in thin-film coating and manufacturing to move into solar panels. China's, Japan's, and Korea's successes stem, at least in part, from their deep expertise in processing ultrapure **crystalline** silicon into wafers and applying thin films of silicon onto large glass sheets—capabilities developed by their semiconductor foundries and their manufacturers of flat-panel displays. (China has another advantage: It is the production base for the mundane components like power semiconductors, controllers, and housings that are needed to produce full panels.)

⑯ Although the U.S. still produces about 14% of the world's photovoltaic cells, it no longer is a significant player in crystalline silicon-based solar panels, the prevailing technology. Some U.S. manufacturers, such as Tempe, Arizona-based First Solar, are trying to become players in thin-film solar, the newest technology. But the decline of the domestic infrastructure in thin-film deposition and electronics manufacturing puts them at a big disadvantage.

(1487 words)

Notes

trade balance: 贸易差额，贸易平衡。The trade balance, also known as the balance of trade (BOT), is the calculation of a country's exports minus its imports. A country's trade balance is positive if the value of exports exceeds the value of imports. Conversely, a country's trade balance is negative, or registers a deficit, if the value of imports exceeds that of exports.

light-emitting diode: 发光二极管（体）。A light-emitting diode (LED) is a two-lead semiconductor light source. It is a p–n junction diode that emits light when activated.

Kindle e-reader: 电子书阅读器。The Amazon Kindle is a series of e-readers designed and marketed by Amazon. Amazon Kindle devices enable users to browse, buy, download, and read e-books, newspapers, magazines, and other digital media via wireless networking to the Kindle Store.

***The World Is Flat*:**《世界是平的》。*The World Is Flat* is Thomas L. Friedman's account of the great changes taking place in our time, as lightning-swift advances in technology and communications put people all over the globe in touch as never before—creating an explosion of wealth in India and China, and challenging the rest of the world to run even faster just to stay in place.

4.3 Read Text B. Write a summary in the following form and take notes according to the table below.

Subject: _____
Key words: _____
Organization types: _____
Thesis statement (or main ideas): _____
_____
_____

Conclusion (or major findings): _____
_____
_____

No.	Paragraph(s)	Structure	Content
1)		Problems	
2)		Problem in general	
3)		Supporting evidence	
4)		Solutions	
5)		Solution 1	
6)		Solution 2	
7)		Closing statement	

4.4 Read Text B again and answer the following questions.

1) How does Text B differ from Text A in its attitude towards offshoring and outsourcing?
2) How does Text B differ from Text A in its description of the phenomenon against offshoring?
3) How does Text B differ from Text A in its discussion of employment?
4) What aspect of outsourcing does Text A mention which Text B fails to take into account?
5) What's your view on outsourcing based on the comparison of two texts?

UNIT PROJECT

Read Text B and Text A again, form two groups, and hold a debate on the topic "Offshoring and outsourcing". Give evidence to support your arguments and refute your opponents'.

Unit 5 Outsourcing

5 Practice for Enhancement

5.1 Read the four words in each group and cross the word which is not a synonym for the bold word. An example is given for you.

e.g. **ephemeral**

    × perpetual   ☐ momentary   ☐ transient   ☐ fleeting

1) **restore**

    ☐ recover   ☐ regain   ☐ recollect   ☐ bring back

2) **approach**

    ☐ method   ☐ manner   ☐ mode   ☐ walk

3) **stipulate**

    ☐ specify   ☐ claim   ☐ state   ☐ require

4) **reconcile**

    ☐ cease   ☐ resolve   ☐ settle   ☐ adjust

5) **embrace**

    ☐ accept   ☐ receive   ☐ reject   ☐ welcome

6) **talent**

    ☐ intelligence   ☐ aptitude   ☐ gift   ☐ ability

7) **verification**

    ☐ validation   ☐ proof   ☐ confirmation   ☐ extraordinary

8) **specify**

    ☐ state   ☐ speak   ☐ stipulate   ☐ designate

9) **deposition**

    ☐ removal   ☐ dismissal   ☐ reception   ☐ ousting

5.2 Match the word in the box with the words in each column that regularly go together. An example is given for you.

brand, information, high, circles, business, margin, trade, product, finance, investment			
e.g. margin	1) _____	2) _____	3) _____
low-	-tech	-name	-endorsement
small-	-risk	-loyalty	-launch
profit-	-pressure	-awareness	-range
safety-	-end	-image	-placement

4) _____	5) _____	6) _____	7) _____
academic-	real-	-policy	-cards
business-	speculative-	-style	-plan
government-	net-	-accounting	-insider
political-	fix-interest-	-science	-analyst
8) _____	9) _____		
-talks	-age		
-war	-flow		
-union	-technology		
-fair	-desk		

5.3 Paraphrase the following sentences. An example is given for you.

e.g. Critically, the policies and their implementation must be subject to verification for credibility—either by inside or outside auditors, or in public reports from independent third party auditors.

<u>The key point is that the credibility as to their policies and their subsequent implementation must be verified, either by inside or outside auditors, or by independent third party auditors by way of public reports.</u>

1) It is therefore vital for global businesses, which may be subject to exacting scrutiny, to defend offshoring with clear positions and clear actions regarding purpose, global standards, and assistance for displaced workers.

   _____

   _____

2) Companies must step up and honestly explain why they offshore business functions and employment in a broad array of product and service activities to compete in a truly global economy.

   _____

   _____

3) In response to that criticism, international corporations have set—or should set—policies to assure decent working conditions overseas, both in their own facilities and in facilities of third party suppliers.

   _____

   _____

4) Aimed specifically at training, job placement, income support, and health care for workers

laid off due to international trade, this 50-year-old program was reauthorized last fall by bipartisan majorities in both the House and the Senate.

5) Beginning in 2000, the country's trade balance in high technology products—historically a bastion of the U.S. strength—began to decrease. By 2002, it turned negative for the first time and continued to decline through 2007.

6) This undoubtedly is one reason that Americans have attempted to borrow their way to prosperity, a strategy that clearly is no longer tenable.

7) Experts flock there because that's where the jobs and knowledge networks are. Firms do the same to tap the talent pool, stay abreast of advances, and be near suppliers and potential partners.

8) China's, Japan's, and Korea's successes stem, at least in part, from their deep expertise in processing ultrapure crystalline silicon into wafers and applying thin films of silicon onto large glass sheets—capabilities developed by their semiconductor foundries and their manufacturers of flat-panel displays.

5.4 Translate the following sentences into Chinese.

1) However, given partisan divisions about proper public or private roles, these issues will stay in flux—and will be distorted or obfuscated as the campaigns jockey for position—until after the election.

2) They are key both to cash flow which finances dividends, and to "net income" that drives

stock price which, in turn, benefits shareholders (heavily American)—especially older individuals who are either direct investors or who rely on pension funds.

_____
_____

3) These policies must be made real by implementing systems and processes in education and training, in leadership development, in protocols for qualifying and requalifying suppliers as well as for assessing second and third tier suppliers, and by imposing real sanctions when suppliers violate standards.

_____
_____

4) While we agree with the general idea that geographic boundaries to trade are falling and that the global economy is more intertwined than ever, the evidence suggests that when it comes to knowledge, distance does matter.

_____
_____

5) China has another advantage: It is the production base for the mundane components like power semiconductors, controllers, and housings that are needed to produce full panels.

_____
_____

6) It began in the late 1800s in Switzerland and Germany because the earliest drugs were based on synthetic dye chemistry and the two countries were home to large chemical companies with strong research labs and deep technical expertise in synthetic dye production.

_____
_____
_____

6 Movie Exploration: *Too Big to Fail* (2011)

Cast

Directed by: Curtis Hanson
Starring: William Hurt as Henry Paulson

Unit 5 Outsourcing

Paul Giamatti as Ben Bernanke
James Woods as Dick Fuld
Peter Hermann as Christopher Cox

Plot

- News reports are all over the TV about the mortgage industry crisis and the forced sale of the troubled giant companies, such as Bear Stearns and JP Morgan.
- Dick Fuld, CEO of Lehman Brothers, is seeking any help to prevent the company from falling down.
- The U.S. Treasury Secretary Henry Paulson gathers the CEOs of major banks to find a private market solution to support the Lehman sale to Bank of America.
- Paulson instructs SEC Chairman Christopher Cox to direct the Lehman board to declare bankruptcy before the market opens.
- Paulson receives phone calls from key persons who criticize him for the turmoil Lehman's bankruptcy has caused.
- Ben Bernanke and Paulson lobby Congress to pass TARP, but fail.
- Paulson succeeds in making the participating banks receive mandatory capital injections.

6.1 Search for the meanings of the following terms from the movie.

1) **Federal Reserve System:** _____
2) **regulatory agency:** _____
3) **Glass-Steagall Act:** _____
4) **Warren Buffett:** _____
5) **Treasury Secretary:** _____
6) **401(k):** _____
7) **toxic asset:** _____
8) **capital injection:** _____

Web Resources

https://en.wikipedia.org/wiki/Federal_Reserve_System
https://en.wikipedia.org/wiki/Regulatory_agency
https://www.investopedia.com/articles/03/071603.asp
https://www.forbes.com/profile/warren-buffett/

> https://en.wikipedia.org/wiki/United_States_Secretary_of_the_Treasury
> https://en.wikipedia.org/wiki/401(k)
> https://en.wikipedia.org/wiki/Toxic_asset
> http://www.investinganswers.com/financial-dictionary/businesses-corporations/capital-injection-5747

6.2 While watching, listen to how Bernanke and Paulson lobby Congress to pass TARP and complete it by filling in the blanks.

> In this part, Paulson (P for Paulson) and Bernanke (B for Bernanke) lobby Congress (C for congressmen) to pass TARP.

C: Troubled Asset Relief Program?

P: TARP. We are calling it.

C: This is your draft of the bill?

P: 1)_____ revision certainly.

C: Well, I've only got three pages here. Am I missing something?

P: No.

C: You're just looking for a big 2)_____ in a hurry.

C: It's all for the banks. You don't want a penny for the 3)_____ that's about to lose his house?

C: There's not a scrap of 4)_____ built into this, nor for the banks or for you for that matter. You want us to simply hand over $700 billion and trust you?

C: How is it possible you didn't see this coming?

P: If you want to 5)_____ the tape, we can do that. But right now the one thing we don't have is time. We need an announcement tonight to 6)_____. We need legislation next week.

B: I spent my entire academic career studying the Great Depression. The Depression may have started because of a 7)_____, but what hit the general economy was a 8)_____: average citizens unable to borrow money to do everything, to buy a home, start a business, stock their shelves. Credit has the ability to build a modern economy, but lack of credit has the power to destroy it, 9)_____. If we do not act boldly and immediately, we will 10)_____ the Depression of the 1930s. Only this time it will be far far worse. We don't do this now; we won't have an economy on Monday.

Unit 5　Outsourcing

6.3 After watching, cross the word or phrase that is closest in meaning to the bold one in each of the following sentences from the movie. An example is given for you.

e.g. The housing market has reached **frantic** proportions. It seems that everybody is building, buying, or selling.

　　☐ dangerous　　　　　　　✗ uncontrollable　　　　　☐ excellent

1) The Dow and the S & P both broke records, and the profits **soared** 93% at Goldman Sachs this year.

　　☐ accumulated　　　　　　☐ amounted　　　　　　　☐ increased

2) In the wake of Bear's collapse, Lehman Brothers is **scrambling** to reassure investors about the impact of the mortgage crisis.

　　☐ struggling　　　　　　　☐ stopping　　　　　　　　☐ wondering

3) He suggests us to buy up all the **vacant** houses.

　　☐ luxury　　　　　　　　　☐ inexpensive　　　　　　　☐ unoccupied

4) The amount of debt your country carries is a terrible **vulnerability**.

　　☐ disaster　　　　　　　　☐ weakness　　　　　　　　☐ lesson

5) We have two **potential** buyers, Bank of America and Barclays. Neither will take the company unless someone else finances part of the deal.

　　☐ wealthy　　　　　　　　☐ well-known　　　　　　　☐ possible

6) We understand the Barclays deal has **imploded**. We were hoping you might have some options that we haven't thought of yet.

　　☐ failed　　　　　　　　　☐ postponed　　　　　　　　☐ collapsed

7) Just minutes ago, CNN has confirmed that the Federal Reserve is negotiating to rescue insurance giant AIG, including an $85 billion temporary loan to **stave off** AIG's imminent collapse.

　　☐ delay　　　　　　　　　☐ prevent　　　　　　　　　☐ help

8) For those who supported the $700 billion Wall Street bailout, it was a **stunning** failure.

　　☐ unavoidable　　　　　　☐ huge　　　　　　　　　　☐ surprising

9) Even if Neel could **expedite** the process, the system is crumbling. The banks need money.

　　☐ accelerate　　　　　　　☐ maintain　　　　　　　　☐ handle

6.4 Work in groups and discuss the following questions.

1) What leads to the housing bubble according to the movie?
2) What does "too big to fail" mean?

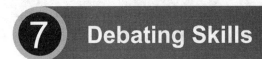

7 Debating Skills

Debate Roles[1]

The best teams are made up of debaters who understand the roles and responsibilities as well as the complexities associated with each speaker's position. With this understanding, the speakers can appreciate how the roles complement each other and thus put the team in the best position to win.

Speaker role myths

- **Myth 1:** Some speakers' positions are more important than others'.
  Truth: Each speaker's position is just as important as the other's and contributes the same number of points for the team.
- **Myth 2:** The "best" debaters should always be used in the most important positions.
  Truth: Different speakers have different attributes and they should be assigned to different positions based on how these attributes match up with each position.
- **Myth 3:** Once committed to a certain position, the speakers should never change.
  Truth: Although all speakers should specialize to a certain extent, especially during tournaments, they should not get into the mindset that they are unable to step into the other positions. This flexibility is especially useful when teammates may be unable to speak due to illness and other reasons. Many of the best speakers are often comfortable speaking in two or more positions and will switch roles even during a tournament.

First Speakers

The First Speakers in the debate are critical because they establish the definitions and the clarifications for the debate. This action creates the foundation for a good debate to build upon.

1) First Proposition

- Provides the team's definitions;
- Provides the clarifications and parameters;
- Outlines case division for Proposition;
- Delivers two or three substantive arguments in support of the motion.

First Proposition Speakers have the onus to provide a fair and comprehensive definition for the debate. They have an additional challenge to inject the necessary energy into the audience and the room in order to bring the debate to life at the beginning.

---

1 Adapted from Debateable. (unknown publication date). *Speaker roles*. Retrieved from http://debateable.org/debate-topics/speaker-roles

Unit 5 Outsourcing

First Proposition Speakers usually take advantage of the ability to open the debate by delivering the strongest argument for the Proposition's side. Unlike the other speakers, they will not have the opportunity to respond directly to the opponents' arguments. Thus, First Proposition Speakers should make the best use of opportunities, such as the giving and taking of POIs to showcase their ability to engage and rebut their opponents.

2) First Opposition
- Accepts/Challenges/Expands definition (if necessary);
- Delivers Opposition's clarifications;
- Rebuts First Proposition's substantive arguments;
- Outlines case division for Opposition;
- Delivers two or three substantive arguments opposing the motion.

The First Oppositions' position can be challenging as the speakers have the least amount of time to prepare to respond to two major components, i.e. the Proposition's definition and the First Proposition's substantive arguments. The First Opposition Speakers will have to make decisions quickly on whether the definition is to be accepted, challenged, or expanded. If the definition is to be challenged, the First Opposition Speakers will then have to explain why there is a need to challenge, provide the counter definition, and still rebut the argumentation provided by Proposition. They also have the responsibility of delivering the Opposition's strongest argument against the motion. These speakers will also be responsible for providing the first attack on the Proposition's strongest argument within the debate.

Second Speakers

The Second Speakers' position is special as it provides an ideal opportunity to evaluate the overall stance taken by the opposing team and provide critique on the general approach taken by the opponents. This evaluative process is especially useful for the Third Speakers in framing their rebuttals and for the Summary Speakers to frame their Reply speeches.

The Second Speakers are also in a good position to add new dimensions to the debate by developing their argumentation further. This allows the team to broaden the scope of the debate and demonstrate that its approach to the motion does not rest on a single line of argumentation or logic.

1) Second Proposition
- Defends definition (if challenged);
- Rebuts First Opposition's substantive arguments;
- Defends First Proposition's substantive arguments (if necessary);
- Delivers two substantive arguments in support of the motion.

2) Second Opposition
- Rechallenges definition (if already challenged);
- Rebuts Second Proposition's substantive arguments;

- Rebuts First Proposition's substantive arguments (if necessary);
- Defends First Opposition's substantive arguments (if necessary);
- Delivers two substantive arguments opposing the motion.

Third Speakers

The Third Speakers' primary role is to attack the substantive arguments raised by the opposing team. Although the Third Proposition Speakers have the option of delivering a small substantive argument, most find it more useful to devote the time allocated to rebutting their opponents' substantive arguments. Although some of these substantive points may already have been rebutted by the Second Speakers or the First Opposition Speakers, the Third Speakers can add value to the debate by developing the rebuttals further, e.g. from a different perspective or a different dimension.

The Third Opposition Speakers are not allowed to bring up new constructive arguments within a debate as the Proposition will no longer have an opportunity to rebut these points, but they can address the key examples in their opponents' cases while adding more examples in their own rebuttals. Moreover, the Third Speakers should avoid merely listing the arguments in chronological order. Rather, they should reorganize the points into two or three distinct categories and deliver them based on their order of importance.

1) Third Proposition
- Defends definition (if challenged);
- Rebuts Opposition's substantive arguments;
- Defends Proposition's substantive arguments (if necessary);
- Provides quick summary of Proposition's case;
- Has option to run a constructive argument.

2) Third Opposition
- Rechallenges definition (if challenged);
- Rebuts Proposition's substantive arguments;
- Defends Opposition's substantive arguments (if necessary);
- Provides quick summary of Opposition's case.

Reply/Summary Speakers
- Summarize the key points raised by both teams;
- Focus on the key areas of clash between the two teams;
- Analyze and evaluate why the debate was won by their team;
- May only be delivered by the First or Second Speaker from each team.

Reply Speakers should not take the view that it will be enough to merely list out the arguments and rebuttals presented in the debate. Listing out the points already delivered does not provide much value to the debate. The Reply Speakers will therefore add value to the debate in the

following two ways: first, they demonstrate their understanding of the core issues of the debate by summarizing and grouping the arguments into broad areas of clash; second, they bring the biggest value to the debate with evaluative analysis. This means that the speakers look at the debate with a critical eye and describe how the debate was won by their teams. They will have to highlight the flaws in their opponents' approach, arguments, and rebuttals while pointing out the strength of their own case and refutations. Reply Speakers should note that no new arguments or refutations may be brought up during their speeches.

In most debates, the judges will have made their decisions on which team has won by the end of the Third Opposition Speaker. However, the Reply Speeches are absolutely critical as they have some ability to influence how a judge evaluates the match and decides on the winner.

ACADEMIC ENGLISH FOR BUSINESS

Unit 6
Sharing Economy

商务学科英语

1 Search for Background Information

1.1 Search for the meanings of the following terms from texts or about the subject.

1) sharing economy: _____
2) P2P business/service: _____
3) crowd-based capitalism: _____
4) access economy: _____
5) platform economy: _____
6) collaborative consumption: _____
7) pure collaboration: _____
8) sourcing collaboration: _____
9) trading collaboration: _____
10) product-service systems: _____
11) Generation Share: _____
12) Uber: _____
13) Lyft: _____
14) Airbnb: _____
15) mobile app: _____

Web Resources

https://en.wikipedia.org/wiki/Sharing_economy

https://www.investopedia.com/terms/p/peertopeer-p2p-service.asp

http://www.gothamgazette.com/city/6965-as-cities-wrestle-with-the-sharing-economy-a-new-alliance

https://en.wikipedia.org/wiki/Access_economy

https://en.wikipedia.org/wiki/Platform_economy

https://en.wikipedia.org/wiki/Collaborative_consumption

http://www.linkedin.com/pulse/product-service-systems-sensible-fundamental-change-michel-bosman

http://www.thepeoplewhoshare.com/blog/generation-share-who-is-sharing-the-people-driving-the-sharing-economy/

https://en.wikipedia.org/wiki/Uber

https://en.wikipedia.org/wiki/Lyft

Unit 6　Sharing Economy

https://en.wikipedia.org/wiki/Airbnb
https://en.wikipedia.org/wiki/Mobile_app

1.2 Present what you've found to the class orally with or without PowerPoint in three minutes.

2　Discuss the Words' Meaning

2.1 Define the following underlined words. An example is given for you.

e.g. By the end of 1989, the group had assets of 3.5 billion dollars.
   asset: all the things that a company or a person owns.
1) Our aim is to achieve greater market penetration and succeed in selling our products.
   penetration: _____
2) The new airport will facilitate the development of tourism.
   facilitate: _____
3) Guests should feel at liberty to avail themselves of your facilities and services.
   avail: _____
4) If you are selling your property, why not call us for a free valuation without obligation?
   valuation: _____
5) The city has trebled the number of its prisoners from 7,000 to 21,000.
   treble: _____
6) Often physical appearance is indicative of how a person feels. That is how lie detector works.
   indicative: _____
7) The flexibility of distance learning would be particularly suited to busy managers.
   flexibility: _____
8) The association has seen explosive growth since 2016, doubling its membership to more than 20,000 media and entertainment professionals worldwide.
   explosive: _____
9) All candidates are required to be 18 years old with a valid citizenship and a permanent resident card.
   valid: _____

10) The past three months saw a decrease of 10% in property investment compared with the equivalent period last year.
    equivalent: _____
11) Diploma and certificate courses normally require the submission of a dissertation.
    submission: _____
12) All the items sold out are not refundable and exchangeable, expect for quality issue.
    refundable: _____
13) I want to make sure that I could buy it outright and wouldn't need to pay anymore fees later.
    outright: _____
14) There is considerable ambiguity about what this part of the agreement actually means.
    ambiguity: _____
15) A sovereign state could not be subject to another country's laws and regulations.
    subject: _____
16) The company says it is in full compliance with Chinese Labor Contract Law.
    compliance: _____
17) The huge income gap shows the great disparity of wealth between rich and poor countries.
    disparity: _____
18) Scientists believe that man diverged from the apes between five and seven million years ago.
    diverge: _____
19) The government will provide temporary accommodation for up to three thousand homeless people.
    accommodation: _____
20) Artificial intelligence has found an increasingly wide utilization in all fields.
    utilization: _____
21) Without his encouragement and help, I could not have finished the work; thus I attribute my success to him.
    attribute: _____
22) Young people are the most susceptible to celebrity advertisements and excessively consume.
    susceptible: _____
23) To judge from his productivity, Mozart clearly enjoyed robust good health throughout his twenties.
    robust: _____
24) It seemed difficult for the celebrity couple to get rid of the ubiquitous paparazzi who pursue them wherever they travel.
    ubiquitous: _____
25) These people obsess over what they perceive as a terrible defect in their physical appearance and seek plastic surgery.
    obsess: _____

26) All the people present agreed that this decision was fully justified by economic conditions.
   justify: _____
27) The official promise to compensate farmers for their loss of land has been worked out properly.
   compensate: _____
28) There is a firm belief that we need to bring prisons back under firmer control, reversing recent trends of escalating violence and spreading disorder.
   escalating: _____
29) The newspaper released the name of the victim and breached the code of conduct on privacy.
   breach: _____
30) The government will not seek to disrupt the legitimate business activities of the defendant.
   legitimate: _____

2.2 Fill in the following blanks with various forms of each word. An example is given for you.

No.	Base form	Variations in the word family
e.g.	legal	legally, illegal, illegally, legalize, legalization
1)	indicate	
2)	innovate	
3)	contract	
4)	defend	
5)	submit	
6)	complete	
7)	qualify	
8)	class	
9)	regulate	
10)	operate	
11)	able	
12)	ensure	
13)	produce	
14)	satisfy	
15)	justify	

商务学科英语

2.3 Explain the meaning of the following roots or affixes. Add at least five similar derivatives with their Chinese definitions. An example is given for you.

No.	Roots/Affixes	Meaning	More derivatives with Chinese translation
e.g.	cent	sure	certain肯定的；concert音乐会；ascertain确定；certify证明；certitude确信
1)	ab-/abs-		
2)	se-		
3)	quit		
4)	fore-		
5)	dia-		
6)	cata-		
7)	dict		
8)	equ		

3 Watch the Video

Difficult Words and Expressions

★ millennial /mɪˈlenɪəl/ *adj./n.* 千禧年的 / 千禧世代
★ baby boomer /ˈbeibi ˈbuːmə/ *n.* 婴儿潮时期出生的人
★ freelancer /ˈfriːlɑːnsər/ *n.* 自由职业者

3.1 Watch the first part of the video and answer the following questions.

1) What is the video about?
2) What changes in the city have been witnessed by the mayor?
3) What are the different places of residence favored by the three generations?
4) What examples are given to show the waste of resources in people's daily life?

Unit 6 Sharing Economy

5) What problem that is conducive to the sharing economy emerges when millennial generation moves back to the cities?

3.2 Watch the second part of the video and take notes according to the following outline.

Outline	Detailed information
Roles of computers and smartphones	As a consumer, you can _____. If you have a house to share, you can _____.
Changes	One in three workers _____. More than three out of four would rather _____ over _____. It changes how we _____, how we _____ and _____.
Things to be shared	People share not only _____ and _____, but also _____, _____, _____, and _____.
Impacts	Currently, _____ Americans earn money through the sharing economy. The sharing economy global revenues reaches _____ today and _____ by 2025.
Problems	Old industries are _____. Bad apples bring bad image to _____.

3.3 Watch the whole video again and write a short summary of it according to your answers and notes.

_____
_____
_____
_____

3.4 Work in groups and give a report to the class on "Sharing economy" according to the following clues in five minutes.

1) What impact does the sharing economy have on people's life?
2) What potential benefits and problems are brought about by the sharing economy?

4 Read for Information

TEXT A

The Current and Future State of the Sharing Economy[1]

Niam Yaraghi and Shamika Ravi

① The world has witnessed a steep rise and **penetration** of the sharing economy **facilitated** by the growing digital platform and willingness of consumers to try mobile apps that facilitate peer-to-peer business models, shared **entrepreneurial** enterprises, etc. We are moving from the 20th century model where the corporation **accumulates** resources and produces goods and services toward the 21st century model where we can **avail** ourselves of certain platforms. These platforms are large companies but draw resources from a distributed crowd with digital spaces on the rise. Sharing economies allow individuals and groups to make money from **underutilized** assets. We are moving toward an economy where physical assets are shared as services.

② In order to understand the future of a sharing economy, let us consider a study from Professors Arun Sundararajan and Scott Galloway at New York University. As their study shows, in the next ten years, the increase in revenues from the traditional **rental** industry will be **modest** in comparison to the explosion in revenues in the sharing economy. The growth projections from the shared economy will be significantly higher in sectors, such as crowdfunding, online staffing, car sharing and others, than those in traditional sectors, such as equipment, cars, and DVD rentals.

③ The rapidly growing **valuation** of Uber and Airbnb, two of the leading firms in the sharing economy, is an **indicator** of the potential of this sector. Both these firms have witnessed **trebling** of their valuation in the last three years. These massive increases, however, are also **indicative** of the nascent stages of a firm's life cycle. Such increase in valuations can only be **sustained** through fundamental innovations in their businesses. Given the global nature to these firms, their future growth potential will also depend on their ability to adapt to local conditions.

⑤ There are multiple reasons for the growth of sharing economy platforms.

Flexibility

⑥ One of the unique characteristics of sharing economy platforms is the level of **flexibility** that they provide to their **contractors**. The U.S. Office of the Chief Economist focuses on this

---

1 Adapted from Yaraghi, N., & Ravi, S. (2016, December 29). The current and future state of the sharing economy. Brookings India. Retrieved from https://www.brookings.edu/research/the-current-and-future-state-of-the-sharing-economy/

Unit 6 Sharing Economy

aspect of the sharing economy platforms and defines them as "digital matching firms" that use IT and user-ratings to provide self-employed workers with flexible schedules. Currently, 2.7 million Americans work as independent contractors (i.e. 15+ hours per week) via such firms, a 4,700% increase since 2012. This massive growth is reflected in Uber's 2015 valuation at $62.5 billion, which would have put it in the top 20% of firms in the Standard and Poor's 500 **index** if it had gone public. While **explosive**, the growth should come with little surprise, given the industry's rates; across the globe, Airbnb offers rates that range from 30%–60% cheaper than traditional hotels.

Low entry barrier for workers

❼ The New York City Taxi Application requires applicants to be 19 years old with a valid social security number and a **chauffeur**-class or **equivalent** driver's license. Additional documentation requirements include a state driving record, certificate of completion for a driving course, and a medical exam. All drivers must complete a drug test, background check, training, fingerprint, and photo **submission**. There is a $252 non-**refundable** application fee.

❽ Uber and Lyft drivers must be at least 21 years old with a three-year history on driving record, a valid in-state driver's license, auto insurance, and vehicle registration. Drivers must pass a background check, and own a **qualifying** vehicle. Drivers must have a current smartphone with a data plan to use the apps, and a bank account to receive payments for rides.

A shift from valuing ownership to renting

❾ Smartphone users in the U.S. numbered 207 million in 2016, or 64% of the total population. Digital technologies now enable sharing by lowering **transaction** costs. Sharing has long been a way for communities with few resources to spread those resources among their members. Now, the sharing economy allows a community to share its resources by choice rather than out of **necessity**.

❿ In the broadest sense, the sharing economy represents a transformation of products, once bought **outright** by consumers, into services that can be accessed on demand. Wanting the service that the product offers would lead someone to rent that product for a short period of time. Until recently, the transaction costs of sharing goods for short periods of time between peers were greater than the costs of buying them outright. Peer-to-peer sharing makes the most sense for expensive, underutilized items like cars and spare rooms.

Lax regulations

⓫ Online platforms perhaps benefit from **ambiguity** about how they should be **regulated**. Internet companies that exist solely online are subject to one set of regulations, while transportation companies like taxis are subject to another. Thirty-nine states now have laws that specifically apply to transportation network companies (TNCs), such as Uber and Lyft. California, home to many sharing economy companies, was the first state to pass a TNC law in September 2014.

⓬ Critics complain that companies, such as Uber and Lyft, are skirting regulations that represent significant costs for traditional taxi companies. Dave Sutton, a spokesman for the

"Who's Driving You?" anti-ride sharing campaign, estimates that 35%–40% of **operational** costs for taxis come from regulatory **compliance**. To overcome the **disparity** in regulations, Rebecca Elliot recommends that app-based companies work with regulators to balance innovation with public interest. In addition, taxi commissions should look for ways to lower the costs of regulatory compliance to better compete with TNCs. No one will invest in taxi licenses if the costs of regulation exceed the value of the license.

Operational efficiency

⑬ Unsurprisingly, the Airbnb model diverges from trends in the hotel industry in a number of categories. On average, Airbnb **accommodations** have **occupancy** rates that are a fraction, ranging from one-half to two-thirds, of their city's average hotel occupancy. As hotels range from 70% to 85% occupancy across large cities globally, the average Airbnb accommodation will find itself book for around four to six months of the year. In the majority of these cities, however, with San Diego, Nashville, and Austin remaining notable exceptions, Airbnb accommodations tend to beat hotels in price.

⑭ When comparing the relative **efficiencies** of Ubers and taxis, the capacity **utilization** rate serves as the determining factor to measure the fraction of time a driver has a fare-paying passenger in his vehicle. Research has found that this measurement is significantly higher, both in terms of time and distance, for Uber drivers than that for taxi drivers.

⑮ This difference is most noticeable in San Francisco, where Uber drivers can expect capacity utilization rates of 54% on average, 16% higher than their taxi driving **counterparts**. This efficiency gap is **attributed** to the scale, **surge** pricing, passenger-driver matching **algorithm**, and lack of regulation that Uber benefits from. Indeed, the inability for taxi systems to **coordinate** system-wide data sharing on when and where potential passengers tend to be results in fleets 50% larger than what is needed for **sufficiency**. While the vast majority of Uber drivers are part-time, taxi drivers are mostly full-time, suggesting that taxi drivers may be more **susceptible** to **diminishing** returns on efficiency.

⑯ As the sharing economy reaches new **heights**, it will **inevitably** become a major part of the global economy. Examples of the sharing economy are not limited to Uber and Lyft. People have shown a **robust** appetite for all ranges of services provided by sharing economy in hospitality and dining, automotive and transportation, labor, delivery, short-term loans, and retail and consumer goods. In the future, this crowd-based capitalism model is expected to **penetrate** into many sectors.

(1253 words)

Notes

digital platform: 数字平台。Digital platform usually refers to a custom website at the heart of an organization's digital operations to update in order to keep up with technology advances, business needs, and user expectations.

Unit 6 Sharing Economy

shared entrepreneurial enterprises: 共有创业企业。Shared entrepreneurial enterprises are business partners who share a business and are willing to take risks in order to make a profit.

crowdfunding: 众筹。Crowdfunding is a way to raise capital through a large number of investors.

IT: 信息技术。IT is an abbreviation for "information technology". IT defines an industry that uses computers, networking, software programming, and other equipment and processes to store, process, retrieve, transmit, and protect information.

the U.S. Office of the Chief Economist (OCE): 美国农业部首席经济学家办公室。The OCE advises the Secretary of Agriculture on the economic implications of policies and programs affecting the U.S. food and fiber system and rural areas. It supports USDA's policy decision-making by analyzing the impact of proposals and coordinating a response among several USDA agencies.

the Standard and Poor's 500 index (S & P 500): 标准普尔500指数，一个由1957年起记录美国股市的一个股票指数，观察范围达美国的500家上市公司。A stock market index tracking 500 companies in various industries with a large amount of market capitalization. It is a capitalization-weighted index, meaning that stocks with higher market caps affect the average more. The companies included on the S & P 500 are decided by committee and are updated periodically. It also scales its averages to account for stock splits and other changes in the companies tracked. Next to the Dow Jones Industrial Average, it is considered one of the premier securities indices in the United States.

4.1 Read Text A and answer the following questions.

1) What facilitate the steep rise and penetration of the sharing economy?
2) What change would take place in the next ten years according to the study of Professors Arun Sundararajan and Scott Galloway at New York University?
3) What are the reasons for the growth of sharing economy platforms?
4) Who have a more rigid requirement? The New York taxi drivers? Or the Uber and Lyft drivers?
5) What makes the capacity utilization rate of Uber drivers higher than that of taxi drivers?

4.2 Read Text A again and write a summary.

Summary (about 100 words): _____

TEXT B

The Dark Side of Uber: Why the Sharing Economy Needs Tougher Rules[1]

Greg Jericho

① A report **released** last week by the Grattan Institute on services like Uber and Airbnb finds that such peer-to-peer services can provide large benefits to the economy, but that governments need to **ensure** that both consumers and providers are protected. Hoping the services will just go away is not an option governments can afford to take.

② It's amazing how quickly peer-to-peer services have become part of our lives. The phrase "It's Uber, but for…" has become so **ubiquitous** that it has almost reached a dad-joke level of humor. We're now not so much worrying about whether to use Uber or not, but instead **obsessing** over our Uber rating.

③ But with this "new" economy comes challenges—will it improve **productivity** at the expense of safety and wages? How should governments react, given the biggest resistance from established players, such as the taxi companies and owners?

④ The Grattan Institute's latest report, "Peer-to-Peer Pressure: Policy for the Sharing Economy", examines the policy issues involved. The report notes that there certainly are clear economic benefits from the sharing economy. The report estimates Uber can cut more than $500 million from Australian taxi bills—close to 10% of the $5.5 billion spent each year by Australians catching a taxi.

⑤ The report's author Jim Minifie argues that other sharing platforms are "boosting employment and incomes for those on the **fringe** of the labor market, and putting thousands of underused homes and other assets to work". This point is one that certainly has **import** in light of continued concerns about productivity. A person's spare room or granny flat that is unused is essentially an economic asset going to waste—renting it out via Airbnb puts that asset to work.

⑥ But a major concern for those who compete with these new sharing operators—especially the 68,000 taxi drivers around the nation—is that the playing field is not **level**. Taxi regulations and license fees force taxi fares to be higher than Uber's, and certainly the evidence in the Grattan Institute report backs this up. A short trip from Canberra Civic to Parliament House costs more in a taxi, even when including a 1.5x Uber surge charge.

---

1 Adapted from Jericho, G. (2016, April 18). *The dark side of uber: Why the sharing economy needs tougher rules*. Retrieved from https://www.theguardian.com/business/grogonomics/2016/apr/18/uber-airbnb-sharing-economy-tougher-rules-australia

Unit 6   Sharing Economy

❼ Amid all the issues regarding unfair competition, the reality is that many taxi drivers provide good service in a dangerous occupation—the report suggests driving a taxi is possibly 15 times as dangerous as the average job (in 2013–14 in Victoria for example, there were 51 assaults in taxis).

❽ But there has also long been a very real sense of customer **dissatisfaction** with the service. When a survey in Western Australia finds that "only 41% of women feel safe catching a taxi alone at night", you know the industry has an image problem—**justified** or not.

❾ Uber, however, gives customers some power. Customers can estimate fares and car arrival times, view the approach of a driver, monitor actual versus advised routes, **streamline** payments, and review each trip's route, time, driver, and fare.

❿ But the ability to rate someone on an app is the very lightest form of consumer protection, and the report argues that while some taxi regulations should be reduced, mostly these relate to licensing and pricing. Instead, it argues that not only should the safety regulations remain in place, Uber drivers should also be required to meet certain standards—such as passing a criminal history and driving history check, a need to have zero blood-alcohol **concentration**, and for their cars to **undergo** an initial roadworthy inspection and appropriate follow-up **inspections**.

⓫ The introduction of Uber certainly does lead to a drop in taxi drivers' income and the value of taxi licenses. The report notes that even in states where Uber is not legal, the value of taxi licenses has fallen. But the report argues that while the new entrant will reduce taxi drivers' and license owners' income, they should not for the most part be compensated—instead, only those suffering economic hardship should be assisted.

⓬ Similarly, the Grattan Institute recommends only light regulation of accommodation services like Airbnb. The service, which has grown exponentially in recent years, allows people to rent out rooms in their own house or other properties for short-term periods.

⓭ The Grattan Institute report finds that a majority of Airbnb activity is not in people's primary residence—thus investment properties that would have been used for long-term renters are now being used as **de facto** serviced apartments.

⓮ Two concerns which arise from this are that it may increase rents in these areas due to a shortage and that short-term stayers are more likely to cause disruption to neighbors.

⓯ The report suggests that the impact of Airbnb on rents would at worst be very localized—inner city and more touristy suburbs—and that mostly it would be minimal, given Airbnb residents only account for about 2% of Sydney's current rental capacity.

⓰ However, concerns about the disruption to neighbors appear to be well founded—especially within apartment complexes. Within the Melbourne CBD and inner-city, short-term residents are more than three times more likely to be subject to complaints about behavior than long-term ones.

⓱ Unfortunately, in many states—such as New South Wales—the legal **remedies** to neighborhood disruptions are more **geared** for complaints against long-term residents. One better example perhaps is that of Queensland where "party house" legislation enables local governments to require some or all "party house" owners to obtain permits, which can include conditions, such as occupancy limits and noise controls.

⑱ Certainly, it is clear that both state and local governments need to adapt to the Airbnb growth by ensuring the ability to "quickly identify the property that is the subject of a complaint, to contact the operator, and to impose **escalating** penalties, up to bans, on landlords if they **breach** conditions repeatedly".

⑲ While the peer-to-peer economy may bring with its improved competition, lower prices, and better services for consumers, there is some concern that it will reduce wages. This was an issue noted by the shadow assistant treasurer, Andrew Leigh, last year when he released the ALP's sharing economy policy.

⑳ But the Grattan Institute's report would suggest this concern can be **overstated**. The report notes that for the most part peer-to-peer services are in areas that already mostly involve independent contractors, such as household repair and construction, household services and **errands**, writing, website design, IT services, and data entry.

㉑ The report notes that "few large platform workforces in manufacturing, retail and wholesale trade, healthcare, or financial services". The report does, however, see the possibility for such apps to be abused and recommends "**sham** contracting provisions in the Fair Work Act, to deter **misclassification** of legitimate employees as independent contractors".

㉒ The sharing economy is here to stay. For governments to ignore it and hope services like Uber will just go away would be like media organizations pretending that social media is just a passing **fad**.

㉓ There are clear economic benefits from this new economy, but also issues for consumers and providers of these new services—the Grattan Institute's report provides some good recommendations for governments to follow.

(1169 words)

Notes

Grattan Institute: 格拉坦研究所，澳大利亚的公共政策智库。Established in 2008, the Melbourne-based institute defines itself as contributing "to public policy in Australia as a liberal democracy in a globalized economy". It is partly funded by a $34 million endowment, with major contributions from the Australian Federal Government, the State Government of Victoria, the University of Melbourne, and BHP Billiton. It currently focuses on seven key policy areas: budget policy, transport, energy, health, school education, higher education, and productivity. These programs were chosen with the belief that research into these areas, in line with principles of evidence-based policy, could make a demonstrable difference to Australia's public policy.

dad-joke:（俚语）毫无幽默感、让人尴尬的笑话。Dad-joke (slang) is a lame, embarrassing or

unfunny joke.

Western Australia (WA): 西澳大利亚州，澳大利亚最大的州。Western Australia is the largest state in Australia. The state covers an area of about 976,790 square miles, and occupies a large part of the western part of the country.

de facto:（拉丁）事实上的，实际上的。De facto is used to indicate that something is a particular thing, even though it was not planned or intended to be that thing.

Melbourne CBD: 墨尔本中央商务区。Melbourne Central Business District refers to the Melbourne City Centre, a locality surrounded by metropolitan Melbourne in Victoria, Australia which comprises the original settlement, the central business district, parkland, and other built-up areas. It is the most heavily developed area of Melbourne and represents the financial center of Melbourne, with a vast majority of corporate headquarters. Located within the locality, it has played host to a number of significant international and national events, including 1956 Summer Olympics, Commonwealth Heads of Government Meeting in 1981, World Economic Forum in 2000, 2006 Commonwealth Games, and G20 Summit in the same year.

ALP: 澳大利亚劳动党。Australian Labor Party, one of the major Australian political parties, a centre-left party, is committed to protecting and promoting the rights of workers and the socially disadvantaged. The ALP believes that the government must play a vital role in ensuring the public welfare, and it has strongly supported gender and racial equality and Aboriginal rights.

Fair Work Act: 澳大利亚公平工作法案。The Fair Work Act 2009 is the primary piece of legislation governing Australia's workplaces where rules and obligations for employees and employers are outlined. It is the foundation to all standards and regulations for employment in Australia.

4.3 Read Text B. Write a summary in the following form and take notes according to the table below.

Subject: _____

Key words: _____

Organization types: _____

Thesis statement (or main ideas): _____

_____

_____

Conclusion (or major findings): _____

_____

_____

Paragraphs	Structure		Content
	The phenomenon:		The attitude of the report:
	Concerns in ride service		
	Concerns in acco-mmodation service		
	Wage concerns		
	Author's voice	On the sharing economy:	
		On the report:	

4.4 Read Text B again and answer the following questions.

1) According to clues given in their titles, how does Text B differ from Text A in its attitude towards sharing economy?
2) How does Text B differ from Text A in its description of the benefits of sharing economy?
3) How does Text B differ from Text A in its discussion of low entry barriers of Uber drivers?
4) What problems of the accommodation service Airbnb does Text B mention which Text A fails to take into account?
5) What's your view on the future of the sharing economy based on the comparison of two texts?

UNIT PROJECT

Read Text B and Text A again, form two groups, and hold a debate on the topic "The benefits of sharing economy outweighs its risks". Give evidence to support your arguments and refute your opponents'.

5 Practice for Enhancement

5.1 Read the four words in each group and cross the word which is not a synonym for the bold word. An example is given for you.

e.g. **indicate**

  × approve   ☐ suggest   ☐ signify   ☐ express

1) **diminish**

  ☐ decrease   ☐ lessen   ☐ reduce   ☐ delete

2) **robust**

  ☐ strong   ☐ sound   ☐ vigorous   ☐ elegant

3) **utilize**

  ☐ use   ☐ employ   ☐ export   ☐ apply

4) **disparity**

  ☐ difference   ☐ solidarity   ☐ discrepancy   ☐ disagreement

5) **outright**

  ☐ downright   ☐ thoroughly   ☐ completely   ☐ properly

6) **barrier**

  ☐ dilemma   ☐ obstruction   ☐ obstacle   ☐ barricade

7) **ubiquitous**

  ☐ everywhere   ☐ omnipresent   ☐ universal   ☐ extraordinary

8) **react**

  ☐ respond   ☐ reply   ☐ answer   ☐ resist

9) **notable**

  ☐ respectable   ☐ famous   ☐ renowned   ☐ celebrated

5.2 Match the word in the box with the words in each column that regularly go together. An example is given for you.

transaction, economy, revenue, valid, balance, inevitable, massive, breach, sustain, regulation

e.g. transaction	1) _____	2) _____	3) _____
honest-	annual-	self-	-consequence
cigarette-	deferred-	safety-	-choice
start-	-collection	government-	-risk
business-	unearned-	-infringement	-accident

4) _____	5) _____	6) _____	7) _____
-coal	-system	-of the peace	-life
-fraud	industrialized-	-of copyright	-economic growth
-scale	market-	-of protocol	-social conscience
-change	to bolster its-	-of contract	-a loss

8) _____	9) _____
keep-	-argument
-the two needs	-idea
-supply and demand	-point
ecological-	-ticket

5.3 Paraphrase the following sentences. An example is given for you.

e.g. Governments need to ensure that both consumers and providers are protected.
<u>The interest of both consumers and providers shall be protected by the authorities.</u>

1) Both these firms have witnessed trebling of their valuation in the last three years.
_____
_____

2) Such increase in valuations can only be sustained through fundamental innovations in their businesses.
_____
_____

3) While explosive, the growth should come with little surprise, given the industry's rates.
_____
_____

4) Smartphone users in the U.S. numbered 207 million in 2016, or 64% of the total population.
_____
_____

5) As hotels range from 70% to 85% occupancy across large cities globally, the average Airbnb accommodation will find itself book for around four to six months of the years.
_____
_____

6) The report notes that there certainly are clear economic benefits from the sharing economy.

7) But a major concern for those who compete with these new sharing operators—especially the 68,000 taxi drivers around the nation—is that the playing field is not level.

8) However, concerns about the disruption to neighbors appear to be well founded—especially within apartment complexes.

5.4 Translate the following sentences into Chinese.

1) The world has witnessed a steep rise and penetration of the sharing economy facilitated by the growing digital platform and willingness of consumers to try mobile apps that facilitate peer-to-peer business models, shared entrepreneurial enterprises, etc.

2) As their study shows, in the next ten years, the increase in revenues from the traditional rental industry will be modest in comparison to the explosion in revenues in the sharing economy.

3) In the broadest sense, the sharing economy represents a transformation of products, once bought outright by consumers, into services that can be accessed on demand.

4) While the vast majority of Uber drivers are part-time, taxi drivers are mostly full-time, suggesting that taxi drivers may be more susceptible to diminishing returns on efficiency.

5) The report suggests the impact of Airbnb on rents would at worst be very localized—inner city and more touristy suburbs—and that mostly it would be minimal given Airbnb residents

only account for about 2% of Sydney's current rental capacity.

6) The report does, however, see the possibility for such apps to be abused and recommends "sham contracting provisions in the Fair Work Act, to deter misclassification of legitimate employees as independent contractors".

6 Movie Exploration: *Barbarians at the Gate* (1993)

Cast

Directed by: Glenn Jordan
Starring: James Garner as F. Ross Johnson
              Jonathan Pryce as Henry Kravis
              Leilani Sarelle as Laurie Johnson

Plot

- RJR Nabisco CEO F. Ross Johnson holds a party expecting a boost of the company's stock.
- After receiving news of the likelihood of the failure of the company's new product Premier, smokeless cigarette, Johnson decides to take the tobacco and food conglomerate company private.
- Johnson meets Henry Kravis for the buyout, but turns Kravis down.
- Johnson makes the potentially enormous deal with another firm, which angers Kravis who feels betrayed.
- Kravis and Johnson are unable to reconcile their differences.
- There is a leak of information and other bidders emerge. The bidding goes to an unprecedented height.
- Johnson loses the bidding even if his bid is higher.
- Johnson receives fifty-three million dollars for settlement.

Unit 6 Sharing Economy

6.1 Search for the meanings of the following terms from the movie.

1) LBO: _____
2) junk bonds: _____
3) credit market: _____
4) cash flow: _____
5) bidding: _____
6) win-win: _____
7) FDA: _____
8) Insider Trading Sanctions Act of 1984: _____

> **Web Resources**
>
> https://en.wikipedia.org/wiki/Leveraged_buyout
> https://www.investopedia.com/terms/j/junkbond.asp
> https://www.investopedia.com/terms/c/credit_market.asp
> https://en.wikipedia.org/wiki/Cash_flow
> https://en.wikipedia.org/wiki/Bidding
> http://www.wisegeek.org/what-is-a-win-win-situation.htm
> https://en.wikipedia.org/wiki/Food_and_Drug_Administration
> https://www.investopedia.com/terms/i/insider-trading-sanctions-act-of-1984.asp

6.2 While watching, listen to the conversation between Ross Johnson and his wife and complete it by filling in the blanks.

> In this conversation, Ross Johnson (J for Johnson) explains to his wife Laurie (L for Laurie) how he sees the buyout.

(Background news) In New York, further shock waves hit the financial world as investigators revealed that junk-bond specialist Michael Milken whose earnings this year 1)_____ the $500 million mark and 26 other members of Milken's investment firm of Drexel Burnham Lambert were owners of a stake in the company owned by dethroned financial wizard Ivan Boesky. Boesky, 2)_____ insider trading was recently sentenced to 18 months in jail and fined a record $100 million.

J: You know the three rules of Wall Street? Never play by the rules, never tell the truth, and never pay in cash. They earn their money the old-fashioned way. They steal it.

L: You promise you won't think I'm stupid.

J: Of course not. Although I have been known to break my promises.

L: There's just so much about this I don't get, insider trading, junk bonds. Even this buyout thing you're talking about.

J: Sweetheart, half the people involved don't know what's going on. The buyout aren't all that hard really. Basically, all a buyout means is that management, the team that runs the company, they buy out 3)_____ and the company goes 4)_____.

L: Doesn't that take 5)_____ money?

J: That's where the Kravis types come in. They help you borrow that you need against the assets of the company and use the business as 6)_____.

L: It's just like 7)_____.

J: I hate to tell you this, baby, but you got a lot to learn about being stupid. Now the problem is you get guys like Henry as your partner…with a power tool making sure you do thing their way…Nobody gets that rich letting anyone 8)_____ with them.

L: How are you gonna handle that?

J: Nothing to handle. There's no way I'd 9)_____ Henry Kravis. If we ever made a deal he'd have my desk in the men's room in five seconds flat. All we have to do is just 10)_____ until Ed gets the test results on Premiers. You just watch those babies are gonna turn the whole company around.

6.3 After watching, cross the word or phrase that is closest in meaning to the bold one in each of the following sentences from the movie. An example is given for you.

e.g. The stock hasn't **budged**. We are still stuck in the 40s!

  ☐ stopped   ✗ changed   ☐ sold

1) My shareholders are **antsy** about the lower price of their RJR stock.

  ☐ annoyed   ☐ confident   ☐ angry

2) He can **outline** the whole deal probably when you are down in Palm Beach in 15 minutes.

  ☐ complete   ☐ brief   ☐ bargain

3) We'll throwing numbers at the board that no one else can. We're **knocking out** all conceivable competition.

  ☐ pleasing   ☐ challenging   ☐ eliminating

4) At that price, how long will it be before your counters **pare down** the company expense?

  ☐ raise   ☐ cover   ☐ decrease

5) You just **floored** us with the RJR thing. Are you aware that we gave that idea to Johnson in the first place?

  ☐ humiliated   ☐ defeated   ☐ irritated

Unit 6　Sharing Economy

6) We must **gauge** his intention to see if he is going to stay out of it or if he can be a part of it.
   ☐ weigh   ☐ gain   ☐ ignore
7) You don't think the shares will get a big **boost** once we start selling Premiers?
   ☐ promotion   ☐ increase   ☐ failure
8) How much of the company will he own? Obviously, those figures are **confidential**.
   ☐ considerable   ☐ unexpected   ☐ secret
9) After exploring every **conceivable** option, we feel that the best possible way is through a leveraged buyout.
   ☐ imaginary   ☐ feasible   ☐ ideal

6.4 Work in groups and discuss the following questions.

1) Are the three rules of Wall Street, i.e. never play by the rules, never tell the truth, and never pay in cash, gold rules in the business world?
2) When deciding the future of the company, to what extent does a businessman care about his employees?

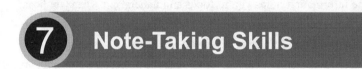

7　Note-Taking Skills

How to Take Notes While Listening[1]

Taking notes while you are listening is very different from when you are reading. When you are reading, you can easily flip the pages if you missed key information. That is not the case when you are attending lectures and speaker events. And even if you are taking a course online, it is annoying when you often have to rewind or pause.

Six good reasons to take notes

Taking effective notes in lectures and tutorials is an essential skill for university study. Good note-taking allows a permanent record of key information that you can integrate with your own writing, and use for exam revision. Taking reliable, accurate notes also reduces the risk of plagiarizing. It helps you distinguish where your ideas come from and how and what you think about those ideas. The following are good reasons for taking notes:

• Notes are a useful record of key information, and the sources of that information.

1　Adapted from University of South Wales. (unknown publication date). *Listening note taking strategies*. Retrieved from https://student.unsw.edu.au/note-taking-skills

- Notes inscribe information kinesthetically and help you remember what you heard.
- Taking notes helps you to concentrate and listen effectively.
- Selecting what to note down increases your understanding.
- Notes create a resource for exam preparation.
- Notes taken in classes often contain information that can't be found elsewhere.

Before the lecture: Be prepared

Preparation before the lecture provides the background knowledge which helps you to be an effective listener and an effective student. Here are some tips for good preparation:

- Know what the lecture will be about. Check the course outline for weekly topics.
- Do any required pre-reading.
- If lecture slides are available before class, download them.
- Review notes from previous lectures.
- Set up notebooks or documents for note-taking.
- Arrive on time and sit near the front—in order to take good notes, you need to hear and see clearly.

During the lecture: Taking notes effectively

Analyzing and questioning the information helps you to focus and understand what you hear. Don't try to write down everything being said, because it is impossible! You need to know common abbreviated words and use them to save time. Rephrase what you are hearing, which speeds up your note-taking. On an ongoing basis, work on improving your vocabulary, so you never have to think about which words to use when taking notes.

Effective listening note-taking also involves recognizing key concepts and identifying and selecting what is relevant. Listen for the overall argument and note the main points and key information. Here are tips for how to recognize what is important:

- Introductory remarks. Lectures often begin with a useful overview of the key ideas or themes of a particular topic. This helps you grasp the "big picture".
- Verbal signposts. These signposts indicate something important is about to be said. Lecturers often signal key information with phrases like: "There are four main aspects", "This is important…", or "To sum up".
- Repetition. Important points will often be repeated, especially in introductions and conclusions.
- Phonological cues. Cues, such as voice emphasis, change in volume, speed, and emphasis, often indicate important information.
- Non-verbal cues. Facial expressions, hand and body signals often indicate something important is being said.
- Final remarks. Most lectures conclude with a summary, a restatement of the main ideas and an

Unit 6 Sharing Economy

indication of how the topic connects with upcoming materials.

After the lecture: Review and reengage actively

Review your notes while the lecture is fresh in your mind. Reviewing helps you remember what was said, builds up your understanding, and helps identify gaps in your knowledge. Here are tips for reviewing actively:

- Read through your notes. Make sure they are clear and legible. Clean them up—fix spelling errors, expand on abbreviations, tidy up handwriting (if necessary).
- Fill in missing words or information and add anything extra that you may have thought of since the lecture.
- Code your notes—use color and symbols to mark structure and emphasis, highlight major sections, main points, and diagrams. Use different colors to emphasize main points, classify different topics, and link concepts or information.
- Explain and clarify diagrams by writing a simple version of their meanings.
- Identify anything that needs further clarification.

The following are tips for re-engaging with notes:

- Try "chunking" similar pieces of information into categories that you can remember more easily.
- Transcribe key concepts in your own words.
- Add your own questions to the notes to help you recall the key ideas.
- Write a brief overall summary of the notes.
- Reflect on the learning process itself—what do you find confusing? How do you solve problems or clarify your understanding?

ACADEMIC ENGLISH FOR BUSINESS

Unit 7
Corporate Social Responsibility

商务学科英语

1 Search for Background Information

1.1 Search for the meanings of the following terms from texts or about the subject.

1) sustainable business: _____
2) externality: _____
3) monopoly: _____
4) business case: _____
5) minimum wage: _____
6) hedge fund: _____
7) carried interest: _____
8) tax inversion: _____
9) overdraft protection: _____
10) cash hoard: _____
11) stock buyback: _____
12) mutual funds: _____
13) TARP: _____
14) CSV: _____
15) competitive advantage: _____

Web Resources

https://www.sustainabilitydegrees.com/what-is-sustainability/sustainable-business/
http://lexicon.ft.com/Term?term=business-sustainability
https://financial-dictionary.thefreedictionary.com/Externality
https://www.investopedia.com/terms/m/monopoly.asp
https://en.wikipedia.org/wiki/Business_case
https://en.wikipedia.org/wiki/Minimum_wage
https://www.investopedia.com/terms/h/hedgefund.asp
https://tax.findlaw.com/federal-taxes/what-is-carried-interest-.html
https://en.wikipedia.org/wiki/Tax_inversion
https://www.thebalance.com/what-does-overdraft-protection-mean-for-your-credit-960738
https://www.investopedia.com/terms/c/cash-hoard.asp
https://www.investopedia.com/ask/answers/042015/why-would-company-buyback-its-own-shares.asp

Unit 7　Corporate Social Responsibility

https://www.investor.gov/investing-basics/investment-products/mutual-funds
https://www.thebalance.com/tarp-bailout-program-3305895
https://en.m.wikipedia.org/wiki/Creating_shared_value
https://www.thebalance.com/what-is-competitive-advantage-3-strategies-that-work-3305828

1.2 Present what you've found to the class orally with or without PowerPoint in three minutes.

2　Discuss the Words' Meaning

2.1 Define the following underlined words. An example is given for you.

e.g. Their diseases were then passed on to domestic cattle with catastrophic effect.
   catastrophic: causing a lot of destruction, suffering, or death.
1) It is therefore in many ways more akin to an art rather than a science.
   akin: _____
2) And more public schools incorporate hands-on learning that educators say can help children better absorb some concepts.
   incorporate: _____
3) Welfare benefits and the public sector payroll are far beyond the ability of the economy to sustain.
   payroll: _____
4) It would also help ministers to ensure that resource allocation was aligned to policy goals.
   align: _____
5) The school gives incentives such as more play time to kids who work hard.
   incentive: _____
6) The data management system tracks the complete record of every transaction with a customer from the point that his name is entered in its order books..
   transaction: _____
7) I mean, I've heard a story, though I wasn't sure how apocryphal it was.
   apocryphal: _____

8) The company was slow to restructure, and its problems could carry over into another substantial profit decline.
   substantial: _____
9) Yet teacher shortages are acute, turnover is high and morale is low.
   turnover: _____
10) The entrance tests for people wishing to enter the diplomatic service are particularly rigorous.
    rigorous: _____
11) To reduce traffic accident, there should be improved driver training and stricter enforcement of road traffic law.
    enforcement: _____
12) The prison system does not work because many of the younger offenders are being corrupted by older, long-term prisoners.
    corrupt: _____
13) The financial community is expected to continue lobbying Congress to introduce new legislation.
    lobby: _____
14) The studies demonstrate a clear link between smoking and heart disease.
    demonstrate: _____
15) It is not to be inferred that all scientists are antagonistic to religion.
    antagonistic: _____
16) Once plugged into western markets, poor countries are better able to compete squarely with the rest of the world.
    squarely: _____
17) The company's refusal to hire him was a blatant act of discrimination.
    blatant: _____
18) Today an estimated 150,000 people are stung each year but less than 1% of these attacks prove fatal.
    fatal: _____
19) The merger proposal calls for the three companies to be combined into a new entity.
    merger: _____
20) Shareholders of a corporation are legally separate from the corporation itself.
    shareholder: _____
21) The training promises to provide empirical evidence of incremental improvements in staff effectiveness.
    incremental: _____
22) In Japan in the 1990s, a financial collapse led to economic stagnation.
    stagnation: _____

Unit 7 Corporate Social Responsibility

23) The unequal treatment of men and women in the labor market is deeply <u>entrenched</u> in our culture.
    entrenched: _____
24) The pictures are similar, but there are <u>subtle</u> differences between them.
    subtle: _____
25) Staff saw costs <u>escalating</u> and sales slumping as the effect of the recession hit the company.
    escalate: _____
26) Many hoped he would renew the country's <u>atrophied</u> political system.
    atrophy: _____
27) A recession could mean huge losses at state-run factories, requiring a <u>bailout</u> from the state of billions of dollars.
    bailout: _____
28) <u>Fluctuations</u> in profits resulted from differences between the volume of sales and the volume of production.
    fluctuation: _____
29) The crackdown and arrests by the government are getting worse and are going to prompt a <u>rebellion</u> against the government.
    rebellion: _____
30) To the extent that religions provide their <u>adherents</u> with a common set of norms and values, they are an important source of social solidarity.
    adherent: _____

2.2 Fill in the following blanks with various forms of each word. An example is given for you.

No.	Base form	Variations in the word family
e.g.	integrate	integrative, integration, integrable, integrability, integrated
1)	perceive	
2)	sustain	
3)	include	
4)	accelerate	
5)	substance	
6)	corrupt	
7)	polarize	

No.	Base form	Variations in the word family
8)	emit	
9)	invert	
10)	cumulate	
11)	enforce	
12)	rebel	
13)	social	
14)	recede	
15)	adhere	

2.3 Explain the meaning of the following roots or affixes. Add at least five similar derivatives with their Chinese definitions. An example is given for you.

No.	Roots/Affixes	Meaning	More derivatives with Chinese translation
e.g.	corpor/corp	body	corporal身体的；corporate公司的；corporation公司；incorporate包含；corpse尸体
1)	mono-		
2)	ant-/anti-		
3)	eco-		
4)	intra-		
5)	tract		
6)	quart-		
7)	spect		
8)	vid/vis		

Unit 7　Corporate Social Responsibility

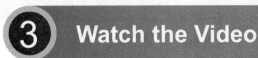

3　Watch the Video

Difficult Words and Expressions

★ unscrupulously /ʌnˈskruːpjələslɪ/ adv. 无道德原则地；不客气地
★ compliance /kəmˈplaɪəns/ n. 合规
★ societal /səˈsaɪətəl/ adj. 社会的
★ ecological /ˌiːkəˈlɒdʒɪkl/ adj. 生态（学）的
★ materiality /məˌtɪərɪˈælɪtɪ/ n. 物质性；重要性

★ matrix /ˈmeɪtrɪks/ n. 矩阵
★ orientation /ˌɔːrɪənˈteɪʃn/ n. 取向；方向，目标
★ integration /ˌɪntɪˈɡreɪʃn/ n. 结合；整合
★ procurement /prəˈkjʊəmənt/ n. 采购
★ facilitation /fəˌsɪlɪˈteɪʃn/ n. 简易化

3.1　Watch the first part of the video and answer the following questions.

1) Could you cite two examples of the dark side of our economic activity mentioned at the beginning of the video?
2) What is the seemingly obvious approach of CSR?
3) What is risk management aimed at?
4) What is a code of conduct often called? Could you give an example?
5) What is CSR mainly about according to the video?

3.2　Watch the second part of the video and take notes according to the following outline.

	Four steps that help companies implement CSR
Step 1	"A good company _____" • It includes the _____ of their business activity, the _____ the company want to accomplish through its business, the activities that is _____ under any circumstances. • Examples: 1) It's not about cars, but about _____. 2) An insurance company does not sell insurance policies, but _____.

(Continued)

	Four steps that help companies implement CSR
Step 2	"The identification of _____ and _____ issues and exchange with the stakeholders of the company" • To systemize this, companies often use _____, which structures the relevant aspects in a single matrix from the point of view of both the stakeholders and the company. • CSR is not a blueprint but rather _____ in different sectors and companies.
Step 3	"The _____ towards general standards such as UN global compact, or the ISO26000" • The Global Compact contains ten principles concerned with human rights, _____, _____, environmental protection. and _____. • The ISO26000 distinguishes seven ranges of topics including human rights, labor practices, environmental protection, _____, consumer concerns and the integration of companies into society, and also _____ which addresses the systematic and strategic dimension of responsibility.
Step 4	"The concrete _____ at all levels of activity and in all departments of a company" • It includes procurement, production, _____, human resources, marketing, sales and distributions, advertisement and so on. • Examples: 1) In procurement the _____ turned into a criterion for the choice of suppliers. 2) In the area of sales and distribution, there are _____ for fair consulting services, and absolutely "no go" approaches for _____.

3.3 Watch the whole video again and write a short summary of it according to your answers and notes.

_____
_____
_____
_____

3.4 Work in groups and give a report to the class on "How companies implement corporate social responsibility" in five minutes.

Unit 7 Corporate Social Responsibility

4 Read for Information

More and More CEOs Are Taking Their Social Responsibility Seriously[1]

Rebecca M. Henderson

❶ JANA Partners, the activist hedge fund, isn't known as a tree-hugging hippie sort of firm. Yet, last month it joined with the California State Teachers' Retirement System to send a letter to Apple's board warning about the effects of the company's devices on children. The same month, BlackRock CEO Larry Fink sent a letter telling companies that his firm would consider social responsibility when making investments. And Mark Zuckerberg told investors that Facebook would be making changes to its platform that would help users in the long-term, even though, he warned, in the short-term the result would be users spending less time on it.

❷ We are witnessing a big, transitional moment—**akin** to the transition from analog to digital, or the realization that globalization is a really big deal. Companies are beginning to realize that paying attention to the longer term, to the **perceptions** of their company, and to the social consequences of their products is good business.

❸ This realization is arriving not a moment too soon. The world badly needs a more sustainable form of capitalism if we're going to build a more **inclusive**, prosperous society and avoid **catastrophic** climate change. Of course, many of us have been saying this for a while—that we need to think more about the long-term, consider social context, and **incorporate** sustainability into business. The question, then, is: Why now? Why are more and more mainstream players taking this seriously?

❹ In my discussions with executives and in my teaching at Harvard Business School, two answers come to mind. The first is millennials' growing role in the workforce. My students today are more likely to focus on a business's impact on the environment or society at large, and to insist that companies have a positive social mission. The second is a declining confidence on the part of executives that governments will step in and fix some of our biggest problems—from climate change to inequality. (This decline mirrors a decline among the broader population.) Both of these

---

1 Adapted from Henderson, R. M. (2018, February 01). More and more CEOs are taking their social responsibility seriously. *Harvard Business Review*. Retrieved from https://hbr.org/2018/02/more-and-more-ceos-are-taking-their-social-responsibility-seriously

trends existed before Trump became president, but his election has **accelerated** them both.

❺ Even so, the fundamental question around sustainable business remains how companies can bridge the gap between their own apparent self-interest and the broader needs of society. If a company decides to do the right thing, won't its competitors take advantage? That question remains critical. It's hard work to run a firm and to consistently make **payroll**, much less save the world. As I tell my students, rule one is: Don't crash the company. We can't expect managers to primarily focus on anything other than building a thriving, profitable enterprise.

❻ That said, there is growing recognition that over the long- or even the medium-term, the interests of companies and the interests of society are more **aligned** than many people once thought. In some industries and under some conditions, socially and environmentally responsible firms are at least as profitable and sometimes more profitable than their conventional rivals, and there is some evidence to suggest that a focus on the long-term pays off. Moreover, many shareholders care about more than short-term profits.

❼ But there is one other reason for all of this is happening now, one that perhaps represents a silver lining within a more worrying trend. It's no coincidence that the firms I mentioned above are Apple, Facebook, and BlackRock. Apple is an enormously powerful firm, and its actions can set the agenda for an entire industry. If an individual developer sets out to make an app that is better for kids, it may or may not gain any **traction**; if Apple makes this issue a priority, an entire ecosystem will shift. The same is true of Facebook. It has such a high share of the market that when there's a problem with fake news, it becomes, in large part, Facebook's problem. BlackRock is a giant, too, and finance is another industry where a small number of big players dominate.

❽ Big firms face different incentives, for a few reasons. To the extent that these firms have market power, they're less subject to quarter-to-quarter competitive pressure. That means it's easier for them to focus on the long-term. And, to some degree, they have room to use that market power to pursue social objectives—especially if their investors or their employees pressure them to do so.

❾ Big firms can also internalize certain externalities. An externality is a cost from a transaction that doesn't fall on the buyer or the seller. If I pollute the air to make a product I sell to you, the cost of that pollution is spread out across society, and isn't incorporated in the price I charge you for the product. Externalities pose problems for markets, since neither buyers nor sellers have any incentive to deal with the costs. But sometimes, for really large firms, things work differently.

❿ A somewhat **apocryphal** story about Henry Ford illustrates the principle. One example of an externality comes when firms pay their workers too little. The firm doesn't necessarily bear the full cost from doing so (though it might bear some) nor does the firm's customers. Society, on the other hand, might pay **substantial** costs. For one thing, if workers don't have money to spend, the entire economy could suffer. Ford supposedly raised wages in his factories in part because he believed that if his workers had more money in their pockets, they'd buy more Ford cars. The Ford story doesn't add up, if you assume that Ford believed that his move alone was enough to raise

Unit 7 Corporate Social Responsibility

overall demand for cars.

⓫ But if you think instead that he was signaling to his competitors that if they all moved, none of them would be at a disadvantage and that aggregate demand for the industry would increase, then the principle arguably holds in other contexts for some of today's giants. (And, of course, there's some evidence that he was also hoping to reduce **turnover**—which is entirely consistent with the idea that firms that handle this well look for short-term wins at the same time they're looking for longer-term changes.)

⓬ Consider Facebook and news. If you log into Facebook, read some fake news, and later tell several of your friends what you read, there's a clear negative externality. The cost to your friends of hearing that fake news wasn't considered in that interaction between you and Facebook. But what if instead of telling your friends in person, you shared the fake news on Facebook? There are still costs from fake news that are externalized. However, the higher the share of such discussion that happens on Facebook, the more that Facebook is forced to bear the cost. This dynamic is increasingly giving Facebook a significant incentive to take action.

⓭ This isn't an argument for **monopoly**. There's considerable research suggesting the U.S. economy is too concentrated, and I'm in favor of **rigorous enforcement** of **antitrust** laws. Nonetheless, I believe we must push the sustainability agenda as hard as we can, wherever we can. And right now, we are in a moment where big companies are waking up to the business case for social responsibility, and to the wisdom of taking a longer-term view. There are good reasons why large firms can be leaders in sustainability, and by doing so change the standards of entire industries. Big retailers and textile firms can make supply chains greener, safer, and less **corrupt**. And though this sort of self-regulation is seldom sufficient, it can lay the groundwork for systemic change.

⓮ We need more big companies to commit to renewable energy and to **lobbying** for legislation that imposes the real cost of burning fossil fuels on the buyers of fossil fuels. We need more big companies to commit to paying more than the minimum wage and to lobbying for minimum wage legislation. To say they're not going to dump stuff in the river, or buy from those who do. To insist that they won't corrupt local authorities in the developing world. And to **demonstrate** that you can be a successful business not just in spite of but because of these commitments. The top 500 firms' revenues equate to nearly 37% of world GDP. What would happen if you could convince 100 of them to commit to going carbon-free and to taking a less **antagonistic** view of their labor force?

⓯ That scenario isn't likely. Nor is it a substitute to good public policy and healthy democratic governance. But it's more likely than it was just a few years ago. And it's a start.

(1413 words)

Notes

JANA Partners: 加纳伙伴基金。It is an investment manager specializing in event-driven investing. It was founded in 2001 by Barry Rosenstein. JANA engages in traditional shareholder activism and socially responsible investing.

from analog to digital: 模拟到数字转换。The difference between analog and digital technologies is that in analog technology, information is translated into electric pulses of varying amplitude; in digital technology, translation of information is into binary format (zero or one) where each bit is representative of two distinct amplitudes.

Ford: 福特汽车公司。Ford Motor Company is a multinational automaker that has its main headquarter in Dearborn, Michigan, a suburb of Dctroit. It was founded by Henry Ford and incorporated on June 16, 1903. The company sells automobiles and commercial vehicles under the Ford brand and most luxury cars under the Lincoln brand.

4.1 Read Text A and answer the following questions.

1) According to the article, why are more big companies taking social responsibility seriously now?
2) Can those companies survive competition when they do more sustainable business? Why?
3) What changes can big companies bring to the whole industry when they take action?
4) What different incentives do big firms have compared to small ones?
5) What hope does the writer of the article have from big companies?

4.2 Read Text A again and write a summary.

Summary (about 100 words): _____
_____
_____
_____
_____

How Big Business Created the Politics of Anger[1]

Mark R. Kramer

❶ Companies are not **squarely** to blame for the anger and frustration that have so **warped**

---

1 Adapted from Kramer, M. R. (2016, March 08). How big business created the politics of anger. *Harvard Business Review.* Retrieved from https://hbr.org/2016/03/how-big-business-created-the-politics-of-anger.

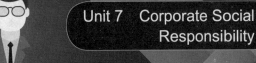

Unit 7 Corporate Social Responsibility

this presidential primary season. Nor are they entirely innocent. The growing economic inequality that **polarizes** U.S. politics is not merely the inevitable result of our free-market system; it is also a consequence of the choices our business leaders make. And those choices have contributed to the anti-business attitude that both parties have **embraced**.

❷ **Blatant** examples of illegal and immoral behavior, such as Volkswagen's emissions test cheating and Takata's **fatal** airbags, are one part of the problem. These are not U.S. companies, but their wrongdoing affected millions of U.S. consumers and certainly fueled some of the frustration that drives the current political climate in America.

❸ A far greater factor is U.S.-based companies using questionable corporate practices that are entirely legal. When Disney **compels** its employees to train lower-paid foreign replacements before being laid off, when hedge fund managers fiercely protect the carried interest **loophole**, when major companies undertake complex **mergers** to create tax inversions that **strip** their domestic earnings with **intracompany** debt, or when banks impose **overdraft** protection fees on unsuspecting low-income clients, they undermine the long-term welfare of the United States.

❹ They transfer money away from public treasuries and wage earners to provide a short-term **incremental** benefit that does nothing to improve the company's long-term prospects. Although the impact of each company's decision is small, this **cumulative** trend contributes to the growing inequality of wealth and the **stagnation** of middle-class earnings, reinforcing the deeply **entrenched** poverty of nearly 50 million Americans. These corporations may not have done anything wrong, but that doesn't mean what they have done is right.

❺ There is an even **subtler** harm in capital-allocation decisions when companies **hoard** $1.9 trillion in cash, hold foreign profits overseas, and use their capital to buy back stock. Escalating wealth driven by a bull market cannot be divorced from the **atrophying** of the middle class when stock repurchases and cash reserves **nudge** earnings per share and stock prices higher but do nothing to create employment or increase national productivity. Given that the wealthiest 10% of Americans own 81% of all stocks and mutual funds, these uses of corporate cash are a direct transfer of corporate profits away from creating jobs and capital investment, increasing income inequality. And the repurchase trend has accelerated **radically**. Stock buybacks as a percent of capital spending have risen to an all-time high of 113% in the last five years, compared to 60% in 2000 and 38% in 1990.

❻ The $520 billion that companies spent on 2015 stock repurchases alone is enough to pay the average U.S. wage to 11 million workers—considerably more than our 7.8 million citizens who are currently unemployed. To put this in a different perspective, the amount corporations spent on stock repurchases in 2015 that went to the wealthiest 10% of the population was $60 billion more than the total federal government spending on all safety net programs combined.

❼ I do not mean to suggest that corporations have any obligation to redistribute their profits to those in need. But neither should they make capital-allocation decisions without regard to the long-term consequences for their own success. Authoritative studies have shown that inequality and stagnating wages hurt corporate growth. And the choice to hold on to cash or use it to repurchase shares, rather than invest profits in new opportunities for innovation and expansion, has had real consequences for our economy that have contributed to the current political upheaval.

❽ Counting cash reserves, dividend payments, and stock repurchases, corporate America has had the opportunity to invest nearly $3 trillion in capital since the 2008 Great Recession—more than six times the size of the TARP bank **bailout**. Had corporate executives made that choice, the shape of the economic recovery, average wages, and economic inequality would look very different today. And so would this election cycle.

❾ It is easy to understand why share repurchases are so popular: The high percentage of CEO compensation that is linked to stock price, the sensitivity of that price to minor **fluctuations** in earnings per share, and the relatively short **tenure** of many CEOs mean that CEOs have a strong incentive to pump up the stock price and fine-tune quarterly earnings.

❿ Of course, corporate leaders claim that they are legally bound to do everything possible to maximize shareholder value. Share repurchases immediately and directly impact price and earnings in a way that longer-term investments in growth and innovation do not. Whether that kind of leadership positions a company for long-term success is a different question. Short-sighted decisions that increase quarterly earnings do not create shareholder value if they also undermine a company's reputation and long-term worth. Nor does political **rebellion** serve companies or their shareholders well.

⓫ Professor Michael Porter of Harvard Business School and I have argued that companies have an opportunity and obligation to create shared value by pursuing profits and competitive advantage in ways that strengthen the communities where they operate. We wrote:

"All profit is not equal, an idea that has been lost in the narrow, short-term focus of financial markets and in much management thinking. Profits involving a social purpose represent a higher form of capitalism—one that will enable society to advance more rapidly while allowing companies to prosper even more. When profits embody societal benefits, a positive cycle of company and community prosperity will lead to profits that endure."

⓬ **Visionary** CEOs understand the strategic link between social benefits and shareholder returns. In February 2014, CVS CEO Larry Merlo announced that, as a part of CVS's strategic shift into providing health care, the company would stop selling tobacco products. The company walked away from $2 billion in annual revenue. This represented a huge short-term hit to shareholder returns for the sake of a long-term shared value strategy, yet CVS's stock price rose by 38% in the months that followed and is still 22% above the price at the time of the announcement. Nor was this a purely symbolic action: A year later, CVS reported that in states where it had at least a 15%

Unit 7 Corporate Social Responsibility

market share, total cigarette sales from all types of retailers had dropped by 95 million packs.

⑬ More recently, the 100,000 Opportunities Initiative, led by Starbucks, the Aspen Institute, and FSG, a non-profit strategy consulting firm that Professor Porter and I founded, has brought together three dozen leading U.S. companies to create employment opportunities for disadvantaged youth. These companies are committed to going beyond their usual hiring practices in order to fill the jobs they need by identifying new sources of talent in communities that have been left out of the national recovery. The initiative's first three events have already resulted in 2,350 job offers.

⑭ None of this is charity. Creating shared value is a corporate strategy that delivers social benefits in order to increase profits and gain competitive advantage. Its **adherents** see opportunities in the synergy between corporate and societal interests that their more narrow-minded competitors miss.

⑮ One hundred thousand jobs will not change the political climate, but 11 million sure would have. America's corporate leaders can stand back **appalled** at today's political **spectacle**, or they can acknowledge that the means to "make America great again" are already at their disposal if they embrace a strategy to create shared value.

(1212 words)

Notes

Volkswagen: 大众汽车公司。Volkswagen is a German automaker founded on May 28, 1937 by the German Labor Front, and headquartered in Wolfsburg. It is the flagship marque of the Volkswagen Group, the largest automaker by worldwide sales in 2016 and 2017.

Takata: 高田公司。Takata Corporation was a Japanese automotive parts company. The company had production facilities on four continents, with its European headquarters located in Germany, where it also had nine production facilities. In 2013, a series of deaths and injuries associated with defective Takata airbag inflators manufactured by their Mexican subsidiary in Coahuila led Takata to initially recall 3.6 million cars equipped with such airbags. Further fatalities caused by the airbags have led the National Highway Traffic Safety Administration (NHTSA) to order an ongoing, nationwide recall of more than 42 million cars, the largest automotive recall in the U.S. history. In June 2017, Takata filed for bankruptcy and was acquired by Key Safety Systems.

corporate America: 美国公司。It is an informal (and sometimes derogatory) phrase describing the world of corporations and big business within the United States.

CVS (Pharmacy): 西维士药店。CVS (Pharmacy) is a subsidiary of the American retail and health care company CVS Health, headquartered in Woonsocket, Rhode Island. It was also known as, and originally named, the Consumer Value Store and was founded in Lowell, Massachusetts, in 1963.

Starbucks: 星巴克。Starbucks Corporation is an American coffee company and coffeehouse chain. Starbucks was founded in Seattle, Washington in 1971. As of 2018, the company operates

28, 218 locations worldwide.

Aspen Institute: 阿斯彭研究所。The Aspen Institute is an international non-profit think tank founded in 1949 by the Aspen Institute for Humanistic Studies. The organization is a non-partisan forum for values-based leadership and the exchange of ideas. The Institute and its international partners promote the pursuit of common ground and deeper understanding in a non-partisan and non-ideological setting through regular seminars, policy programs, conferences, and leadership development initiatives. The institute is headquartered in Washington, D.C., the United States, and has campuses and partner Aspen Institutes in many cities.

FSG: FSG商业咨询公司。Facility Solution Group is a non-profit strategy consulting firm set up by Michael E. Porter and Mark R. Kramer. The company helps companies design social impact strategies that strengthen their businesses, and helps funders and non-profits develop and evaluate strategies that advance their missions.

4.3 Read Text B. Write a summary in the follow form and take notes according to the table below.

Subject: _____
Key words: _____
Organization types: _____
Thesis statement (or main ideas): _____
_____
_____

Conclusion (or major findings): _____
_____

No.	Paragraph(s)	Structure	Content
1)		Problem	
2)		Examples of irresponsible corporate behavior and the consequences	
3)		Reasons for the behavior	
4)		Solution	
5)		Conclusion	

4.4 Read Text B again and answer the following questions.

1) How does Text B differ from Text A in its attitude towards big companies in America?
2) What corporate wrongdoing does Text B mention which Text A does not?
3) What factors behind the responsible corporate behavior does Text A consider which Text B does not?
4) On what aspect do Text A and Text B agree on?
5) What's your view on the performance of big companies in regard to social responsibility based on the two texts?

UNIT PROJECT

Read Text B and Text A again, form two groups, and hold a debate on the topic "Should big companies be held accountable for social problems?" Give evidence to support your arguments and refute your opponents'.

5 Practice for Enhancement

5.1 Read the four words in each group and cross the word which is not a synonym for the bold word. An example is given for you.

e.g. **catastrophic**
□ disastrous × rigorous □ devastating □ calamitous

1) **incorporate**
□ entrench □ include □ embrace □ integrate

2) **incentive**
□ motivation □ priority □ encouragement □ stimulus

3) **apocryphal**
□ dubious □ legendary □ doubtful □ conventional

4) **substantial**
□ sizable □ significant □ considerable □ sustainable

5) **antagonistic**
□ hostile □ opposed □ resistant □ fatal

6) **squarely**

☐ quarterly ☐ directly ☐ straight ☐ precisely

7) **blatant**

☐ obvious ☐ apparent ☐ subtle ☐ plain

8) **adherent**

☐ supporter ☐ demonstrator ☐ advocate ☐ follower

9) **cumulative**

☐ collective ☐ aggregate ☐ strategic ☐ amassed

5.2 Decide what words can go with the following verbs. An example is given for you.

e.g. enforce: a law, a ban, a specification, a practice, constitution, a limit, etc.

1) corrupt:
2) undermine:
3) demonstrate:
4) polarize:
5) stagnate:
6) hoard:
7) escalate:
8) atrophy:
9) fluctuate:

5.3 Paraphrase the following sentences. An example is given for you.

e.g. The second is a declining confidence on the part of executives that governments will step in and fix some of our biggest problems—from climate change to inequality.
Secondly, corporate executives are increasingly doubtful whether the government will intervene to solve the big issues including climate change and inequality.

1) We are witnessing a big, transitional moment—akin to the transition from analog to digital, or the realization that globalization is a really big deal.

2) It's hard work to run a firm and to consistently make payroll, much less save the world.

Unit 7 Corporate Social Responsibility

3) But there is one other reason all of this is happening now, one that perhaps represents a silver lining within a more worrying trend.

4) Externalities pose problems for markets, since neither buyers nor sellers have any incentive to deal with the costs.

5) Companies are not squarely to blame for the anger and frustration that have so warped this presidential primary season.

6) But neither should they make capital-allocation decisions without regard to the long-term consequences for their own success.

7) Share repurchases immediately and directly impact price and earnings in a way that longer-term investments in growth and innovation do not.

8) Its adherents see opportunities in the synergy between corporate and societal interests that their more narrow-minded competitors miss.

5.4 Translate the following sentences into Chinese.

1) In some industries and under some conditions, socially and environmentally responsible firms are at least as profitable and sometimes more profitable than their conventional rivals, and there is some evidence to suggest that a focus on the long-term pays off.

2) But if you think instead that he was signaling to his competitors that if they all moved none of

them would be at a disadvantage and that aggregate demand for the industry would increase, then the principle arguably holds in other contexts for some of today's giants.

3) And right now, we are in a moment where big companies are waking up to the business case for social responsibility, and to the wisdom of taking a longer-term view.

4) Although the impact of each company's decision is small, this cumulative trend contributes to the growing inequality of wealth and the stagnation of middle-class earnings, reinforcing the deeply entrenched poverty of nearly 50 million Americans.

5) Escalating wealth driven by a bull market cannot be divorced from the atrophying of the middle class when stock repurchases and cash reserves nudge earnings per share and stock prices higher but do nothing to create employment or increase national productivity.

6) The high percentage of CEO compensation that is linked to stock price, the sensitivity of that price to minor fluctuations in earnings per share, and the relatively short tenure of many CEOs mean that CEOs have a strong incentive to pump up the stock price and fine-tune quarterly earnings.

 Movie Exploration: *Rouge Trader* (1999)

Directed by: James Dearden
Starring: Ewan McGregor as Nick Leeson
               Anna Friel as Lisa Leeson

Unit 7　Corporate Social Responsibility

Plot

- Nick Leeson, an employee of Barings Bank, is sent to Singapore as General Manager of the Trading Floor on the SIMEX exchange.
- Nick meets Lisa Leeson at the office and marries her.
- Nick has his own team and has a chance to flourish.
- Nick opens an 88888 errors account.
- Nick successfully deals with his crisis and becomes a super trader.
- Someone finds out Nick's trick and Nick forges the documents.
- Nick gets away with Lisa from Singapore before Barings Bank is aware of their losses.
- Nick is caught and is sentenced to six and a half years in prison.

6.1　Search for the meanings of the following terms from the movie.

1) **Barings Bank:** _____
2) **balance sheet:** _____
3) **initial margin:** _____
4) **variation margin:** _____
5) **down payment:** _____
6) **error account:** _____
7) **call option:** _____
8) **SIMEX:** _____

Web Resources

https://en.wikipedia.org/wiki/Barings_Bank
https://www.investopedia.com/terms/b/balancesheet.asp
https://www.investopedia.com/terms/i/initialmargin.asp
https://www.investopedia.com/terms/v/variationmargin.asp
https://en.wikipedia.org/wiki/Down_payment
https://en.wikipedia.org/wiki/Error_account
https://www.investopedia.com/terms/c/calloption.asp
https://en.wikipedia.org/wiki/Singapore_International_Monetary_Exchange

6.2 While watching, listen to what Nick says to his wife after he knows Barings Bank is going to collapse and complete it by filling in the blanks.

> In this part, Nick Leeson (N for Nick) is depressed at what he has done and seeks comfort from his wife Lisa (L for Lisa).

(Background news) The Chancellor of the Exchequer is trying to calm fears 1)_____ by the failure of Barings Bank. In a statement to Parliament, he 2)_____ reports that the British banking system is about to collapse. According to him, Barings' failure is a unique situation which he blames on the actions of a rouge trader in Singapore. 3)_____ of potential losses range from 800 million to cover one billion pounds. 4)_____ of knowing how markets will react when they reopen on Monday. As the Bank of England tries to put together a rescue package with the Sultan of Brunei rumored as a buyer, time may be running out for one of Britain's most 5)_____ financial institutions.

L: How could you not tell me? How could you have 6)_____ for all this time, Nick? You must have been through hell!

N: You would have 7)_____ Simon Jones' office.

L: Too bloody right.

N: Then I'd have got fired and I couldn't have made the money back. That's all I was gonna do.

L: No, but you were 8)_____. That's what you were doing with other people's money.

N: I didn't want to 9)_____, you, my dad, the girls in the office, even Ron Bloody Baker. Do you think they're all gonna hate me now?.

L: Well, I don't think you're gonna be 10)_____!

N: It could easily have been the other way, you know. It so nearly was.

6.3 After watching, cross the word or phrase that is closest in meaning to the bold one in each of the following sentences from the movie. An example is given for you.

e.g. He denied reports that the British banking system is about to **collapse** due to the crisis.

  ☐ go panic   ✗ break down   ☐ maintain strong

1) It was my job to **sort out** the certificates so customers wouldn't have any more excuses not to pay.

  ☐ read   ☐ separate   ☐ arrange

2) The **profitability** has been amazing since the reorganization.

  ☐ productivity   ☐ effectiveness   ☐ lucrativeness

Unit 7 Corporate Social Responsibility

3) It's not full of **pompous** ex-colonials thinking they were born to rule the world.

   ☐ wealthy   ☐ arrogant   ☐ stupid

4) We want to **stand out**. We're a new operation. We need to be noticed.

   ☐ leap out   ☐ break out   ☐ fall out

5) It was one thing to **con** people over the phone, another to do it to their face.

   ☐ humiliate   ☐ curse   ☐ deceive

6) They want to check the numbers. Iron out those funding problems **once and for all**.

   ☐ promptly   ☐ conclusively   ☐ temporarily

7) You will realize it's **concealing** losses in the region of £ 200 million.

   ☐ hiding   ☐ increasing   ☐ supplying

8) Nick Leeson runs our operation in Singapore which I want all of you to try to **emulate**.

   ☐ compete   ☐ praise   ☐ imitate

9) Everyone must be connected to our strategy, or we will find you and **weed** you **out**.

   ☐ eliminate   ☐ help   ☐ accuse

6.4 Work in groups and discuss the following questions.

1) Do you think inside trading is dangerous for everyone practicing in the business world?
2) How many traders would resist the temptation of gaining benefits by using their clients' money?

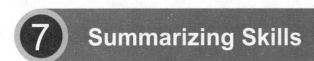

7 Summarizing Skills

How to Write a Summary[1]

A summary is a shortened passage, which retains the essential information of the original. It is a fairly brief restatement—in your own words—of the contents of a passage. Writing a summary is critical to academic studies.

Characteristics of a good summary

- **Briefness:** Omit unnecessary details like examples, explanations, and other unimportant information.
- **Completeness:** Include all the main and supporting points delivered in your own words in a condensed manner.

---

1 Adapted from University of Western Ontario. (2001, Fall). *Summary and precis writing: Characteristics or a good summary*. Retrieved from http://www.sdc.uwo.ca/writing/hangouts/Summary%20writing.pdf

- **Coherence:** Rather than an outline listed as key words and phrases, a summary is a paragraph with necessary transitions and function structures to make it flow.
- **Objectivity:** Contain only the ideas or information of the original. Do not include your own ideas or emotions on the topic. You simply report back what the writer has said, without making any value judgments.

Steps in writing a summary

Firstly, read the article. When reading, you should:
- Divide the article into sections of ideas. Each section deals with one aspect of the central theme;
- Label (classify) each section with a general phrase that captures the subject matter of the section;
- Highlight or underline the main idea and key points.

Secondly, begin your summary with the author's name, type of work, title of work, and the author's thesis statement that conveys the central point of what you are summarizing. For example:
- In his article *Children and Video Games*, Steve Peterson strongly recommends that parents should not allow their children to play video games.

Thirdly, write according to your outlines. After you fully understand the source passage, it is advisable to write an outline, based on which you can write your summary.

Fourthly, use transitions for a smooth and logical flow of ideas. For example:
- **The body:**
  - First of all, the author describes…
  - He then points out that…
  - In addition, the author talks about…
  - Finally, the author suggests…
- **The conclusion:**
  - A summary of the previous analysis;
  - A restatement of the thesis statement;
  - A final statement reflecting the significance of the article (from the author's point of view).
- **The point of view:**
  - The author/passage/text/story/news believes (holds, maintains, claims, argues, points out, suggests) that…

Fifthly, compress supporting details. Control the length of summary within limit. You can:
- Omit the details;
- Reduce the examples;
- Simplify the descriptions;
- Eliminate all repetitions;
- Compress wordy sentences and change clauses or sentences to phrases and phrases to words.

ACADEMIC ENGLISH FOR BUSINESS

Unit 8
Retailing

商务学科英语

1 Search for Background Information

1.1 Search for the meanings of the following terms from texts or about the subject.

1) retailing: _____
2) bricks-and-mortar shop: _____
3) start-ups: _____
4) financial crisis of 2007–2008: _____
5) e-commerce: _____
6) margin: _____
7) premium: _____
8) merchandise: _____
9) click-and-collect: _____
10) Kindle: _____
11) point-of-sale system: _____
12) concept store: _____
13) pop-up shop: _____
14) high street: _____
15) fiscal year: _____

Web Resources

https://www.etymonline.com/word/retail
https://www.bigcommerce.com/blog/brick-and-mortar/
https://www.investopedia.com/ask/answers/12/what-is-a-startup.asp
https://www.investopedia.com/articles/economics/09/financial-crisis-review.asp
http://knowledge.ckgsb.edu.cn/2017/02/27/retail/will-ecommerce-replace-brick-mortar-chinese-retailers/
http://www.businessdictionary.com/definition/margin.html
http://www.businessdictionary.com/definition/premium.html
https://dictionary.cambridge.org/dictionary/english/merchandise
https://www.retailstore.co.uk/7-tips-click-and-collect/
https://hubpages.com/technology/what-are-kindles
https://www.linkedin.com/pulse/point-sale-system-whats-advantage-does-my-business-need-systems

Unit 8 Retailing

> https://www.wisegeek.com/what-is-a-concept-store.htm
> https://www.businessoffashion.com/articles/intelligence/has-the-pop-up-shop-bubble-popped
> https://www.edp24.co.uk/edp-property/is-the-high-street-dead-asks-mike-white-from-martin-co-1-5731618
> https://www.investopedia.com/terms/f/fiscalyear.asp

1.2 Present what you've found to the class orally with or without PowerPoint in three minutes.

2 Discuss the Words' Meaning

2.1 Define the following underlined words. An example is given for you.

e.g. He did not tell his relatives and friends about his woes which he suffered himself.
   woe: the trouble and problem
1) My whole class decided to have a shindig to celebrate our graduation—it was a real blast!
   shindig: _____
2) Fears of a possible faltering of the recovery forced the government to step up stimulus spending.
   faltering: _____
3) Doctors are concentrating on understanding the disease better, and on optimizing the treatment.
   optimize: _____
4) The company needs to improve its competitive edge in attracting investors.
   edge: _____
5) It shows how entrenched habits shape individual lives and analyzes how those habits can be broken and rearranged.
   entrenched: _____
6) Carbon emissions exacerbate the global climate change problem.
   exacerbate: _____
7) Buying in bulk is more economical than shopping for small quantities.
   bulk: _____

商务学科英语

8) Margins are eroding because new products <u>cannibalize</u> older products.
   cannibalize: _____

9) The sale has been held up because the price is <u>reckoned</u> to be too high.
   reckon: _____

10) She's a <u>hotshot</u> broker on Wall Street, admired by others.
    hotshot: _____

11) Even if customers want "solutions", most are not willing to pay a <u>premium</u> for them.
    premium: _____

12) Admittedly, science has created atomic bombs and produced <u>pervasive</u> pollution.
    pervasive: _____

13) It is not an uncommon practice that <u>surplus</u> grain is being sold export.
    surplus: _____

14) We've just appointed a coordinator who will <u>oversee</u> the whole project.
    oversee: _____

15) Species tend to adapt and change—sometimes so much that they <u>morph</u> into a new species.
    morph: _____

16) The staff are <u>crediting</u> him with having saved Hythe's life.
    credit: _____

17) The Monaco Grand Prix started in 1929, under the <u>auspice</u> of the late Prince Louis II, is an event recognized internationally.
    auspice: _____

18) They spotted a <u>niche</u> in the market, with no serious competition.
    niche: _____

19) I had to keep the video camera easily <u>accessible</u> in case I saw something that needed to be filmed.
    accessible: _____

20) While searching for a way to <u>augment</u> the family income, she began making dolls.
    augment: _____

21) The public has an insatiable <u>appetite</u> for stories about the famous.
    appetite: _____

22) In conclusion, walking is a cheap, safe, enjoyable, and <u>readily</u> available form of exercise.
    readily: _____

23) Most travel agents are prepared to <u>tailor</u> travel arrangements to meet individual requirements.
    tailor: _____

24) Can you look back and see a well-defined path, or simply an aimless series of job moves with no <u>coherent</u> structure?
    coherent: _____

Unit 8 Retailing

25) Today our technological connectivity gives us an unprecedented opportunity to <u>harness</u> global creativity for products and services.
   harness: _____
26) Japan's recession has <u>prompted</u> consumers to cut back on buying cars.
   prompt: _____
27) The next year holds much promise as cloud computing moves from <u>buzzword</u> to real technology.
   buzzword: _____
28) Having a tidy desk can seem impossible if you have a busy, <u>demanding</u> job.
   demanding: _____
29) Learning process in college, I realize that my computer science interests and abilities combined <u>seamlessly</u>.
   seamless: _____
30) Fewer than 40% voted—the <u>threshold</u> for results to be valid.
   threshold: _____

2.2 Fill in the following blanks with various forms of each word. An example is given for you.

No.	Base form	Variations in the word family
e.g.	product	produce, production, producer, productive, productivity
1)	sign	
2)	part	
3)	person	
4)	press	
5)	public	
6)	admit	
7)	consume	
8)	invest	
9)	pop	
10)	fact	
11)	intend	
12)	direct	

(Continued)

No.	Base form	Variations in the word family
13)	use	
14)	inform	
15)	habit	

2.3 Explain the meaning of the following roots or affixes. Add at least five similar derivatives with their Chinese definitions. An example is given for you.

No.	Roots/Affixes	Meaning	More derivatives with Chinese translation
e.g.	tent-/tend-	stretch	attend 注意，出席；attentive 注意的；attention 注意力；extent 广度，宽度；tendency 倾向，趋势
1)	over-		
2)	mit		
3)	ann/enn		
4)	aug/auct		
5)	cred		
6)	morph		
7)	duc		
8)	centr		

3 Watch the Video

Difficult Words and Expressions

- ★ exclusive /ɪkˈskluːsɪv/ *adj.* 独家经营的
- ★ downside /ˈdaʊnsaɪd/ *n.* 缺点，不利方面
- ★ preliminary /prɪˈlɪmɪnəri/ *adj.* 初步的，准备的
- ★ snapshot /ˈsnæpʃɒt/ *n.* （快拍）照片
- ★ photogenic /ˌfəʊtəʊˈdʒenɪk/ *adj.* 易上镜的
- ★ get carried away 得意忘形的
- ★ price range 价格幅度，价格承受范围

Unit 8　Retailing

3.1 Watch the video and answer the following questions.

1) What does Emily think about people shopping online?
2) Why does Karl attempt to sell his clothes on the web?
3) What responsibilities do Karl's employees take?
4) Why does Karl think there are certain items to be sold in store?
5) Why is Karl very careful to promote his clothes business online?

3.2 Watch the video again and take notes according to the questions in the left column.

No.	Questions	Notes
1)	Why did Emily order clothes either from the U.S. or China?	She likes to order from the U.S. because they _____; and from China because they _____.
2)	Why does Karl design his products in different colors now?	He produces them in different colors to _____ on the Internet.
3)	Why does Karl take snapshots of his clothes on his phone?	He wants to see they are _____; they have to _____ and _____.
4)	What is the percentage of online fashion stores in Germany?	Every _____ fashion stores in Germany now has its own online shop.
5)	What is the challenge for Karl and his business?	The challenge is _____ while _____.

3.3 Watch the video once more and write a short summary of it according to your answers and notes.

_____
_____
_____
_____

3.4 Work in groups and make a report to the class on "Online shopping" according to the following clues in five minutes.

1) When and why does online shopping emerge as a new mode of shopping?
2) What are strengths and weaknesses of online shopping?

4 Read for Information

Shop till You Drop; Traditional Retailing[1]

① When America's retail bosses gathered in New York earlier this year for the annual **shindig** of their trade association, the National Retail Federation, there were lots of talks about new technology to improve the industry's prospects, from sensors that read consumers' facial expressions to machine-learning software that can **optimize** prices. The ghost at the **banquet** was the company that gave no presentations but made its presence felt everywhere: Amazon.

② Traditional retailing has had a tough time lately. Traffic in shopping centres in Europe's biggest markets has been declining. In America, which has about five times as much space in shopping centres per person as Britain, the pain is acute. Chains that were **faltering** even before Amazon's ascent are now in even deeper trouble. Macy's, a department store, last year said it would close 100 of its 728 shops. Fung Global Retail & Technology, a consultancy, expects nearly 10,000 stores in America to close this year, about 50% more than at the height of the financial crisis in 2008. And there will be more to come.

③ Shops used to compete by offering a combination of selection, price, service, and convenience. E-commerce's most obvious **edge** is in selection and convenience. Even the biggest store cannot hold as many items as Amazon can offer. Walmart conquered America by saving consumers money; Amazon is doing the same by saving them time. Shops still provide immediacy and a personal experience. Though getting attentive service at Gucci may be fun, waiting to pay at the supermarket is not.

④ E-commerce firms are also competing on new kinds of service and pricing. A website knows more about you than any shop assistant can, enabling it to offer personalized recommendations straight away. Online, a shopper can easily compare prices between retailers. More **intriguingly**, merchants can quickly move prices up or down, using bots to match competitors' offerings. **Eventually** this pricing may become more personalized. Alibaba and JD already use their troves of data to offer discounts on particular products to some of their customers.

⑤ All this has meant that consumers are now buying a wider range of goods online. The shift has been most dramatic in America, home to both a relentlessly disruptive e-commerce giant and a herd of entrenched retailers (which China lacks). Consumers still buy certain types of goods

---

1 Adapted from Shop till you drop; Traditional retailing. *The Economist*, 425(9064), 8–10.

Unit 8 Retailing

in stores, such as food and building equipment. But many shops have had no choice but to follow consumers online, setting up their own e-commerce businesses as they maintain their bricks-and-mortar ones. In the short term, this only **exacerbates** their problems. Building an e-commerce business on top of a traditional one is **costly**; firms must create websites and ship products to individual consumers, rather than to stores in **bulk**.

❻ It does not help that Amazon has conditioned consumers to think delivery should be free. Moreover, online sales often **cannibalize** those from existing shops. Analysts at Morgan Stanley **reckon** that for each additional percentage point of shopping that moves online, a retailer's margins shrink by about half a point. Bricks-and-mortar shops also often have trouble recruiting technology staff. For a **hotshot** data scientist, working at a department store is not an obvious choice. Traditional chains must routinely pay a **premium** to lure skilled tech workers. Amazon has no such difficulty.

❼ Start-ups, tech firms, and consultants are offering tools to help smaller retailers adjust. Some of the more interesting ones promise to narrow the gap between what e-commerce sites and physical stores know about their customers. Floor mats can measure store traffic; video analytics will track shoppers' age, sex, and mood; and beacons can gather data about what customers do in the shop once they have signed up for free Wi-Fi. For now, though, many American firms are reluctant to invest in such expensive new technology for shops that may not be there for much longer.

❽ In China, those offering to remedy retailers' **woes** include some of the big e-commerce firms, and retailers may be happy to work with them because their platforms are so **pervasive**. In the West, small merchants already pay Amazon to list products on its site and store goods in its warehouses. The small sellers can reach more consumers more easily; Amazon earns fees and, thanks to sellers' listings, can offer a broader selection.

❾ Big retailers, on the other hand, seem much less likely to team up with Amazon. Target and Toys "R" Us chose Amazon to handle their e-commerce businesses in the early 2000s, but both ended the partnership, with Toys "R" Us doing so in court. Unlike Alibaba, Amazon owns much of the stuff it sells, so competes directly with any seller that uses its services.

❿ Despite such troubles, there are examples of how bricks-and-mortar shops might thrive. One strategy is to offer distinctive products that are not available elsewhere (as does Zara, a clothing chain owned by Inditex), or which are difficult to sell online. A second is to give shoppers a great deal. TJX, an American firm, offers manufacturers' **surplus** goods at **bargain** prices. Another option is a great experience: champagne at Louis Vuitton, perhaps, or personalized advice at Nike. The most difficult route is to try to match Amazon's retail standards and offer more.

⓫ Walmart, once the undisputed king of American retailing, is **mounting** the boldest counteroffensive. It can no longer simply open stores to boost growth; 90% of Americans already live within ten miles of a Walmart. So the company is seeking to protect its margins by making stores even more efficient—saving $7 million by printing shorter receipts, for instance—while investing online. Last year, it spent $3.3 billion buying Jet.com, an e-commerce site founded by Marc Lore, who now **oversees** Walmart's suite of online businesses. He is not trying to match Amazon's breadth. "We are focused on being a retailer," he declares. But Walmart is trying to catch up with Amazon in other ways. The company now offers free two-day shipping. Just as JD's integration with Tencent is helping it challenge Alibaba, Walmart may succeed by partnering with tech giants. In August, it said it would sell through Google's voice assistant, in a bid to counter Amazon's Alexa.

⑫ Walmart can also use its vast network of stores to do things Amazon cannot. In one experiment, Walmart staff drop off customers' orders on their way home. And as America's biggest grocer, it has developed an easy way for customers to order food online, then drive to a Walmart where staff load it into their car.

⑬ Even as Walmart adapts, however, Amazon continues to **morph**. It is using machine learning to measure the ripeness of a peach and to determine how many blue shirts to stock in which size. Constant innovation gives it a huge competitive advantage which many retailers will struggle to match. Too many physical stores lack the strategy or distinctive merchandise that might help them thrive in retail's new era. And in the main, they still rely on the customers coming to them to choose their purchases, whereas their rivals deliver.

(1169 words)

Notes

National Retail Federation: 美国零售联合会。It is the world's largest retail trade association. Its members include department stores, specialty, discount, catalog, Internet, independent retailers, chain restaurants, and grocery stores. Members also include businesses that provide goods and services to retailers, such as vendors and technology providers. NRF represents the largest private-sector industry in the United States that contains over 3.8 million retail establishments with more than 29 million employees contributing $2.6 trillion annually to GDP.

Amazon: 亚马逊。It is the most valuable public company in the world. It is the largest e-commerce marketplace and cloud computing platform in the world as measured by revenue and market capitalization. Amazon.com was founded by Jeff Bezos on July 5, 1994, and started as an online bookstore but later diversified to sell video downloads or streaming, MP3 downloads or streaming, audiobook downloads or streaming, software, video games, electronics, apparel, furniture, food, toys, and jewelry.

Walmart: 沃尔玛。It is an American multinational retail corporation that operates a chain of hypermarkets, discount department stores, and grocery stores. Headquartered in Bentonville, Arkansas, the company was founded by Sam Walton in 1962 and incorporated on October 31,

Unit 8 Retailing

1969. It also owns and operates Sam's Club retail warehouses.

Morgan Stanley: 摩根士丹利。It is an American multinational investment bank and financial services company headquartered at 1585 Broadway in the Morgan Stanley Building, Midtown Manhattan, New York City. With offices in more than 42 countries and more than 55,000 employees, the firm's clients include corporations, governments, institutions, and individuals. Morgan Stanley ranked No. 67 in the 2018 Fortune 500 list of the largest United States corporations by total revenue.

Toys "R" Us: 玩具反斗城。It is an international toy, clothing, video game, and baby product retailer owned by Tru Kids, Inc. It was founded in April 1948, with its headquarters located in Wayne, New Jersey, in the New York metropolitan area.

Louis Vuitton: 路易威登。It is a French fashion house and luxury retail company founded in 1854 by Louis Vuitton. The label's LV monogram appears on most of its products, ranging from luxury trunks and leather goods to ready-to-wear, shoes, watches, jewelry, accessories, sunglasses, and books. Louis Vuitton is one of the world's leading international fashion houses; it sells its products through standalone boutiques, lease departments in high-end department stores, and through the e-commerce section of its website.

4.1 Read Text A and answer the following questions.

1) Why has the traditional retailing had a tough time in recent years?
2) Why do some people firmly believe that physical shops will survive and might thrive?
3) Why does e-commerce seem to be competitive in the new era of retailing?
4) How are technologies used to trace customers' behavior?
5) What will be the difficulties for online retailers to open physical shops? What will be the difficulties for physical shops to try online business?

4.2 Read Text A again and write a summary.

Summary (about 100 words): _____
_____
_____
_____
_____

Let's Get Physical: The New Retailing[1]

Harriet Russell

❶ Regular readers will remember the special in-depth feature we published on e-tailer giant Amazon (U.S.: AMZ) last year and its steady advance on the retail sector. Many industry insiders have **credited** the "e-tailer" with forcing change in the industry, not just in the general evolution of online shopping, but also with **logistics** and technology. And yet, despite Amazon's modern business model, the group is still expanding its physical retail space, opening a bricks-and-mortar bookshop in Seattle in November 2015. At last count, there were plans for five more stores across the United States—to join the three already operating in Seattle, Portland, and San Diego—as well as several pick-up locations across California. Unlike the bookshops, these new locations will allow customers to drive in, park, pick up their items, and leave in under 15 minutes—effectively a click-and-collect depot under Amazon's **auspice**.

❷ Despite ongoing rumours that the group wants to open between 300 and 400 new locations, it's fair to say Amazon is moving slowly with its expansion into physical retail. Amazon is also focused on a **niche** area with this strategy too—namely traditional bookstores as opposed to the hundreds of thousands of product categories currently **accessible** via the website. It's perhaps ironic, given its **primacy** among online booksellers, but Amazon has been forced to **augment** its business model to serve modern consumers that still want to browse books in person prior to purchase. In the Seattle store, books are priced "fluidly", meaning they match the prices offered online, while customers can also browse a range of related technology products, such as Kindle e-readers, the Fire TV, and Echo or "Alexa"—Amazon's voice-controlled home assistant.

❸ Amazon's move into the world of physical retail suggests this **format** still has value, but stores have to evolve to better serve modern shoppers' **appetites**. Amazon is clearly taking direction from its digital business, focusing on what customers value about the online experience before bringing it to the high street. The statistics make for interesting reading. According to Massachusetts-based software firm DemandWare, the number of visits to stores worldwide has increased by 16% since 2014, while another Massachusetts software group, TimeTrade, said 65% of the U.S. consumers would prefer to shop in a store if they knew an item was in stock at a nearby retail location, even if it was **readily** available online. TimeTrade also said the U.S. consumers generally prefer shopping in store, with 85% wanting to touch and feel products before buying

---

1 Adapted from Russell, H. (2017, March 16). *Let's get physical: The new retailing*. Retrieved from https://www.investorschronicle.co.uk/2017/03/16/shares/sectors/let-s-get-physical-the-new-retailing-BLSPg7m1in6L2ITGTfJ46H/article.html

Unit 8 Retailing

them. More than a third also said they didn't like waiting for items to ship, while 30% said they still value advice from sales associates.

❹ According to in-store analytics company RetailNext, the evolution of e-commerce was largely driven by retailers' ability to collect more data on their customers than ever before. Using online analytics tools to track their customers' behavior, online retailers were able to shape marketing campaigns, **tailor** discounts and special offers, and even design product categories in the hope of driving better sales growth. The inability of physical retail locations to provide the same sort of **coherent** insight into customers' behavior put them at a distinct disadvantage to their online competition.

❺ But new technological developments mean this is no longer the case. Analytics companies can now **harness** in-store Wi-Fi systems, video cameras, payment cards, point-of-sale systems, and external factors like weather patterns to gather information on shoppers' habits. This has also proved useful for owners of retail parks, shopping centres, and even manufacturing warehouse sites. And this kind of information gathering can shape consumers' behavior in the future too. For example, their behavior in store means retailers can better tailor what is offered to them online, via web dashboards, mobile apps and even give them the ability to send real-time alerts via e-mail or text message—all this even before the customers have even left the store.

❻ It's not a trend that anyone saw coming. With the arrival of online pure-plays such as Asos (ASC) and the subsequent scale of disruption to the market, you could have been forgiven for thinking that retail was headed in only one direction. But as digital commerce gathered pace, the need to complement online retail with more traditional forms has become increasingly apparent. This has **prompted** other companies to follow Amazon and open "pop-up" or "concept" stores to trial the popularity of physical locations.

❼ One such example is privately-held fitness wear retailer Active in Style. Having started life as an online-only retailer, the company recently opened doors in London's upmarket Chelsea area to take advantage of the growing social trends in health and wellness. Founder Caroline Lucie tells us it's "much harder" to track customer behavior in store, but says she has witnessed an "incredible response" to the brand since opening the physical stores. The company previously experimented with other temporary sites, but Ms. Lucie says she "would not give up" the brand's Chelsea store now. "It's expensive," she admits, "but we've been able to harness the engagement with the brand online to drive customers to the store".

❽ Active in Style is not alone. Although it is not strange to store shopping, luxury retailer Burberry opened what was intended to be a temporary, pop-up shop in Covent Garden. It was designed to play host to the group's new beauty and make-up products. Becoming known as the Burberry Beauty Box, it proved so popular that it's still there.

❾ Interestingly, bosses at fast fashion e-tailer Asos aren't making the same strategy a priority. Chairman Brian McBride has publicly criticized the idea of multi-channel retailing—a modern day

buzzword for the future of the retail sector. Mr. McBride suggests the term was invented by retail groups trying to convince themselves, investors, and the public that something could still be done with physical stores. In his view, the high street is "**demanding**" and "cruel" and "struggles to keep up with change". Instead, Asos will focus its resources on mobile sales, believing e-commerce still has the potential to double its share of the retail market. Last year, 51% of total orders placed on Asos came from mobile platforms following 7.5 million new downloads of the group's mobile app during the financial year.

⑩ But analytics expert ShopperTrak argues blending technology with the human touch offered by retail stores is "the only way" to deliver an omnichannel, "best of both worlds" experience that shoppers will come to expect in the future. This won't be without challenges, however, as retail stores will have to raise their game to become every bit as streamlined, well-stocked, and easy to **navigate** as what's available on the web. What's more, their online offering will be expected to work **seamlessly** with the physical store estate, which means total integration of the distribution network for both online and offline systems. It's not hard to find examples of where this has been difficult. Both Tesco and John Lewis have been forced to increase the **threshold** on minimum spends for their click-and-collect services as prior limits were deemed too costly and inefficient.

(1172 words)

Notes

Burberry: 博柏利（巴宝莉）。It was established in 1856 by Thomas Burberry, originally focusing on the development of outdoor attire, and it has moved into the high fashion market as a British luxury fashion house.

Covent Garden: 考文特花园（科芬花园）。It is a district in Greater London, on the eastern fringes of the West End, between Charing Cross Road and Drury Lane; it is associated with the former fruit-and-vegetable market in the central square, now a popular shopping and tourist site.

Tesco: 特易购（乐购）。It was founded in 1919 by Jack Cohen as a group of market stalls; it is now a British multinational groceries and general merchandise retailer with headquarters in Welwyn Garden City, Hertfordshire. It is the third largest retailer in the world measured by gross revenues and the ninth largest retailer in the world measured by revenues. It has shops in seven countries across Asia and Europe, and is the market leader of groceries in the U.K.

John Lewis: 约翰—路易斯百货店。It is a chain of high-end department stores operating throughout the United Kingdom. The first John Lewis store was opened in 1864 in Oxford Street, London. The chain has promised since 1925 that it is "never knowingly undersold", a phrase used as a slogan—it will always at least match a lower price offered by a "national high street competitor".

Unit 8   Retailing

4.3 Read Text B. Write a summary in the following form and take notes according to the table below.

Subject: _____
Key words: _____
Organization types: _____
Thesis statement (or main ideas): _____
_____
_____

Conclusion (or major findings): _____
_____
_____

No.	Paragraph(s)	Structure	Content
1)		Background	
2)		Reason 1	
3)		Reason 2	
4)		Conclusion 1: A trend	
5)		Conclusion 2: Challenges	

4.4 Read Text B again and answer the following questions.

1) Why did Amazon expand its physical retail space, given its primacy among online booksellers?
2) What do customers value about their online shopping experience?
3) What do customers value about their in-store shopping experience?
4) How do physical retailers and online retailers track the customer's behavior now?
5) What will be challenges for future physical retailers and online retailers?

UNIT PROJECT

Read Text A and Text B again, form two groups, and hold a debate on the topic "Physical shops will be replaced by online shops". Give evidence to support your arguments and refute your opponents'.

5 Practice for Enhancement

5.1 Read the four words in each group and cross the word which is not a synonym for the bold word. An example is given for you.

e.g. **prospect**

    × prosperity   ☐ expectation   ☐ outlook   ☐ view

1) **exacerbate**

    ☐ worsen   ☐ aggravate   ☐ exasperate   ☐ emphasize

2) **woe**

    ☐ misery   ☐ enemy   ☐ trouble   ☐ suffering

3) **oversee**

    ☐ supervise   ☐ monitor   ☐ manage   ☐ negotiate

4) **morph**

    ☐ change   ☐ form   ☐ vary   ☐ shift

5) **format**

    ☐ norm   ☐ arrangement   ☐ design   ☐ plan

6) **harness**

    ☐ control   ☐ rule   ☐ rein   ☐ examine

7) **navigate**

    ☐ pass   ☐ direct   ☐ pilot   ☐ orient

8) **prompt**

    ☐ provoke   ☐ incite   ☐ motivate   ☐ respond

9) **complement**

    ☐ append   ☐ supplement   ☐ compliment   ☐ adding

5.2 Match the word in the box with the words in each column that regularly go together. An example is given for you.

| goods, assistant, load, strategy, retail, site, minimum, service, distinctive, crisis |

e.g. goods	1) _____	2) _____	3) _____
-expensive	-charge	good-	teaching-
unwanted-	-age	customer-	marketing-
paper-	-height	postal-	military-
durable-	at a-	public-	company-

4) _____	5) _____	6) _____	7) _____
work-	manager-	economic-	camping-
heavy-	Chief-	financial-	building-
a big-	shop-	in times of-	construction-
-a truck	sales-	midlife-	web-
8) _____	9) _____		
physical-	-voice		
online-	-style		
-sales	-flavor		
-space	-taste		

5.3 Paraphrase the following sentences. An example is given for you.

e.g. E-commerce's most obvious edge is in selection and convenience.
<u>Selection and convenience are E-commerce's most distinctive advantages.</u>

1) The ghost at the banquet was the company that gave no presentations but made its presence felt everywhere: Amazon.

   _____
   _____

2) Walmart, once the undisputed king of American retailing, is mounting the boldest counteroffensive.

   _____
   _____

3) In China, those offering to remedy retailers' woes include some of the big e-commerce firms, and retailers may be happy to work with them because their platforms are so pervasive.

   _____
   _____

4) Too many physical stores lack the strategy or distinctive merchandise that might help them thrive in retail's new era.

   _____
   _____

5) It's perhaps ironic, given its primacy among online booksellers, but Amazon has been forced to augment its business model to serve modern consumers that still want to browse books in person prior to purchase.

6) The inability of physical retail locations to provide the same sort of coherent insight into customer behavior put them at a distinct disadvantage to their online competition.

7) Using online analytics tools to track their customers' behavior, online retailers were able to shape marketing campaigns, tailor discounts and special offers, and even design product categories in the hope of driving better sales growth.

8) This won't be without challenges, however, as retail stores will have to raise their game to become every bit as streamlined, well-stocked, and easy to navigate as what's available on the web.

5.4 Translate the following sentences into Chinese.

1) A website knows more about you than any shop assistant can, enabling it to offer personalized recommendations straight away.

2) The shift has been most dramatic in America, home to both a relentlessly disruptive e-commerce giant and a herd of entrenched retailers.

3) Many industry insiders have credited the "e-tailer" with forcing change in the industry, not just in the general evolution of online shopping, but also with logistics and technology.

4) Unlike the bookshops, these new locations will allow customers to drive in, park, pick up their items, and leave in under 15 minutes—effectively a click-and-collect depot under Amazon's

auspice.

5) This has prompted other companies to follow Amazon and open "pop-up" or "concept" stores to trial the popularity of physical locations.

6) What's more, their online offering will be expected to work seamlessly with the physical store estate, which means total integration of the distribution network for both online and offline systems.

6 Movie Exploration: *Boiler Room* (2000)

Cast

Directed by: Ben Younger
Starring: Giovanni Ribisi as Seth Davis
               Vin Diesel as Chris Varick
               Nicky Katt as Greg Weinstein
               Nia Long as Abbie Halper
               Taylor Nichols as Harry Reynard

Plot

- Seth Davis earns a successful living by running a casino at his home, but he disappoints his father who is angry at him for dropping out school.
- Greg Weinstein comes to Seth's casino at a night trying to convince him to join J.T. Marlin as a trainee.
- After a group interview, Seth is hired by J.T. Marlin and starts to be familar with corporate business.

商务学科英语

- Seth learns what is going on with J.T. Marlin and has a talk with Abby Halper.
- Seth makes a phone call to Harry Reynard and talks him into buy the stock, but ends up by costing Harrys' savings and family.
- Seth's father refuses Seth first when Seth comes to his office due to the risk of losing his judgeship, but later calls Seth for reconciliation.
- Seth is eventually arrested by the FBI who want him to be their informant.
- Seth returns to J.T. Marlin and makes a copy of the investment files as is instructed by the FBI after he gets Chris Varick' signature to get Harry's money back.

6.1 Search for the meanings of the following terms from the movie.

1) stock option: _____
2) rep number: _____
3) Ivy League: _____
4) IPO: _____
5) lottery: _____
6) NASD: _____
7) Series 7 exam: _____
8) FINRA: _____

Web Resources

https://www.investopedia.com/terms/s/stockoption.asp
https://satraining.com/(X(1)S(pgojr0xn03ly0kcyw43hsqt4))/default.aspx?MenuItemID=462&MenuSubID=41&MenuGroup=1FEED+Training-New+Accounts&AspxAutoDetectCookieSupport=1
https://en.wikipedia.org/wiki/Ivy_League
https://en.wikipedia.org/wiki/Initial_public_offering
https://en.wikipedia.org/wiki/Lottery
https://www.investopedia.com/terms/n/nasd.asp
http://www.finra.org/industry/series7
https://preview.finra.org/

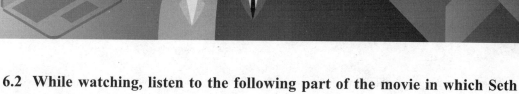

Unit 8 Retailing

6.2 While watching, listen to the following part of the movie in which Seth talks to Abby after he's found out all about the firm and complete it by filling in the blanks.

> In their conversation, Seth (S for Seth) tells everything to Abby (A for Abby) about how much he feels depressed after having learned what the firm does.

A: What's wrong?
S: Nothing.
A: Seth, I know you.
S: Jus...just work.
A: It's your father, isn't it?
S: No, no, everything's great with my dad. He is, you know he is taking me out to lunch next week 1)_____. Do you know how happy that makes me?
A: I do.
S: You know...I mean it's all based on this job, this very 2)_____, respectable job that he can tell his friends about during the Yom Kippur appeal. But you know 3)_____. I mean I'm so close. You know? And I'm screw it up.
A: How would you screw it up?
S: I went to the Med Patent office this morning, and there isn't one. It's cardboard. There's nothing. There're no employees. There's no research and development. Nothing. I found out how Michael's making his money. We're selling stock for companies that don't exist. Do you know what 4)_____ is?
A: No.
S: Basically, it's a way to 5)_____ for a company that's trying to 6)_____. They get money from outside investors. They're the bridge. And it's perfectly legal as long as there's no connection between the investors and the firm. But Michael's 7)_____ his friends as the investors on every IPO we do.
A: So that's why all the names on the contracts are the same.
S: Right. Then he has us push it all on the open market. We're basically selling Michael's shares. That's where the two-dollar rips come in. He can pay us that much, and it's worth it for him because he depends on us to 8)_____ create the market for him. There's no other firm selling this. It's all 9)_____. As soon as we sell off his position, there's no need to maintain the inflated price anymore. We stop pushing and then...
A: And then it 10)_____.
S: Right. But I mean how does that really affect me? I mean no. I'm just selling stock. There's

nothing wrong with that. So I know now how Michael makes his own money. And I know that I'm not working at Goldman Sachs, but we already know that. So how does this really change anything?

A: I don't know, Seth. You tell me.

6.3 After watching, cross the word or phrase that is closest in meaning to the bold one in each of the following sentences from the movie. An example is given for you.

e.g. We used to use the poker chips, and then some kids started **sneaking in** additional funds.

　　☐ stealing boldly　　　　✗ bringing secretly　　　　☐ changing stealthily

1) This is risky business. You don't think you'll **get pinched** in the next couple of years?

　　☐ get arrested　　　　☐ get sued　　　　☐ get exhausted

2) I'm gonna be **blunt**. We are talking about millions of dollars.

　　☐ polite　　　　☐ straightforward　　　　☐ sharp

3) Anyway, the point is I have to **adapt to** the new world.

　　☐ welcome　　　　☐ learn from　　　　☐ adjust to

4) The reason I **capped** him is in case he is piker.

　　☐ beat　　　　☐ laughed at　　　　☐ angered

5) Sometime I have to get in that mode at J.T. Marlin just to **fend** them **off** me.

　　☐ separate…from　　　　☐ distance…from　　　　☐ draw…from

6) I saw John **shredding** a bunch of documents the other day.

　　☐ destroying　　　　☐ hiding　　　　☐ falsifying

7) This is not going to be an **alternative** in the medical world. This is going to be the standard.

　　☐ illusion　　　　☐ opportunity　　　　☐ option

8) Now onto matters of **recreation**, we are going to take a class trip tonight.

　　☐ reproduction　　　　☐ entertainment　　　　☐ encouragement

9) Are you going to release the tape to the press, making your case more **glamorous** with the involvement of a federal judge?

　　☐ appealing　　　　☐ difficult　　　　☐ destructive

6.4 Work in groups and discuss the following questions.

1) Do you believe that there's no such a thing as making too much money or taking too many risks?

2) Do you think that money is the root of all evil?

Unit 8　Retailing

7　Debating Skills

How to Debate[1]

A debate is a structured argument. Two sides speak alternately for and against a particular contention usually based on a topical issue.

Basic debating skills
1) Style

Style is the manner in which you communicate your arguments. This is the most basic part of debating to master. Content and strategy are worth little unless you deliver your material in a confident and persuasive way.

2) Speed

It is vital to talk at a pace which is fast enough to sound intelligent and allow you have time to say what you want, but slow enough to be easily understood.

3) Tone

Varying tone is what makes you sound interesting. Listening to one tone for an entire presentation is boring.

4) Volume

Speaking quite loudly is sometimes a necessity, but it is by no means necessary to shout through every debate regardless of context. There is absolutely no need to speak any more loudly than the volume at which everyone in the room can comfortably hear you. Shouting does not win debates. Speaking too quietly is clearly disastrous since no one will be able to hear you.

5) Clarity

The ability to concisely and clearly express complex issues is what debating is all about. The main reason people begin to sound unclear is usually because they lose the "stream of thought" which is keeping them going. It is also important to keep it simple. While long words may make you sound clever, they may also make you incomprehensible.

6) Use of notes

Notes are essential, but they must be brief and well-organized to be effective. There is absolutely no point in trying to speak without notes. When writing notes for rebuttal during the debate, it is usually better to use a separate sheet of paper so you can take down the details of what the other speakers have said and then transfer a rough outline onto the notes you will actually be using.

1　Adapted from Kidd, A. (2002, August 26). *The Oxford Union rough guide to debating*. Retrieved from http://www.sfu.ca/cmns/130d1/HOWTODEBATE.htm

7) Use of eye contact

Eye contact with the audience is very important, but keep shifting your gaze. No one likes to be stared at.

Debating skills for building argument and rebuttal

In a debate, the arguments used to develop your own side's case and rebut the opposite side's.

1) Argument on the whole

Introduction: The case your group is making must be outlined in the introduction. This involves stating your main arguments and explaining the general thrust of your case. This must be done briefly since the most important thing is to get on and actually argue it. It is also a good idea to indicate the aspects of the subject to be discussed by each of the team members.

Conclusion: At the end, once everyone has spoken, it is useful to briefly summarize what your group has said and why.

2) Argument in the parts

Having outlined the whole of your arguments, you must then begin to build a case (the parts). The best way to do this is to divide your case into between two and four arguments. You must justify your arguments with basic logic, worked examples, statistics, and quotes. Debating is all about the strategy of "proof". Proof, or evidence, supporting your assertion is what makes it an argument.

There are a number of ways of dividing up cases according to groups of arguments (e.g. political/economic/social or moral/practical or international/regional) or just according to individual arguments if you can't group any together. Under each of these basic headings, you should then explain the reasoning behind the argument and justify it. It is usually best to put the most important argument first. Here is an example of a case outline:

- The media exert more influence over what people think than the government does. This is true for three reasons. Firstly, most people base their votes on what they see and hear in the media. Secondly, the media can set the political agenda between elections by deciding what issues to report and in how much detail. Thirdly, the media have successfully demonized politicians over the last ten years so that now people are more likely to believe journalists than politicians.

3) Rebuttal in the parts

Arguments can be factually, morally, or logically flawed. They may be misinterpretations or they may also be unimportant or irrelevant. A team may also contradict one another or fail to complete the tasks they set for themselves. These are the basics of rebuttal and almost every argument can be found wanting in at least one of these respects. Here are a few examples:

- "Compulsory euthanasia at age 70 would save the country money in pensions and healthcare." This is true, but is morally flawed.

Unit 8   Retailing

- "Banning cigarette product placement in films will cause more young people to smoke because it will make smoking more mysterious and taboo." This is logically flawed, the ban would be more likely to stop the steady stream of images which make smoking seem attractive and glamorous and actually reduce the number of young people smoking.
- "My partner will then look at the economic issues…" "Blah…blah…blah…(five minutes later and still no mention of the economic issues)" This is a clear failure to explain a major part of the case and attention should be drawn to it. Even better is when a speaker starts with, "To win this debate, there are three things I must do…". If the speaker fails to do any of those things, you can then hang him by the noose by repeating his exact words—by his own admission he cannot have won the debate.

4) Rebuttal on the whole:

It is very important to have a good perspective of the debate and to identify what the key arguments are. There are a number of things you should do to systematically break down a team's case:

- Ask yourself how the other side have approached the case. Is their methodology flawed?
- Consider what tasks the other side set for themselves (if any) and whether they have in fact addressed these.
- Consider what the general emphasis of the case is and what assumptions it makes. Try to refute these.
- Take the main arguments and do the same thing. It is not worth repeating a point of rebuttal that has been used by someone else already, but you can refer to it to show that the argument has not stood up. It is not necessary to correct every example used. You won't have time and your aim is to show the other side's case to be flawed in the key areas.

ACADEMIC ENGLISH FOR BUSINESS

Unit 9
Bitcoin

商务学科英语

1 Search for Background Information

1.1 Search for the meanings of the following terms from texts or about the subject.

1) digital currency: _____
2) Bitcoin: _____
3) mining: _____
4) cryptocurrency: _____
5) decentralization: _____
6) blockchain: _____
7) deflation: _____
8) inflation: _____
9) hedge (finance): _____
10) monetary policy: _____
11) fiscal policy: _____
12) fraud: _____
13) capital gains tax: _____
14) barter: _____
15) reputational risk: _____

Web Resources

https://en.wikipedia.org/wiki/Digital_currency
https://en.wikipedia.org/wiki/Bitcoin
https://en.wikipedia.org/wiki/Cryptocurrency
https://en.wikipedia.org/wiki/Decentralization
https://en.wikipedia.org/wiki/Blockchain
https://en.wikipedia.org/wiki/Deflation
https://en.wikipedia.org/wiki/Inflation
https://en.wikipedia.org/wiki/Hedge_(finance)
https://en.wikipedia.org/wiki/Monetary_policy
https://en.wikipedia.org/wiki/Fiscal_policy
https://en.wikipedia.org/wiki/Fraud
https://en.wikipedia.org/wiki/Capital_gains_tax
https://en.wikipedia.org/wiki/Barter
https://en.wikipedia.org/wiki/Reputational_risk

Unit 9 Bitcoin

1.2 Present what you've found to the class orally with or without PowerPoint in three minutes.

2 Discuss the Words' Meaning

2.1 Define the following underlined words. An example is given for you.

e.g. Governments may not <u>infringe</u> our basic human entitlements without our consent.
infringe: to do something that is against a law or someone's legal rights.

1) Someone stole my credit card and <u>forged</u> my signature.
   forge: _____
2) Call detail records are used by telecommunication firms to <u>detect</u> fraud in real time.
   detect: _____
3) The sooner people act on <u>accurate</u> information, the sooner the market will set the real price.
   accurate: _____
4) Return your purchase within 14 days for a full <u>refund</u>.
   refund: _____
5) Furniture and carpet <u>retailers</u> are among those reporting the sharpest annual decline in sales.
   retailer: _____
6) The fee charged by the realtor is directly <u>proportional</u> to the price of the property.
   proportional: _____
7) Rather than setting <u>arbitrary</u> prices, public officials force private companies to compete for sales.
   arbitrary: _____
8) Unfortunately, the stock price is easy for executives to <u>manipulate</u>, sometimes over long periods of time.
   manipulate: _____
9) The ruling also forbade the studios and distributors to <u>intervene</u> in ticket pricing by the theaters.
   intervene: _____
10) They agreed to <u>indemnify</u> the taxpayers against any loss.
    indemnify: _____
11) The unexpected and sudden memory briefly <u>panicked</u> her.

商务学科英语

panic: _____

12) This meant that the economy became, and has remained, far more competitive, while corporate performance became far more volatile.
   volatile: _____

13) The oil price increases sent Europe into deep recession.
   recession: _____

14) Consultants say 300 jobs could be created during construction, with 60 permanent posts at the plant.
   permanent: _____

15) Just as multinational corporations establish branches around the world to take advantage of attractive labor or raw material markets, so do illicit businesses.
   illicit: _____

16) The tax puts obstacles in the way of companies trying to develop trade overseas.
   obstacle: _____

17) Highlight only those achievements that make you the best candidate for the job.
   highlight: _____

18) The loss of work means the loss of everything. It affects man spiritually and hence makes him liable to disease.
   liable: _____

19) We should strengthen dialogue and consultation, refrain from taking protectionist measures, and avoid politicizing trade issues.
   refrain: _____

20) Mr. Taylor's critique—while harsher than many businesses would endorse—reflects broader concerns about France's industrial competitiveness.
   critique: _____

21) In economics, status quo bias can cause individuals to make seemingly non-rational decisions to stay with a sub-optimal situation.
   status quo: _____

22) In other situations, there could be more than one interaction between the consumer and the provider, each using a different protocol.
   protocol: _____

23) These are only his business ventures—what does he do in his free time? We took a look into the opulent life of this incredible entrepreneur.
   entrepreneur: _____

24) Good products and smart pricing strategies that drive robust demand can obviously accelerate cycles of innovation.
   accelerate: _____

25) He sold the contracts to another speculator for a profit.

speculator: _____

26) The company's two strongest intangible assets are its technology and how it manages its alliances.
   intangible: _____

27) The main reason for anonymity, however, is a belief that what is written is more important than who writes it.
   anonymity: _____

28) The U.S., in particular, has been trying to apply pressure to OPEC to modify any output cuts.
   modify: _____

29) The paradox is that the region's most dynamic economies have the most primitive financial systems.
   paradox: _____

30) Some stocks and some sectors, however, seem impervious to any speculation about government action.
   impervious: _____

2.2 Fill in the following blanks with various forms of each word. An example is given for you.

No.	Base form	Variations in the word family
e.g.	enforce	enforceable, enforcement, enforced, enforcer
1)	tangible	
2)	conscious	
3)	friction	
4)	authentic	
5)	proprietor	
6)	confederate	
7)	proportion	
8)	manipulate	
9)	intervene	
10)	volatile	
11)	speculate	

(Continued)

No.	Base form	Variations in the word family
12)	anarchy	
13)	modify	
14)	entrepreneur	
15)	critic	

2.3 Explain the meaning of the following roots or affixes. Add at least five similar derivatives with their Chinese definitions. An example is given for you.

No.	Roots/Affixes	Meaning	More derivatives with Chinese translation
e.g.	less	without	frictionless 无摩擦的; aimless 无目的的; baseless 无根据的; boundless 无限的; careless 粗心的
1)	trans-		
2)	-graphy		
3)	il-		
4)	en-/em-		
5)	cor-/col-		
6)	para-		
7)	-hood		
8)	an-		

3 Watch the Video

Difficult Words and Expressions

★ anonymous /əˈnɒnɪməs/ adj. 匿名的
★ fiddly /ˈfɪdlɪ/ adj. 要求高精度的
★ cryptography /krɪpˈtɒgrəfɪ/ n. 密码学
★ ledger /ˈledʒə/ n. 总账，分户总账

Unit 9　Bitcoin

★ scrupulous /ˈskruːpjʊləs/ *adj.* 小心谨慎的　　★ pint /paɪnt/ *n.* 品脱
★ shady /ˈʃeɪdɪ/ *adj.* 不法的　　★ volatile /ˈvɒlətaɪl/ *adj.* 不稳定的

3.1 Watch the first part of the video and answer the following questions.

1) What are the problems of our current paying system?
2) What is the problem of having a payment system without that middleman?
3) Who is Satoshi Nakamoto?
4) What is Nakamoto's proposal?
5) With Bitcoin, can any other party force a fee on a payment or control its flow?

3.2 Watch the second part of the video and take notes according to the questions in the left column.

No.	Questions	Notes
1)	Can you list examples from this clip about the things you can buy with Bitcoin?	
2)	What are the problems involved in Bitcoin?	
3)	Why might Bitcoin have problem in circulation?	
4)	What are people's worries about Bitcoin?	
5)	What is the speaker's attitude towards Bitcoin?	

3.3 Watch the whole video again and write a short summary of it according to your answers and notes.

_____
_____
_____
_____

3.4 Share your summary with your partner and present it to the class.

4 Read for Information

Why Bitcoin Has Value[1]

Van A. Marshall

❶ How can an intangible currency have tangible value? Bitcoin[2] is a currency composed of nothing but bits. Unlike dollars or euros, bitcoins have no physical form, no government backing, and operate with little more than technical regulation. What value can a bitcoin have? If information can be copied or "wants to be free", and bitcoins are nothing but information, why are they not free? As Bitcoin enters popular **consciousness**, the digital economy offers this interesting question.

❷ Consider four answers. First, Bitcoin's technical value lies in solving the double spend problem. Each bitcoin transaction uses public key cryptography to create a **permanent** public record that registers a buyer, a seller, and an amount as a tuple. This shows who can and cannot spend a bitcoin. Even someone who observes the transaction cannot **forge** coin copies. Software keys prevent anyone but the rightful owner from spending them.

❸ Second, the Bitcoin network enables near **frictionless** commerce as transaction fees approach zero. Credit card companies and currency exchanges can take a 2%–3% "rake" from the value of each transaction so companies that currently enjoy this rake might oppose Bitcoin. But any **merchant** competing online and enjoying a 5% margin **chafes at** losing half that margin to transaction fees. These fees represent friction that discourages trade and the movement of money. Just think of your neighborhood shop that refuses credit cards for small transactions because of high fees. After reducing these fees, people will spend more easily, and the economy will grow faster.

❹ Third, Bitcoin is better than credit cards at **detecting** fraud because each transaction requires public **authentication** from buyers and sellers. Years ago, I had the experience of a restaurant putting **fraudulent** charges on my card. I dined there often, so I assumed meal-sized charges were **accurate**. But when I moved to a different city and charges from this restaurant kept appearing on my bill, I knew they were fraudulent. This type of fraud is almost impossible using

---

1 Adapted from Van, A. M. (2014). Why bitcoin has value: Evaluating the evolving controversial digital currency. *Communications of the ACM, 57* (5), 30–32.
2 "Bitcoin" with a capital "B" refers to the network protocol while lowercase "bitcoin" refers to a unit of currency.

Unit 9　Bitcoin

Bitcoin. No waiter can pad bills, no **proprietor** can forge new ones, and no one can delay a **refund** after both parties authenticate. Not even credit cards, which **indemnify** you against fraud, offer this protection. Yet, public transactions do not mean Bitcoin **infringes** privacy. The buyer or seller or amount tuple records an account, not the identity of who owns that account. When properly administered, the Bitcoin protocol guarantees unauthorized parties cannot spend from an account while ownership of that account can remain private.

❺ Fourth, and more practically, Bitcoin has value because people accept it—the same reason for any form of money has value. "Money" is a medium of exchange, a store of value, and a unit of account. Bitcoin has all three **properties**. Money can be wampum, shekels, yen, euros, dollars, rubles, or renminbi. Money can be rock (gold), paper (notes), or scissors as long as people take it in trade, keep it as wealth, and measure it in prices. Overstock.com became the first major **retailer** to accept bitcoins as payments, taking in more than $125,000 the first day. At least 22,000 merchants including Virgin Airlines, Zynga, the Sacramento Kings, and the University of Nicosia accept bitcoins. Accepting money is what gives it value.

❻ Some economists argue that, to have value, money must be backed by a government that has tax and spend authority. Yet, the Iroquois, a **confederation** of pre-colonial tribes, had no income tax policy and traded with polished shell beads (wampum) to settle debts. The Weimar Republic in Germany had tax and spend authority but printed deutsche marks so fast that people and countries stopped accepting paper marks and demanded goods such as gold or coal in exchange.

❼ Such an argument confuses fiscal policy, the authority to tax and spend, with monetary policy, the authority to change the volume of currency in circulation. Both affect the value of money and the health of an economy but for different reasons.

❽ Growing an economy makes each currency unit more valuable, while growing a money supply makes each currency unit less valuable. These properties inform responsible monetary controls. Premodern currencies had built-in control: Gold was rare but could be mined and wampum could be made but only with enough labor. Modern currencies expand under government control to keep prices stable.

❾ Bitcoin has ingeniously engineered non-government control by expanding its supply only at a rate **proportional** to the technological discovery of prime numbers. It also promises that the total supply will never exceed 21 million bitcoins, though it can be subdivided **arbitrarily**. This promise of stable supply is stronger than any promise a government has made when it comes to currency targets. As Weimar Germany showed, politicians can **manipulate** their currencies during a crisis. Citizens of Zimbabwe and Ecuador use U.S. dollars as their national currencies precisely to **reign** in such irresponsible behavior.

❿ The decentralized nature of Bitcoin also means that no central bank can **intervene** to manipulate or stabilize its value when large demand fluctuations occur. Examiners for the U.S. central bank, the Federal Reserve, object to Bitcoin because this makes it volatile and a risky store of value. Bitcoins traded for approximately $1 in April 2011 but above $1,000 in November 2013. In February 2014, it dipped below $550. If Bitcoin had a central bank, it could have stepped in to buy or sell bitcoins as needed. An honest central broker can calm a **panicked** market. The failure of central banks to step in led to the Great Depression of 1929. The success of central banks stepping in avoided a greater **recession** than that of 2008.

⑪ Critics have raised two other objections. The first is that Bitcoin promotes illegal activity. Every transaction is public, but the buyers and sellers listed are simply Bitcoin addresses. The FBI recently shut down Silk Road, a popular market that accepted bitcoins, for facilitating illegal drug sales and other **illicit** transactions. But this is guilt by association. Note that the other preferred currency of criminals is cash. Over time, law enforcement will use the public record of bitcoin transactions to track down **crooks** in ways they never could for dollar bills.

⑫ Critics also point to theft as a risk for Bitcoin, highlighting Mt. Gox, a bitcoin exchange, robbed of $350 million. This problem is not new. Jesse James has just gone digital. Wikipedia lists a history of bank robberies by country. The biggest is nearly $1 billion. In just 10 hours last year, cyber criminals stole $45 million in real currency from real banks. As a start-up, PayPal experienced fraud rates more than five times than that of established credit cards before developing robust systems of control. The real surprise from the Mt. Gox robbery is that anyone thought "Magic: The Gathering Online Exchange"—a place launched to trade game cards—was the best place to store large sums of money.

⑬ Bitcoin is currently **liable** to **hoarding**. With rising values, people **refrain** from trading it in hoping its value will rise further. Critics argue this deflation limits Bitcoin as a medium of exchange. Ironically, this **critique** highlights its use as a store of value and undermines the almost opposite critique that Bitcoin is too volatile. It cannot only go up if it frequently fluctuates down.

⑭ The question is not whether Bitcoin has value; it already does. The question is whether the efficiencies of a cybercurrency like Bitcoin can be merged with the certainties of an honest central bank. I believe it can and will. At some point, a country will step forward and offer its currency as the cybercurrency of choice. Will bitdollars, biteuros, bityen, or bitrenminbi become the new global reserve currency? The first country to fully embrace what Bitcoin offers will do its own economy and the world a favor.

(1283 words)

Notes

Weimar Republic: 魏玛共和国。It is an unofficial historical designation for the German state from 1918 to 1933. The name derives from the city of Weimar, where its constitutional assembly first took place. The official name of the state remaines Deutsches Reich unchanged from 1871. Although commonly translated as "German Empire", the word "Reich" here better translates as "realm", in that the term does not have monarchical connotations per se. In English, the country is

Unit 9 Bitcoin

usually known simply as German.

Federal Reserve: 美国联邦储备系统。The Federal Reserve system (also known as the Federal Reserve or simply the Fed) is the central banking system of the United States. It was created on December 23, 1913, with the enactment of the Federal Reserve Act, after a series of financial panics (particularly the panic of 1907) led to the desire for central control of the monetary system in order to alleviate financial crises. Over the years, events such as the Great Depression in the 1930s and the Great Recession during the 2000s have led to the expansion of the roles and responsibilities of the Federal Reserve system.

FBI: 美国联邦调查局。The Federal Bureau of Investigation (FBI) is the domestic intelligence and security service of the United States, and its principal federal law enforcement agency. Operating under the jurisdiction of the Department of Justice, the FBI is also a member of the U.S. Intelligence Community and reports to both the Attorney General and the Director of National Intelligence. As a leading U.S. counter-terrorism, counterintelligence, and criminal investigative organization, the FBI has jurisdiction over violations of more than 200 categories of federal crimes.

Mt. Gox: It was a Bitcoin exchange based in Shibuya, Tokyo, Japan. Launched in July 2010, by 2013 and into 2014 it was handling over 70% of all Bitcoin transactions worldwide, as the largest Bitcoin intermediary and the world's leading Bitcoin exchange. In February 2014, Mt. Gox suspended trading, closed its website and exchange service, and filed for bankruptcy protection from creditors. In April 2014, the company began liquidation proceedings. Mt. Gox announced that approximately 850,000 bitcoins belonging to customers and the company were missing and likely stolen, an amount valued at more than $450 million at the time. Although 200,000 bitcoins have since been "found", the reasons for the disappearance—theft, fraud, mismanagement, or a combination of these—were initially unclear. New evidence presented in April 2015 by Tokyo security company WizSec led them to conclude that "most or all of the missing bitcoins were stolen straight out of the Mt. Gox hot wallet over time, beginning in late 2011."

PayPal: 贝宝（公司名称）。PayPal Holdings, Inc. is an American company operating a worldwide online payments system that supports online money transfers and serves as an electronic alternative to traditional paper methods like cheques and money orders. The company operates as a payment processor for online vendors, auction sites, and other commercial users, for which it charges a fee in exchange for benefits, such as one-click transactions and password memory.

4.1 Read Text A and answer the following questions.

1) According to the writer, why do credit card companies strongly oppose Bitcoin?
2) Compared with credit card, what advantages does Bitcoin boast?
3) Why does the writer believe that Bitcoin is money?
4) How does decentralized Bitcoin manage to balance its supply and demand?
5) According to the writer, what is the most important issue about Bitcoin?

4.2 Read Text A again and write a summary.

Summary (about 100 words): _____

_____

_____

_____

_____

TEXT B

In Bitcoin We Don't Trust[1]

Vincent Ryan

❶ For businesses, Bitcoin could in theory be used to transmit funds across country or intracompany borders, eliminating the need for traditional bank wires or other automated transfers. And for a nation's financial system, the use of bitcoin (or any other virtual currency) could result in many billions of dollars saved from not having to print, transport, and handle physical money.

❷ But talk to corporate treasurers about Bitcoin, and the conversation quickly turns from the ideal world to mundane reality—to things like settlement risk, security, and price volatility. Can these issues be addressed so that Bitcoin—a digital currency and Internet **protocol** that enables peer-to-peer payment worldwide—can enter the mainstream?

❸ Business adoption, after all, is critical to Bitcoin. Although many entrepreneurs are starting up companies to facilitate bitcoin transactions, there is no evidence that acceptance of the electronic currency in non-financial industries is anywhere close to accelerating. One of the currency's big **obstacles** is the so-called network effect: As with the telephone, the value of bitcoin or any other virtual currency is dependent on the number of other users using it.

❹ "Few retailers accept Bitcoin as a form of payment due to the small user base; and many consumers will not consider using bitcoins until a significant number of retailers accept Bitcoin payments," noted William J. Luther and Josiah Olson of Kenyon College in a June 2013 paper, "Bitcoin Is Memory". "Simply put, network effects favor the status quo…Bitcoin may fail to gain widespread acceptance even if it were superior to existing monies," warned Luther and Olson.

---

1 Adapted from Ryan, V. (2014). In bitcoin we don't trust: Why finance and treasury departments are keeping their distance from the virtual currency. *CFO*, April 24, 36–40. Retrieved from https://www.cfo.com/cash-management/2014/04/corporations-resist-bitcoin-see-lack-of-regulation-as-a-negative-who-will-regulate/

Unit 9 Bitcoin

❺ Besides, the virtues that many see in Bitcoin—especially its lack of regulation—are exactly what many corporate treasurers and investors view as the currency's faults. "Bitcoin is not run by a corporation or non-profit group. In fact, the lack of a central authority means that the Bitcoin payment system is not really run by anyone or anything," written by a law student Nikolei Kaplanov from Temple University in a 2012 paper, "Nerdy Money: Bitcoin, the Private Digital Currency, and the Case Against Its Regulation".

❻ As a result, according to Kaplanov, "there is no contractual relationship between Bitcoin miners and the creator or the provider of the Bitcoin system. Further, unlike virtual worlds that are governed by service agreements, there are no terms of service or any type of user agreements in mining or using bitcoins."

❼ "I don't have a positive view of an unregulated currency being used by corporate treasury departments," comments Gene Neyer, a global payments product manager at vendor Fundtech, "Although there was a small argument made for the foreign exchange efficiency of Bitcoin, it pales in comparison to the negatives: namely, finding and dealing with parties that will accept Bitcoin and not having any regulatory dispute resolution under the Uniform Commercial Code or similar." In addition, says Neyer, the boundaries or limits to inflation or deflation of the currency are unpredictable.

❽ Indeed, **speculators** are jumping into Bitcoin, driving prices to ridiculous heights. The volatility makes bitcoin an unstable store of value. According to John Bird of Atlas Risk Advisory, a foreign exchange risk consultancy, bitcoin is not even useful as a hedge. In a test, his firm found that bitcoin price changes had little or no **correlation** with price changes of assets, such as wheat, corn, oil, the S & P 500, or even the 10-year U.S. Treasury note. The high level of instability in bitcoin price changes "adds an additional degree of difficulty for the structuring of a bitcoin hedge," says Bird.

❾ The Bitcoin community finds the currency's **anarchic** roots attractive, but it will have to build faith in the currency's security and stability to drive adoption. Despite the founder's wishes, the need for trust—in an issuing authority, or any authority—may be impossible to avoid.

❿ Earlier this year, Mt. Gox, a large, Japan-based Bitcoin exchange that once controlled 85% of Bitcoin trading volume, filed for bankruptcy protection in Japan and the United States after 750,000 Bitcoins deposited by users disappeared. In essence, the incident showed, Bitcoin exchanges like Mt. Gox are almost the equivalent of Bitcoin banks. But if that's the case, they are unregulated banks at which depositors have neither protection nor insurance against theft and bank runs, as finance expert Aswath Damodaran points out on his blog *Musings on Markets*.

⓫ At least for now, traditional banks don't seem to be eager to jump into the business. For one thing, Bitcoin's relative **anonymity** would violate U.S. banking laws that require financial institutions to know their customers. So who is going to build trust in Bitcoin?

⓬ Damodaran writes that "Bitcoin's staying power will ultimately depend upon how

impervious its source algorithm is to mischief…If you are a Bitcoin promoter, you want to make sure that even the slightest doubts that the algorithm can be **fudged** or **modified** are dealt with quickly and openly, since those doubts will undo its effectiveness as a currency."

⑬ In addition, while the currency has an advantage in that central banks can't inflate the value of a Bitcoin on a whim and that there is a technical limit on the number of Bitcoins, someone has to work to keep the value of a Bitcoin relatively stable.

⑭ Relying on the Bitcoin community in a kind of "open source" model in which a loosely coordinated group ensures, for example, the algorithm's security, won't be enough for most CFOs. Would regulation help? Governments are still **grappling with** the question of how Bitcoin can and will be regulated. Early on, countries are taking wildly different approaches. Sweden, for one, plans to treat it not like a currency but like a piece of art or an antique, subject to capital gains taxes. Finland's central bank says Bitcoin is not a payment instrument and is more comparable to a commodity, while Canada's Revenue Agency equates Bitcoin payments with barter transactions.

⑮ In the United States, the director of the Financial Crimes Enforcement Network has said the regulator views virtual currency as a kind of money services business, having the same obligation as other businesses in that industry. In early March, the state of New York started accepting proposals and applications for BitLicenses, a certificate that would allow Bitcoin exchanges to operate in the state. A proposal on the regulatory framework won't come until the second quarter.

⑯ For companies, of course, the question of monetary value is no small issue: The accounting for and taxation of Bitcoin and Bitcoin transactions are still a mystery. There are no generally accepted accounting principles for Bitcoin, and no official pronouncements yet about accounting methods for Bitcoin from the Financial Accounting Standards Board. The Internal Revenue Service also has yet to **weigh in**.

⑰ In short, many feel like Fundtech's Neyer does: "Given that the regulations continue to expand, there is just too much reputational risk associated with Bitcoin."

⑱ Bitcoin, meanwhile, is caught in something of a **paradox**. Regulation threatens the principles on which it was founded, but government involvement may be the only way it becomes a standard form of payment or exchange that is widely accepted. If regulators can figure out what Bitcoin is and build confidence in the currency, who knows? Maybe there will be a currency that, without **oversight** from a central bank, can offer the security and convenience of traditional money. But Bitcoin is a long way from that.

(1241 words)

Notes

Internal Revenue Service (IRS): 美国国税局。It is the revenue service of the United States federal government. The government agency is a Bureau of the Department of the Treasury, and

Unit 9　Bitcoin

is under the immediate direction of the Commissioner of Internal Revenue, who is appointed to a five-year term by the President of the United States. The IRS is responsible for collecting taxes and administering the Internal Revenue Code, the main body of federal statutory tax law of the United States. The duties of the IRS include providing tax assistance to taxpayers and pursuing and resolving instances of erroneous or fraudulent tax filings. The IRS has also overseen various benefits programs, and enforces portions of the Affordable Care Act.

4.3　Read Text B. Write a summary in the following form and take notes according to the table below.

Subject: _____
Key words: _____
Organization types: _____
Thesis statement (or main ideas): _____
_____

Conclusion (or major findings): _____
_____

No.	Paragraph(s)	Structure	Content
1)		Question	
2)		Argument 1	
3)		Argument 2	
4)		Argument 3	
5)		Argument 4	
6)		Argument 5	
7)		Argument 6	
8)		Conclusion	

4.4　Read Text B again and answers the following questions.

1) What is the advantage of Bitcoin acknowledged in both Text A and Text B?
2) How does Text B tackle the problem of Bitcoin's business adoption that Text A uses as a

major argument?

3) How do Text A and Text B respectively argue for or against the point of "lack of regulation"?
4) How does Text A differ from Text B on using the case of Mt. Gox to argue for their own opinions?
5) What are the different conclusions drawn by the two articles?

UNIT PROJECT

Read Text B and Text A again, form two groups, and hold a debate on the topic "Bitcoin is nothing but an economic bubble". Give evidence to support your arguments and refute your opponents'.

5 Practice for Enhancement

5.1 Read the four words in each group and cross the word which is not a synonym for the bold word. An example is given for you.

e.g. **intangible**
  ☐ invisible   ☐ discarnate   ✗ imaginable   ☐ untouchable
1) **permanent**
  ☐ eternal   ☐ constant   ☐ perpetual   ☐ external
2) **confederation**
  ☐ confrontation   ☐ alliance   ☐ association   ☐ league
3) **fudge**
  ☐ converse   ☐ manufacture   ☐ concoct   ☐ fabricate
4) **reign**
  ☐ withdraw   ☐ dominate   ☐ rule   ☐ possess
5) **volatile**
  ☐ unstable   ☐ refundable   ☐ mobile   ☐ variable
6) **recession**
  ☐ depression   ☐ downturn   ☐ concession   ☐ decline
7) **obstacle**
  ☐ interference   ☐ disturbance   ☐ interpretation   ☐ bar

8) **correlation**

☐ cooperation ☐ relationship ☐ associations ☐ relevance

9) **impervious**

☐ unaffected ☐ apathetic ☐ unmoved ☐ sympathetic

5.2 Decide what words can go with the following verbs. An example is given for you.

e.g. allocate: resources, time, money, land, funds, etc.
1) forge:
2) detect:
3) manipulate:
4) facilitate:
5) embrace:
6) modify:
7) refund:
8) eliminate:
9) undermine:

5.3 Paraphrase the following sentences. An example is given for you.

e.g. Although there was a small argument made for the foreign exchange efficiency of Bitcoin, it pales in comparison to the negatives.
<u>While there are some minor doubts about Bitcoin's foreign exchange efficiency, they are nothing in the face of its negative effects.</u>

1) But this is guilt by association. Note that the other preferred currency of criminals is cash. Over time, law enforcement will use the public record of bitcoin transactions to track down crooks in ways they never could for dollar bills.

2) Critics argue this deflation limits Bitcoin as a medium of exchange. Ironically, this critique highlights its use as a store of value and undermines the almost opposite critique that Bitcoin is too volatile.

3) The question is whether the efficiencies of a cybercurrency like Bitcoin can be merged with the certainties of an honest central bank.

4) The first country to fully embrace what Bitcoin offers will do its own economy and the world a favor.

5) But talk to corporate treasurers about Bitcoin, and the conversation quickly turns from the ideal world to mundane reality—to things like settlement risk, security, and price volatility.

6) The Bitcoin community finds the currency's anarchic roots attractive, but it will have to build faith in the currency's security and stability to drive adoption. Despite the founder's wishes, the need for trust—in an issuing authority, or any authority—may be impossible to avoid.

7) If you are a Bitcoin promoter, you want to make sure that even the slightest doubts that the algorithm can be fudged or modified are dealt with quickly and openly, since those doubts will undo its effectiveness as a currency.

8) Relying on the Bitcoin community in a kind of "open source" model in which a loosely coordinated group ensures, for example, the algorithm's security, won't be enough for most CFOs.

5.4 Translate the following sentences into Chinese.

1) If information can be copied or "wants to be free", and bitcoin are nothing but information, why is it not free? As Bitcoin enters popular consciousness, the digital economy offers this interesting question.

2) But any merchant competing online and enjoying a 5% margin chafes at losing half that margin to transaction fees. These fees represent friction that discourages trade and the

Unit 9 Bitcoin

movement of money.

3) Yet, the Iroquois, a confederation of pre-colonial tribes, had no income tax policy and traded with polished shell beads (wampum) to settle debts. The Weimar Republic in Germany had tax and spend authority but printed deutsche marks so fast that people and countries stopped accepting paper marks and demanded goods such as gold or coal in exchange.

4) Bitcoin has ingeniously engineered non-government control by expanding its supply only at a rate proportional to the technological discovery of prime numbers. It also promises that the total supply will never exceed 21 million bitcoins, though it can be subdivided arbitrarily.

5) Besides, the virtues that many see in Bitcoin—especially its lack of regulation—are exactly what many corporate treasurers and investors view as the currency's faults.

6) Bitcoin, meanwhile, is caught in something of a paradox. Regulation threatens the principles on which it was founded, but government involvement may be the only way it becomes a standard form of payment or exchange that is widely accepted.

 6 Movie Exploration: *Wall Street 2: Money Never Sleeps* (2000)

Cast

Directed by: Oliver Stone
Starring: Michael Douglas as Gordon Gekko
               Shia LaBeouf as Jacob Moore
               Josh Brolin as Bretton James

商务学科英语

Carey Mulligan as Winnie Gekko
Frank Langella as Louis Zabel
Natalie Morales as Churchill Schwartz

Plot

- Gordon Gekko is released from prison after eight years for insider trading and securities fraud.
- Louis Zabel fails to arrange a bailout from other Wall Street bankers and kills himself after the stock loses.
- Jacob Moore attends Gekko's lecture and introduces himself to Gekko who tells him that it could be Bretton James who has spread rumors about KZI.
- In revenge, Jacob illegally manipulates the market, causing Churchill Schwartz a million dollars.
- Jacob goes to see Bretton who offers him a job.
- Jacob agrees to help Gekko to get him and his daughter Winnie Gekko back together and in return Gekko promises to dig around on Locus Fund.
- With the help of Jacob, Gekko attends a fundraiser and confronts Bretton and luckily he will probably reconcile with his daughter.
- Jacob confronts Bretton when he is told the deal he attempts to make with Chinese is killed.
- Jacob agrees on Gekko's suggestion of using a $100 million trust fund account to fund the fusion research, but he finds himself betrayed by Gekko who leaves the country with the money.
- Jacob gives the details of Bretton's dealings to Winnie who posts them on her website, causing Bretton under intense government scrutiny.
- Jacob successfully reunites with Winnie and Gekko who anonymously has deposited $100 million into the fusion research account.

6.1 Search for the meanings of the following terms from the movie.

1) **nationalization:** _____
2) **money laundering:** _____
3) **proprietary trading:** _____
4) **equity:** _____
5) **Ninja:** _____
6) **SIV:** _____
7) **spot bonus award:** _____
8) **home loan defaults:** _____

Unit 9 Bitcoin

Web Resources

https://en.wikipedia.org/wiki/Nationalization
https://www.int-comp.org/careers/a-career-in-aml/what-is-money-laundering/
https://www.investopedia.com/terms/p/proprietarytrading.asp
https://en.wikipedia.org/wiki/Equity_(finance)
https://en.wikipedia.org/wiki/Ninja
https://en.wikipedia.org/wiki/Structured_investment_vehicle
https://www.salary.com/articles/types-of-bonuses/
https://www.consumer.ftc.gov/articles/0194-trouble-paying-your-mortgage

6.2 While watching, listen to the following part of the movie in which there is a meeting going on after the crisis and complete it by filling in the blanks.

> In this meeting, Bill (B1 for Bill) asks Bretton (B2 for Bretton) and Julie (J for Julie) their suggestions on how to cope with the oncoming crisis.

(Background news) There is carnage on Wall Street. The shares of the major financial stocks 1)_____. It's triggering 2)_____ in the markets. The damage, widespread. The Nasdaq's plunging. The Dow Jones industrial average is plunging and oil is plunging. Literally a 180 points just added to the decline. You can hear the hollering on the floor. We're down 260, literally in a split second. Right now, the Down Jones industrial average is now 500 points on the decline. Headline of the new housing reports is 3)_____ that this is shaping up to be the worst real estate market in a generation. We are now at the highest point there, 724. That was the biggest loss we've seen today. We are now in historic territory. Investors are getting their heads handed to them as another U.S. banking institution nears collapse. The President's working group is going into 4)_____ with the Secretary of the Treasury and the Federal Reserve Board.

B2: This isn't Keller Zabel, Bill. This is 5)_____. This is just an 6)_____ situation. There's about 70-plus trillion out there in credit default swaps held by roughly 17 banks. And we do not know where the bottom is.

B1: How much are you guys thinking?

B2: I think we're talking seven, eight. Selling this to Congress is the problem. They're gonna want to know where the money's going. They'll 7)_____ this to death. The government's got to 8)_____. If we don't stop the bleeding in three days, half the banks in this room are 9)_____. And in five days, we're all gone.

B1: You men realize what you've done here? You're asking for the biggest bailout in the history

233

of this country. We are talking nationalization, Bretton, socialism. I have fought it all my life.

B2: If we don't get it, Bill, they won't be any history. Music stops. Ball's over.

B1: Julie?

J: 1929. It'll get worse now, because it'll go faster. Money markets will 10)_____ around the world by the end of the week. ATMs will stop spitting bills. Federal deposit insurance will collapse. Banks will close. Mobs, panic. It's going to be the end of the world, Bill.

6.3 After watching, cross the word or phrase that is closest in meaning to the bold one in each of the following sentences from the movie. An example is given for you.

e.g. Do me a favor. Don't ask me **dumb** questions.

☐ difficult   ☒ stupid   ☐ lucid

1) I thought maybe the news out of London would've **wreck** the mood.

☐ ruin   ☐ interrupt   ☐ affect

2) We're looking for an **unprecedented** meltdown here.

☐ destructive   ☐ unparalleled   ☐ long-term

3) Stop **bugging** me with irrelevant things.

☐ humoring   ☐ attacking   ☐ annoying

4) If you want us to **bail out** Keller Zabel, we will need substantial guarantees from the U.S. Treasury.

☐ help out   ☐ beat up   ☐ compete with

5) There's no way we can risk that money without a **backstop** from Treasury or the Fed.

☐ criticism   ☐ support   ☐ abuse

6) The stock of Keller Zabel is currently **halted**, pending news that Churchill Schwartz is making out like a bandit right now with government funding.

☐ profited   ☐ ceased   ☐ declined

7) They knew this home loan **fantasy** was going to collapse the market.

☐ illusion   ☐ force   ☐ industry

8) This is only a **preliminary** proceeding. But I want you to know you're under investigation.

☐ simple   ☐ initial   ☐ unimportant

9) The Dow Jones industrial average is **plunging** in response to the crisis.

☐ increasing   ☐ maintaining   ☐ tumbling

6.4 Work in groups and discuss the following questions.

1) To what extent do you agree with Gekko who says "greed is good"?

2) Why did Gekko say that the young generation is Ninja generation according to the movie? Do

Unit 9 Bitcoin

you think that your generation is Ninja generation?

7 Writing Skills

How to Write Good Academic Papers[1]

Academic writing is an important skill for the success in higher education and in any career field but many university students find their written assignments too challenging and often consider them to be a form of a medieval torture. This type of writing is specific and differs a lot from what you were asked to produce in high school because it involves a lot of reading, doing in-depth research of scholarly literature, planning, revising, making changes in content and structure, rewriting, editing, proofreading, and formatting.

Key principles of academic writing

The goal of completing written assignments is to show that you have a profound knowledge of a specific topic and to share your own thoughts about a scientific question or an issue that may be of interest to your audience—students, your professor, and other scholars. You have to demonstrate your critical thinking skills by following the key principles:

- Your papers must have a clear purpose (inform, analyze, synthesize, or persuade) and answer your topic question.
- Your papers must present your original point of view.
- Your writing must have a single focus—all paragraphs have to include relevant evidence (facts, expert opinions, quotations, and examples) to support your thesis statement.
- You must follow a standard organizational pattern. Every academic text must include the following parts: an introduction, the main body, and a conclusion. Some papers may require an abstract.
- As an author, you need to provide clear, logical, and simple explanations to your readers.
- You should refer to a number of scholarly sources. You need to integrate source materials into your discussion. Take care to include all sources (books, articles from a scientific journal, and publications on online resources) that you cite, introduce, analyze, or explain on a reference list in the bibliography page.
- To ensure academic integrity, all college essays should be formatted in accordance with the requirements of one of the specific citation styles—APA, MLA, Harvard, and Chicago that

---

1 Adapted from Pro Academic Writers. (unknown publication date). *How to write good academic papers: Easy guide for beginners*. Retrieved from https://pro-academic-writers.com/blog/academic-paper-writing

determine the rules for in-text citations, paper sections, format, and reference list.

Essential steps of the writing process

Writing an academic paper can be done step by step. If you are a beginner, you can follow these steps below that have worked for millions of college students; they can save you a lot of time.

- Select an interesting topic. If you lack ideas, you may search the Internet, look through your lecture notes, and consider your course readings or current news.
- Do research and record sources' information. Keep in mind that you may need to continue your research as you discover a thesis, make an outline, write and revise the document.
- Formulate a strong thesis statement that you will argue.
- Plan your essay and make a basic outline. Take notes from your sources and add details to your outline to make sure that you have supporting evidence for your points.
- Write the first draft of your essay. You can start from any part and you should not worry about grammar, punctuation, and spelling as you construct your sentences. You will fix them later.
- Revise your first draft and improve the content, logic, and the flow. Make transitions between your ideas. Make changes to improve the content and rewrite your draft. You may need to do it more than once.
- Edit and proofread your final draft to ensure that your essay is flawless.

Thesis statement

A thesis statement determines the main argument of your essay. A good thesis statement expresses the main idea of your essay, presents your own point of view, and gives an answer to your research question. The success of your entire project depends on your thesis and you need to do your best to ensure that it is debatable, specific, and concise. Try to write your thesis early. It will help you stay focused when you do research and take notes.

Introduction

Introductions and conclusions are very important. The introduction introduces your argument to your readers and convinces them why they should care about reading your paper. Start your introduction with attention grabber and provide background information about the significance of your topic, introduce a subject, and give some definitions of the key terms. End your introduction with a thesis statement.

Body paragraphs

Start each body paragraph with a topic sentence; do not begin a paragraph with a fact. The topic sentence should present the main idea of the paragraph and express your point of view. In the next sentences, you should support the topic sentence with additional supporting ideas, specific details, interesting facts, statistics, clear explanations, and relevant examples. All supporting

Unit 9 Bitcoin

sentences should be logical. You should make sure they are connected with connection words to help your readers follow your argument.

Finish every paragraph with a concluding sentence. It should be your own idea and not a source citation. The last sentence in a paragraph should review the key points you have discussed in it, emphasize your main idea or your thesis statement, and prepare your audience to the points that you are going to discuss in the next paragraph.

Do not make your paragraphs too long. People find it difficult to focus on large blocks of text. If you discover that your paragraph is very long, divide it logically into two separate paragraphs.

Conclusion

This part of your paper is the most important. Actually, readers remember the first and the last parts of what they read; a conclusion is your last chance to make an impression and show the significance of your findings. How can you achieve that? When writing a conclusion, you need to provide connections to the previous ideas, briefly summarize your findings, or restate the thesis. Finish your essay with a strong concluding statement that your readers will remember.

Revising

No one can write a perfect first draft. It's impossible—revising is critical if you want to impress your professor and get a high grade for your work. You should start revising the content before your paper is due. You can use another strategy as well—revise individual paragraphs as you write them. Be ready that you may need to write more than one draft or revise your paper several times.

Read your paper and make changes to fix it and make it impeccable. You can do it in a number of ways:
- Eliminate irrelevant ideas and unnecessary information.
- Add new explanations, details, and points to ensure additional support for your argument.
- Rewrite paragraphs and sentences to present your ideas better.
- Reorganize paragraphs and sentences to make your paper logical.

Editing and proofreading

The goal of editing is making your writing clearer, more precise to ensure that your readers will be able to understand it. Follow the editing strategies to make your essay as best as it can be:
- Fix sentences with the passive voice.
- Improve word choice by replacing long words with shorter ones.
- Improve sentence structure and word order—correct run-ons and fragments.
- Fix the logic, flow, and connections between ideas.
- Rewrite long sentences and make them concise; eliminate unnecessary sentences in paragraphs if they do not convey new messages.
- Fix repetition and use thesaurus to find synonyms.

When you finish editing, proofread your essay and fix minor errors, careless mistakes, and typos. Check punctuation and spelling. Use the printed copy to notice mistakes you may overlook on a computer screen.

Citation

To avoid plagiarism, you must give credit to other people whose ideas you use in your own work. You have the right to express your opinions. You have the right to use ideas of people to support your argument and draw conclusions, but it's your responsibility to inform your audience which ideas in your essay are not yours and which are your own. With proper citations, you demonstrate that you understand the significance of other people's research, findings, and ideas in developing your own argument.

ACADEMIC ENGLISH FOR BUSINESS

Unit 10
Trade War

商务学科英语

1 Search for Background Information

1.1 Search for the meanings of the following terms from texts or about the subject.

1) trade war: _____
2) WTO: _____
3) balanced trade: _____
4) subsidy: _____
5) gold reserve: _____
6) currency depreciation: _____
7) trade deficit: _____
8) trade surplus: _____
9) TPP: _____
10) USITC: _____
11) mercantilism: _____
12) Dow Jones Industrial Average: _____
13) quota: _____
14) America First: _____
15) OECD: _____

Web Resources

https://www.investopedia.com/terms/t/trade-war.asp
https://www.wto.org/english/thewto_e/thewto_e.htm
https://www.investopedia.com/terms/b/balanced-trade.asp
https://www.investopedia.com/terms/s/subsidy.asp
https://en.wikipedia.org/wiki/Gold_reserve
https://www.investopedia.com/terms/c/currency-depreciation.asp
https://www.investopedia.com/terms/t/trade_deficit.asp
https://www.investopedia.com/terms/t/trade-surplus.asp
https://en.wikipedia.org/wiki/Trans-Pacific_Partnership
https://www.usitc.gov/press_room/about_usitc.htm
https://en.wikipedia.org/wiki/Mercantilism
https://en.wikipedia.org/wiki/Dow_Jones_Industrial_Average

Unit 10 Trade War

https://www.investopedia.com/terms/q/quota.asp https://en.wikipedia.org/wiki/America_First_(policy)

http://www.oecd.org/about/

1.2 Present what you've found to the class orally with or without PowerPoint in three minutes.

2 Discuss the Words' Meaning

2.1 Define the following underlined words. An example is given for you.

e.g. Trump's invocation of national security to justify some of his moves could open a Pandora's box of similar claims by other nations.
   justify: to show or prove that somebody or something is right or reasonable.

1) Officials say they will intensify health screening measures at airports and ports.
   intensify: _____
2) Seven of the nine states that do not levy an income tax grew faster than the national average.
   levy: _____
3) Washington would not take such a step without its allies' approval.
   ally: _____
4) This action was undoubtedly in retaliation for last week's bomb attack.
   retaliation: _____
5) He vowed to act on climate change himself if Congress failed to enact legislation.
   enact: _____
6) The advantages of this system are too numerous to mention.
   numerous: _____
7) I know that the Prime Minister's invocation of "education, education, education" has become a political cliché, but he is right.
   invocation: _____
8) Initially, I thought I would only stay there for a year.
   initially: _____
9) Shoppers were scrambling to get the best bargains.
   scramble: _____
10) She was a person accustomed to having eight hours' sleep a night.

accustomed: _____

11) The new governor pledged to reduce crime.
    pledge: _____

12) The company's new policy backfired when a number of employees threatened to quit.
    backfire: _____

13) Barnet was desperate for money to resolve his financial problems.
    resolve: _____

14) Her argument was grounded in fact.
    grounded: _____

15) The government hiked up the price of milk by over 40%.
    hike: _____

16) Microsoft's code—millions of lines long in the case of Windows—is known to be extremely intricate.
    intricate: _____

17) They are warning of impending collapse in the Dow Jones Industrials and the NASDAQ.
    impending: _____

18) The meeting will take place at an unspecified date in the future.
    unspecified: _____

19) He is confined in isolation because of his vulnerability to infection.
    vulnerability: _____

20) The fall in the number of deaths from heart disease is generally attributed to improvements in diet.
    attribute: _____

21) The government has failed to halt economic decline.
    halt: _____

22) In many respects, private non-profit programs were intermediate between public and for-profit programs.
    intermediate: _____

23) Hotels often inflate prices at particular times of the year.
    inflate: _____

24) As commodities such as coffee or soya flooded into the world market, prices slumped, causing more economic chaos.
    slump: _____

25) Measures need to be taken to mitigate the environmental effects of burning more coal.
    mitigate: _____

26) Most investments are expected to appreciate at a steady rate.

appreciate: _____

27) Caffeine is the active constituent of drinks, such as tea and coffee.
    constituent: _____
28) His position as mayor gives him leverage to get things done.
    leverage: _____
29) The house had many drawbacks, most notably its price.
    notably: _____
30) I am a strong and resilient person and the fact that I can easily adapt to any situation made me a survivor.
    resilient: _____

2.2 Fill in the following blanks with various forms of each word. An example is given for you.

No.	Base form	Variations in the word family
e.g.	intention	intentional, intentionally, unintentional, intend, intentionality
1)	intensify	
2)	retaliate	
3)	enact	
4)	numerous	
5)	invoke	
6)	initial	
7)	vulnerable	
8)	resolve	
9)	mediate	
10)	specific	
11)	inflate	
12)	note	
13)	adverse	
14)	escalate	
15)	optical	

2.3 Explain the meaning of the following roots or affixes. Add at least five similar derivatives with their Chinese definitions. An example is given for you.

No.	Roots/Affixes	Meaning	More derivatives with Chinese translation
e.g.	bi-	two/double	bilateral 双边的；bisexual 两性的；bilingual 双语的；bipolar 两极的；bimonthly 双月刊
1)	dent		
2)	dis-		
3)	under-		
4)	vers/vert		
5)	fin		
6)	pos		
7)	inter-		
8)	ven		

3 Watch the Video

Difficult Words and Expressions

★ ignite /ɪgˈnaɪt/ v. 燃烧；点燃
★ jazz up 使变得有趣；使活泼
★ spoiler /ˈspɔɪlə/ n. 剧透
★ subsidize /ˈsʌbsɪdaɪz/ v. 资助，补贴
★ fray /freɪ/ n. 争论；打架

3.1 Watch the first part of the video and answer the following questions.

1) What is the video about?
2) What are some examples of the "weapons" in a trade war?
3) What are tariffs?
4) What is a trade war?
5) Why does a country start a trade war?

3.2 Watch the second part of the video and take notes according to the questions in the left column.

No.	Questions	Notes
1)	How do some economists predict who "wins" a trade war?	
2)	What countries benefit from trade wars?	
3)	Why did the U.S. enact the Smoot-Hawley Tariff Act?	
4)	What are the consequences of the Smoot-Hawley Tariff Act?	
5)	Why are trade wars harmful for almost everyone involved, particularly for poorer consumers?	

3.3 Watch the whole video again and write a short summary of it according to your answers and notes.

_____

_____

_____

3.4 Work in groups and give a report to the class on "Trade war" according to the following clues in five minutes.

1) What are advantages and disadvantages of trade war?
2) Can trade war be avoided? If yes, how? If no, why?

4 Read for Information

TEXT A

Can Trump Win if He Escalates His China Trade War?[1]

① U.S. President Donald Trump is threatening to **intensify** an ongoing trade war by rolling out tariffs on $267 billion worth of Chinese exports to the U.S., on top of the $200 billion worth that he could soon hit with duties. He previously had imposed tariffs, which act like a tax on imports, on $50 billion worth of Chinese products, and could soon run out of ways to **levy** more duties: The total of imposed and threatened tariffs is now $517 billion, yet the U.S. only bought $505 billion of goods from China last year.

② China has hit back with tariffs on U.S. goods. The U.S. also has levied duties on steel and **aluminum** imports from most countries, including **allies** Canada, Mexico, and the European Union. They also reacted with tariffs of their own. It adds up to an **all-out** trade war, one that risks gumming up global supply chains, raising consumer prices, stalling economic growth, and tying the World Trade Organization in knots. What's less clear is whether it will end the way Trump wants.

③ What is a trade war? The dictionary says it's "an economic conflict in which countries impose import restrictions on each other in order to harm each other's trade". Trump's tariffs and the **retaliation** by other countries, both threatened and **enacted**, meet this definition. But so do centuries of protectionist **skirmishes** by **numerous** countries in countless sectors. What make this a **full-blown** trade war are Trump's singling out of China for retaliation, the tit-for-tat actions by the U.S. and its closest allies over metals tariffs, and Trump's **invocation** of national security to justify some of his moves—which could open a Pandora's box of similar claims by other nations.

④ One of the most **notorious** examples of previous trade wars is the Smoot-Hawley Act passed by Congress in 1930 that is often blamed for deepening the Great Depression. The law, which effectively **hiked** U.S. tariffs by an average of 59%, **initially** was meant to protect American farmers. But many other industries lobbied for protection, and Congress agreed. The tariffs caused other countries to retaliate against the U.S. and each other, which resulted in higher prices on many manufactured and consumer goods. As demand collapsed, countries **scrambled** to maintain their

---

1 Adapted from Bloomberg. (2018, September 08). *Can Trump win if he escalates his China trade war?* Retrieved from http://fortune.com/2018/09/08/trump-china-trade-war-2/

Unit 10 Trade War

gold reserves by devaluing their currencies or imposing even more trade barriers. Global trade fell off a cliff.

⑤ Trump has said the U.S. will win because it has a stronger economy and can outlast China in a trade war. The U.S. economy is booming and China's is showing signs of stress. But the longer the dispute goes on, the more both sides will see casualties. For Trump, those could include key **constituencies**, such as consumers who are **accustomed** to buying lower-priced goods made in China. Already, many companies are warning of lower profits because of higher prices for raw materials, supply-chain disruptions, and sales declines. The U.S. also has begun a $12 billion program to bail out farmers hurt by China's and other countries' retaliatory tariffs on U.S. exports of soybeans, corn, and other crops. Tit-for-tat tariffs "so far have only produced increased costs for American businesses, farmers, importers, exporters, and consumers", a **coalition** of about 150 business and trade organizations told the Trump administration.

⑥ The reason why Trump is inviting this fight was stated in a March 2 Twitter post. He declared trade wars "good, and easy to win". Trump later said duties on Chinese imports are justified after decades in which China tilted the playing field, including by devaluing its currency and forcing American companies to share their technology. He has repeatedly **pledged** to reduce the U.S. trade deficit—the difference between what the U.S. imports and what it exports. But by the end of 2017, the deficit had risen to $568 billion from $505 billion in 2016, and it has kept on rising. Stepping back from trade deals like the North American Free Trade Agreement and the Trans-Pacific Partnership also appeals to Trump's base of voters in America's Rust Belt. But talk of a trade war is alarming to many U.S. business leaders, who largely support existing trade deals, and the securities markets, which fear lower profits and slower economic growth.

⑦ Also, tariffs could **backfire** on the U.S. Take steel, for instance. Many more people are employed in industries, such as auto manufacturing, that buy steel to make products than in steel-making itself. President George W. Bush's higher steel tariffs, imposed from 2002 to 2005 to protect against a surge in imports, created a $30 million drag on U.S. gross domestic product, according to the U.S. International Trade Commission. Workers' wages fell economy-wide; investors saw lower returns on capital and about 200,000 jobs were lost. Trade tensions could boost inflation more than desired by Federal Reserve policymakers, who might feel the need to raise rates more aggressively than planned.

⑧ Some may ask whether the World Trade Organization could help **resolve** the situation. The WTO is supposed to be the arbiter of international trade disputes. It was created in 1995 out of a set of agreements struck by countries trying to reduce trade barriers. If a government's complaint about another nation's trade barriers is seen as **grounded**, the WTO recommends acceptable retaliation. But the U.S. and China both propose justifying tariffs under domestic law, rather than following established WTO procedures, limiting the WTO's ability to **mediate**. In the case of aluminum and steel, Trump is invoking a seldom-used clause of a 1962 law that gives him the authority to curb imports if they undermine national security. His administration is studying whether to use the same law to justify restricted automobile imports. Other nations could copy the U.S. move.

❾ Actually, tariffs are not the only weapon in trade wars. There are many others, including clamping down on Chinese investments in the U.S., as Trump has also done. Intentionally weakening one's currency, which he accuses China of doing, is another. One worry for the U.S. is that China, the U.S.'s biggest creditor, will **scale back** purchases of Treasuries, an option that China's ambassador to the U.S. doesn't rule out. China could also retaliate against the U.S. in non-trade matters. Trump has accused China, for example, of undermining North Korea denuclearization talks in retaliation for hitting China's exports with tariffs. Countries through the years have used other means to keep foreign goods out and protect homegrown companies, a practice known as mercantilism. Some practices are blatant, such as quotas and subsidies for domestic industries (which Trump also accuses China of doing); others are less obvious, such as unusual product specifications, lengthy inspections of goods at entry ports, and **intricate** licensing requirements.

(1115 words)

Notes

Pandora's box: 潘多拉盒子。The expression is from the Greek Mythology in which Pandora was created by the God Zeus and sent to the earth with a box containing many evils. When she opened the box, the evils came out and infected the earth. It refers to a process that, if started, will cause many problems that cannot be solved.

Great Depression: 经济大萧条。The Great Depression was a severe worldwide economic depression that took place mostly during the 1930s, beginning in the United States. The timing of the Great Depression varied across nations; in most countries, it started in 1929 and lasted until the late-1930s. It was the longest, deepest, and most widespread depression of the 20th century. In the 21st century, the Great Depression is commonly used as an example of how intensely the world's economy can decline.

4.1 Read Text A and answer the following questions.

1) How serious is the U.S. President Donald Trump about the U.S.-China trade war?
2) What does the U.S. trade war with China and other countries risk?
3) What happened in previous trade wars?

Unit 10 Trade War

4) Why is Trump inviting this fight?
5) Could the WTO help resolve the situation?

4.2 Read Text A again and write a summary.

Summary (about 100 words): _____

_____
_____
_____
_____

Why China Will Win the Trade War[1]

Philippe Legrain

❶ Trump thinks he has a strong hand. In fact, Washington is far more vulnerable than Beijing.

❷ "When you're already $500 billion down, you can't lose!" U.S. President Donald Trump tweeted on April 4. He seems to believe that because the U.S. has a huge trade deficit with China—actually $337 billion in 2017, not $500 billion—he is bound to win the **impending** trade war between the two countries. But even though China sells more to America than it buys in return, Beijing's position is actually much stronger, both economically and politically, than that crude **calculus** suggests.

❸ Economically, both the U.S. and China would lose from a trade war. Punitive tariffs would push up import prices, **dent** exports, cost jobs, and **crimp** economic growth, so both sides would do best to avoid an outbreak of hostilities. But now that the Trump administration is threatening to impose 25% tariffs on $46 billion of U.S. imports from China and China has responded in kind, a trade war looms. Trump has since raised the stakes by threatening tariffs on a further $100 billion of imports (so far **unspecified**), which Beijing promptly said it would match. Trump's calculation appears to be that China has more to lose and so will back down. He is wrong.

❹ Headline statistics greatly overstate China's economic **vulnerability**—and understate America's. Focusing on trade in goods, as most observers do, U.S. imports from China last year totaled $506 billion, nearly four times its exports in the other direction. But the U.S. also sold $38

---

1 Adapted from Legrain, P. (2018, April 13). *Why China will win the trade war*. Retrieved from https://foreignpolicy.com/2018/04/13/why-china-will-win-the-trade-war/

billion more in services to China than it bought in return, its biggest **bilateral** surplus. And whereas U.S. goods exports to China are mostly agricultural produce and finished products consisting of mostly American content and sold by U.S. firms, China's exports to the U.S. are typically Chinese-assembled goods that contain many foreign parts and components—and are often American-branded to boot.

⑤ Take Apple's iPhone for example. When iPhones are shipped from Chinese factories to the U.S., the full import cost is attributed to China. Yet, these phones include many other foreign components. According to one estimate, assembly in China accounts for only 3%–6% of the $370 manufacturing cost of an iPhone X. Since that smartphone retails for $999, the bulk of the value added is American: Apple's margin and that of U.S. retailers.

⑥ Admittedly, that is an extreme example, and Trump isn't yet targeting iPhone imports. So, consider instead the $46 billion in imports that Trump is threatening, of which $26 billion are electronic goods. **Ostensibly** designed to **stymie** the Chinese government's drive to develop its own high-tech products, his tariffs would mainly affect lower-tech products that China actually exports to America right now. And according to estimates by the Organization for Economic Cooperation and Development (OECD), nearly half of the content of Chinese exports of computer, electronic, and **optical** equipment to the U.S. is foreign. Even if the proposed tariffs were to slash China's exports of these products by a quarter, the direct hit to China would be $6.5 billion—roughly 0.05% of the country's GDP. For an economy growing at 6.8% per year, that would be a pin prick.

⑦ Even a blanket U.S. tariff on all Chinese goods exports would be bearable for China. The OECD reckons that around a third of the content of U.S. imports from China is actually of foreign origin. So the Chinese value added of its exports to the U.S. is perhaps $329 billion—some 2.7% of China's $12 trillion economy. So even if a blanket Trump tariff slashed China's exports to the U.S. by 25%, the direct hit to GDP would be 0.7%. That would hurt. But it would still leave the Chinese economy growing at 6.1% a year.

⑧ It is very unlikely to come to that, precisely because the U.S. is much more vulnerable to a trade war than Trump thinks. Imagine the consumer **uproar** if Trump slapped a tariff on iPhones! Indeed, because so many U.S. firms outsource production to China, they are acutely vulnerable to Chinese tricks, such as **halting** production for a while on **spurious** regulatory grounds.

⑨ The threat isn't just to American-branded products that American consumers love. A trade war also poses a threat to U.S.-based manufacturers that rely on Chinese parts and components to be globally competitive. Trump's $46 billion list already targets aircraft propellers, machine tools, and other **intermediate** goods. Pushing up their costs would threaten manufacturing jobs in America's heartland. And while those tariffs avoid consumer staples, such as clothing and footwear, they will **inflate** the prices of some consumer goods, such as televisions and dishwashers.

⑩ In contrast, China's potential retaliation is much better targeted. First in line is $16 billion

Unit 10 Trade War

of U.S. **civilian** aircraft exports. Boeing's share price **slumped** when the Chinese move was announced. But Chinese airlines are expanding so fast that Boeing may be willing to slash prices to hang on to sales there, in which case none of the cost of the tariffs would fall on China. And the Chinese already have a reliable alternative supplier: Europe's Airbus.

⑪ Second in line is $12.8 billion of U.S. soybean exports. China accounts for more than half of American soybean exports, giving it market power. Indeed, as talk of a trade war heated up, the hit to U.S. farmers was immediate: Soybean prices **plunged**. Here, too, China has an alternative supplier: Brazil.

⑫ In short, the United States' trade deficit with China scarcely gives it an advantage.

⑬ China also has much more scope to **mitigate** any economic damage than the Trump administration does. Unlike the U.S. Federal Reserve, China's central bank is not independent, so the People's Bank of China can be ordered to cut interest rates to boost domestic demand if necessary. State-owned banks can likewise be told to extend more credit. And while China has allowed its currency to **appreciate** against the dollar considerably since Trump took office, it could nudge the renminbi down instead, making Chinese exports more competitive.

⑭ The Chinese government also has a much healthier fiscal position and is free to compensate any industries harmed by a trade war. By contrast, the U.S. government is facing a large budget deficit of some 4% of GDP that is set to rise in the next few years.

⑮ Finally, the Chinese government can absorb the political costs of a trade war much more easily than the Trump administration can. Every time Trump **lashes out** at China, U.S. stock markets plunge. That is particularly **problematic** for a president who treats the Dow Jones Industrial Average as his personal approval rating, especially because the single biggest **constituent** of the Dow is Boeing. Because the president has tied himself to the Dow; every time stocks fall, the Trump administration feels compelled to reassure markets that it is seeking a negotiated solution to the trade conflict, a move that undercuts its **leverage**.

⑯ With mid-term elections coming up in November, the Republicans are particularly vulnerable politically. China is capitalizing on that by targeting products such as soybeans that are mostly produced in Trump-supporting states in the Midwest. China also plans to retaliate against U.S. whiskey exports, which come mostly from Kentucky, the home state of Senate Majority Leader Mitch McConnell.

⑰ On top of all that, Trump doesn't seem to have a strategy. An international alliance would be more effective in pressuring China to open its markets and respect foreign intellectual property rights than going it alone. Last year, the U.S., the EU, and Japan agreed to make common cause on this. But Trump has now **alienated** those allies by slapping tariffs on Japan's steel and aluminum exports on bogus national security grounds and threatening to do the same to EU allies. Since his threatened tariffs against China would also hit its foreign suppliers, **notably** in Asia, that further undermines any potential for a united front.

⑱ Trump has made matters worse by acting **unilaterally** against China in a way that would appear to breach WTO rules. Indeed, potential allies find Trump's America First rhetoric repulsive. All this has given China the political high ground—"China doesn't want a trade war, but we're not afraid to fight a trade war" has become Beijing's official line.

⑲ For all his bragging about his negotiating skills, Trump is a **bungling** amateur. He has opted for a solo fight against a smarter, more patient, and more **resilient** adversary. So far, this is mostly political theater. But since Trump is overestimating his leverage and underestimating Chinese resolve, there is a real danger that the conflict will escalate.

⑳ In any case, China can afford to play for time and probably win the trade war.

(1446 words)

Notes

intermediate goods: 中间产品。Intermediate goods or producer goods or semi-finished products are goods, such as partly finished goods, used as inputs in the production of other goods including final goods. A firm may make and then use intermediate goods, or make and then sell, or buy and then use them. In the production process, intermediate goods either become part of the final product, or are changed beyond recognition in the process. This means intermediate goods are resold among industries. Intermediate goods are not counted in a country's GDP, as that would mean double counting, as the final product only should be counted, and the value of the intermediate good is included in the value of the final good.

consumer staples: 消费者日常用品，必需消费品。Consumer staples are essential products, such as food, beverages, tobacco, and household items. Consumer staples are goods that people are unable or unwilling to cut out of their budgets regardless of their financial situation. Consumer staples are considered to be non-cyclical, meaning that they are always in demand, no matter how well the economy is performing. People tend to demand consumer staples at a relatively constant level, regardless of their prices.

Senate Majority Leader: 参议院多数党领袖。The Senate Majority Leader is a United States Senator and member of the party leadership of the United States Senate. The leader serves as the chief Senate spokesperson for the political party holding the majority in the United States Senate, and manage and schedule the legislative and executive business of the Senate. By rule, the Presiding Officer gives the Majority Leader priority in obtaining recognition to speak on the floor of the Senate. The Majority Leader customarily serves as the chief representative of their party in the Senate, and sometimes even in all of Congress if the House of Representatives and thus the office of Speaker of the House is controlled by the opposition party.

Unit 10 Trade War

4.3 Read Text B. Write a summary in the following form and take notes according to the table below.

Subject: _____
Key words: _____
Organization types: _____
Thesis statement (or main ideas): _____
_____
_____

Conclusion (or major findings): _____
_____
_____

No.	Paragraph(s)	Structure	Content
1)		Argument	
2)		America's economic vulnerability to a China-U.S. trade war	
3)		China's strengths in the trade war	
4)		Strength 1	
5)		Strength 2	
6)		Strength 3	
7)		Strength 4	
8)		Trump's weaknesses and mistakes in the trade war	
9)		Closing statement	

4.4 Read Text B again and answer the following questions.

1) According to the author, why does U.S. President Donald Trump believe that he is bound to win the impending China-U.S. trade war?

2) Why does the author say that Trump's calculation that China has more to lose is wrong?
3) How does Text B differ from Text A in its prediction of the China-U.S. trade war?
4) How does Text B differ from Text A in its discussion of a trade war?
5) What's your view on the China-U.S. trade war after reading and comparing the two texts?

UNIT PROJECT

Read Text B and Text A again, form two groups, and hold a debate on the topic "China/the U.S. will win the China-U.S. trade war". Give evidence to support your arguments and refute your opponents'.

Practice for Enhancement

5.1 Read the four words in each group and cross the word which is not a synonym for the bold word. An example is given for you.

e.g. **overstate**

    × restate   ☐ exaggerate   ☐ overemphasize   ☐ amplify

1) **uproar**

    ☐ noise   ☐ upright   ☐ chaos   ☐ disturbance

2) **plunge**

    ☐ plenty   ☐ drop   ☐ fall   ☐ plummet

3) **adversary**

    ☐ opponent   ☐ enemy   ☐ advocate   ☐ rival

4) **alienate**

    ☐ estrange   ☐ distance   ☐ unify   ☐ isolate

5) **ostensibly**

    ☐ actually   ☐ apparently   ☐ seemingly   ☐ superficially

6) **problematic**

    ☐ difficult   ☐ tricky   ☐ challenging   ☐ booming

7) **backfire**

    ☐ backup   ☐ fail   ☐ miscarry   ☐ boomerang

Unit 10 Trade War

8) **stymie**

   ☐ thwart   ☐ foil   ☐ prevent   ☐ succeed

9) **lash**

   ☐ hit   ☐ blow   ☐ confuse   ☐ criticize

5.2 Match the word in the box with the words in each column that regularly go together. An example is given for you.

> alternative, bilateral, import, approval, mitigate, slash, crude, deficit, tariff, fiscal

e.g. bilateral	1) _____	2) _____	3) _____
-relations	-estimate	-costs	restrict-
-agreements	-workmanship	-prices	-control
-trade	-pictures	-fares	-license
-talks	-language	-the workforce	increase-
4) _____	**5) _____**	**6) _____**	**7) _____**
budget-	-barriers	-year	-rating
trade-	levy-	-policy	government-
reduce-	raise-	-revenue	obtain the-
financial-	import-	-crisis	written-
8) _____	**9) _____**		
-approaches	-risks		
seek-	-the effects		
offer an-	-the damage		
have no-	-symptoms		

5.3 Paraphrase the following sentences. An example is given for you.

e.g. Headline statistics greatly overstate China's economic vulnerability—and understate America's.

Front-page figures seriously play down the weakness of American economy and exaggerate the susceptibility of China's economy.

1) The U.S. also has begun a $12 billion program to bail out farmers hurt by China's and other countries' retaliatory tariffs on U.S. exports of soybeans, corn, and other crops.

_____

_____

2) Trump later said duties on Chinese imports are justified after decades in which China tilted

the playing field, including by devaluing its currency and forcing American companies to share their technology.

3) Trade tensions could boost inflation more than desired by Federal Reserve policymakers, who might feel the need to raise rates more aggressively than planned.

4) But the U.S. and China both propose justifying tariffs under domestic law, rather than following established WTO procedures, limiting the WTO's ability to mediate.

5) Punitive tariffs would push up import prices, dent exports, cost jobs, and crimp economic growth, so both sides would do best to avoid an outbreak of hostilities.

6) But now that the Trump administration is threatening to impose 25% tariffs on $46 billion of U.S. imports from China and China has responded in kind, a trade war looms.

7) But Chinese airlines are expanding so fast that Boeing may be willing to slash prices to hang on to sales there, in which case none of the cost of the tariffs would fall on China.

8) Because the president has tied himself to the Dow, every time stocks fall, the Trump administration feels compelled to reassure markets that it is seeking a negotiated solution to the trade conflict, a move that undercuts its leverage.

5.4 Translate the following sentences into Chinese.

1) U.S. President Donald Trump is threatening to intensify an ongoing trade war by rolling out

Unit 10　Trade War

tariffs on $267 billion worth of Chinese exports to the U.S., on top of the $200 billion worth that he could soon hit with duties.

2) It adds up to an all-out trade war, one that risks gumming up global supply chains, raising consumer prices, stalling economic growth, and tying the World Trade Organization in knots.

3) What make this a full-blown trade war are Trump's singling out of China for retaliation, the tit-for-tat actions by the U.S. and its closest allies over metals tariffs, and Trump's invocation of national security to justify some of his moves—which could open a Pandora's box of similar claims by other nations.

4) And whereas U.S. goods exports to China are mostly agricultural produce and finished products consisting of mostly American content and sold by U.S. firms, China's exports to the U.S. are typically Chinese-assembled goods that contain many foreign parts and components—and are often American-branded to boot.

5) Ostensibly designed to stymie the Chinese government's drive to develop its own high-tech products, his tariffs would mainly affect lower-tech products that China actually exports to America right now.

6) The OECD reckons that around a third of the content of U.S. imports from China is actually of foreign origin. So the Chinese value added of its exports to the U.S. is perhaps $329 billion—some 2.7% of China's $12 trillion economy.

商务学科英语

6 Movie Exploration: *Jerry Maquire* (1996)

Cast

Directed by: Cameron Crowe
Starring: Tom Cruise as Jerry Maguire
               Cuba Gooding Jr. as Rod Tidwell
               Renée Zellweger as Dorothy Boyd
               Jerry O'connell as Frank Cushman

Plot

- Jerry Maquire, a rich and popular sports agent, writes a mission statement about the problems arising in this business and gives everyone in the company a copy of it, which causes him to be fired.
- Most of Jerry's clients leave him except Rod Tidwell.
- When Jerry announces that he will start his own agency, Dorothy Boyd agrees to go with him.
- Jerry fails to convince Frank Cushman to sign the contract.
- Jerry becomes closer to Dorothy who finally agrees to marry him.
- Jerry has an argument with Rod who takes Jerry's advice later.
- Dorothy decides to divorce Jerry.
- Rod plays well and helps his team to win.
- Jerry comes back to Dorothy.
- Rod appears on a sports show and extends his gratitude to Jerry.

6.1 Search for the meanings of the following terms from the movie.

1) **celebrity endorsement:** _____
2) **NFL:** _____
3) **ESPN:** _____
4) **ABC:** _____
5) **Super Bowl:** _____
6) **sports agent:** _____
7) **market orientation:** _____
8) **sport management:** _____

Unit 10 Trade War

Web Resources

http://www.businessdictionary.com/definition/celebrity-endorsement.html
https://en.wikipedia.org/wiki/National_Football_League
https://simple.wikipedia.org/wiki/ESPN
https://en.wikipedia.org/wiki/American_Broadcasting_Company
https://en.wikipedia.org/wiki/Super_Bowl
https://en.wikipedia.org/wiki/Sports_agent
http://www.businessdictionary.com/definition/market-orientation.html
https://en.wikipedia.org/wiki/Sport_management

6.2 While watching, listen to the following part of the movie in which Jerry Maquire suddenly figures out what's wrong with his business and complete it by filling in the blanks.

> In this monologue, Jerry Maquire realizes that there's something missing in his job and he startes to write a mission statement which leads to his unemployment later.

    Who had I become? Just another 1)_____? With the 2)_____ salaries and you are one of the guys responsible…Two days later, at our corporate conference in Miami, a 3)_____…I already had 18 million on the table, but I couldn't 4)_____ one simple thought. I hated myself. No, here's what it was. I hated my place in the world. I had so much to say and no one to listen. And then it happened. It was the 5)_____, most unexpected thing. I began writing what they call a mission statement. Not a memo, a mission statement. You know, a suggestion for the future of our company. A night like this doesn't come along very often. I 6)_____ it. What started out as one page became 25. Suddenly, I was my father's son again. I was remembering the simple pleasure of this job, how I 7)_____ here out of law school, the way a stadium sounds when one of my players performs well on the field, the way we are meant to protect them in health and in injury. We had forgotten what was important. I wrote and wrote and wrote and wrote and I'm not even a writer. I was remembering even the words of the original sports agent, my mentor…who said "the key to this business is 8)_____." Suddenly it was all pretty clear. The answer was fewer 9)_____, less money. More attention. Caring for them. Caring for ourselves. And the games too. Just starting our lives really. I will be the first to admit it what I was writing was somewhat touchy and feely…It was the me I'd always wanted to be. I took it to a copymat in the middle of the night and printed 110 copies… And I 10)_____ it The Things We Think and Do Not Say: The Future of Our Business.

6.3 After watching, cross the word or phrase that is closest in meaning to the bold one in each of the following sentences from the movie. An example is given for you.

e.g. **A:** We gotta win Super Bowls.
B: I **hail** you.

☐ doubt ✗ adore ☐ support

1) **A:** You are a single mom. You have given up the right to be **frivolous**.
B: If you had read what he wrote, you would have left with him too.

☐ thoughtless ☐ serious ☐ sensitive

2) You know, next time when you decide to **lecture** me, don't leave my boy with that divorced women's group.

☐ admonish ☐ ridicule ☐ suggest

3) **A:** Meet me at the pub at 8:00.
B: You bet.

☐ No way ☐ Sure ☐ Who knows

4) **A:** We're two people working together. We can't have atmosphere.
B: No, I'm really **relieved** that you said that.

☐ surprised ☐ confused ☐ pleased

5) I guess I got **revved up** at the date of an evening among adults.

☐ exhausted ☐ excited ☐ nervous

6) The Cardinals just refuse to go quietly into the desert night as their seemingly **interminable** season winds down.

☐ endless ☐ glorious ☐ busy

7) Here's the guy who most of the season had been **truculent** with the media.

☐ enthusiastic ☐ hostile ☐ indifferent

8) America still **sets the tone for** the world.

☐ criticizes ☐ speaks for ☐ leads

9) She is **picturing** her ex-boyfriend when boxing.

☐ taking a photo of ☐ imagining in her mind ☐ drawing the attention of

6.4 Work in groups and discuss the following questions.

1) Do you agree with what Jerry says in his mission statement?
2) Do you believe "show me the money" is the motto of the business world?

Unit 10 Trade War

7 Referencing Skills

Citation Styles and How to Reference[1]

A citation style, sometimes called a reference style, is a set of rules on how to refer to your sources in academic writing. Often, style guidelines are published in an official handbook containing explanations, examples, and instructions.

There are many different citation styles. In the past, each discipline followed its own referencing rules, but today there's a growing tendency among universities and colleges to choose one single style. The most common citation styles in English include APA, Chicago, Harvard, and MLA. These styles, among others, are widely used throughout many different academic disciplines.

Choosing a citation style is important as universities and academic journals have specific requirements. You can find the required citation style for your target journal or field of study in the corresponding submission guidelines, style guide or style manual.

The APA citation style, currently in its 6th edition, is one of the most common citation styles in academic writing. The APA style was created by the American Psychological Association and was originally used in psychology and social sciences. Today many other disciplines are using it.

Type 1: How to reference a book

A basic APA format structure is as follows:
- Author, A. (Year of Publication). *Title of work*. Publisher City, State: Publisher.
  Here comes an example:
- Finney, J. (1970). *Time and again*. New York, NY: Simon and Schuster.
  When citing a book in APA, keep notes in mind:
- Capitalize the first letter of the first word of the title and any subtitles, as well as the first letter of any proper nouns.
- The full title of the book, including any subtitles, should be stated and italicized.

Type 2: How to reference an e-book from an e-reader

A basic APA format structure is as follows:
- Author, A. (Year of Publication). *Title of work* [E-Reader Version]. Retrieved from http://xxxx or DOI:xxxx
  Here comes an example:

---

1 Adapted from B:bMe™. (unknown publication date). *APA citation guide*. Retrieved from http://www.bibme.org/citation-guide/apa/

- Eggers, D. (2008). *The circle* [Kindle Version]. Retrieved from http://www.amazon.com/

Type 3: How to reference a website article
1) Citing a general website article with an author
A basic APA format structure is as follows:
- Author, A. (Year, Month Date of Publication). Article title. Retrieved from URL

Here comes an example:
- Simmons, B. (2015, January 09). The tale of two Flaccos. Retrieved from http://grantland.com/the-triangle/the-tale-of-two-flaccos/

2) Citing a general website article without an author
A basic APA format structure is as follows:
- Article title. (Year, Month Date of Publication). Retrieved from URL

Here comes an example:
- Teen posed as doctor at West Palm Beach hospital: police. (2015, January 16). Retrieved from http://www.nbcmiami.com/news/local/Teen-Posed-as-Doctor-at-West-Palm-Beach-Hospital-Police-288810831.html

Type 4: How to reference a journal article
1) Citing a journal article in print
A basic APA format structure is as follows:
- Author, A. (Publication Year). Article title. *Periodical Title, Volume*(Issue), pp.–pp.

Here comes an example:
- Nevin, A. (1990). The changing of teacher education special education. *Teacher Education and Special Education: The Journal of the Teacher Education Division of the Council for Exceptional Children, 13*(3–4), 147–148.

2) Citing a journal article found online
A basic APA format structure is as follows:
- Author, A. (Publication Year). Article title. *Periodical Title, Volume*(Issue), pp.–pp. DOI:XX.XXXXX or Retrieved from journal URL

Here comes an example:
- Jameson, J. (2013). E-Leadership in higher education: The fifth "age" of educational technology research. *British Journal of Educational Technology, 44*(6), 889–915. DOI: 10.1111/bjet.12103

When creating your online journal article citation, keep notes in mind:
- APA does not require you to include the date of access or retrieval date or database information for electronic sources.
- You can use the URL of the journal homepage if there is no DOI assigned and the reference was retrieved online. For example: Retrieved from http://onlinelibrary.wiley.com/journal/10.1111/

Unit 10　Trade War

(ISSN)1467-8535; jsessionid=956132F3DE76EEB120577E99EE74CE9C.f04t01
- A DOI (digital object identifier) is an assigned number that helps link content to its location on the Internet. It is therefore important, if one is provided, to use it when creating a citation. All DOI numbers begin with a 10 and are separated by a slash.

Type 5: How to reference a newspaper
1) Citing a newspaper article in print

　　A basic APA format structure is as follows:
- Author, A. (Year, Month Date of Publication). Article title. *Newspaper Title,* pp. xx–xx.

　　Here comes an example:
- Rosenberg, G. (1997, March 31). Electronic discovery proves an effective legal weapon. *The New York Times*, p. D5.

　　When creating your newspaper citation, keep notes in mind:
- Precede page numbers for newspaper articles with p. (for a single page) or pp. (for multiple pages).
- If an article appears on discontinuous pages, give all page numbers, and separate the numbers with a comma (e.g. pp. B1, B3, B5–B7).

2) Citing a newspaper article found online

　　A basic APA format structure is an follows:
- Author, A. (Year, Month Date of Publication). Article title. *Newspaper Title*, Retrieved from newspaper homepage URL

　　Here comes an example:
- Rosenberg, G. (1997, March 31). Electronic discovery proves an effective legal weapon. *The New York Times*, Retrieved from http://www.nytimes.com

　　When citing a newspaper in APA, keep notes in mind:
- APA does not require you to include the date of access for electronic sources. If you discovered a newspaper article via an online database, that information is not required for the citation either.
- Multiple lines: If the URL runs onto a second line, only break URL before punctuation (except for http://).

Type 6: How to reference an online lecture notes or presentation slides

　　A basic APA format structure is as follows:
- Author, A. (Publication Year). Name or title of lecture [file format]. Retrieved from URL

　　Here comes an example:
- Saito, T. (2012). Technology and me: A personal timeline of educational technology [Powerpoint slides]. Retrieved from http://www.slideshare.net/Bclari25/educational-technology-ppt

Type 7: How to reference an encyclopedia entry

    A basic APA format structure is as follows:

- Author, A. (Publication Year). Entry title. In *Encyclopedia title*, (Vol. xx, pp. xx). City, State of publication: Publisher.

    Here comes an example:

- Kammen, C., & Wilson, A.H. (2012). Monuments. In *Encyclopedia of local history*. (pp. 363–364). Lanham, MD: AltaMira Press.

Type 8: How to reference a photograph

1) Citing a photograph

    A basic APA format structure is as follows:

- Photographer, A. (Photographer). (Year, Month Date of Publication). *Title of photograph* [photograph]. City, State of publication: Publisher/museum.

    Here comes an example:

- Roege, W.J. (Photographer). (1938). *St. Patrick's cathedral, fifth avenue from 50th street to 51st street* [photograph]. New York, NY: New-York Historical Society.

2) Citing a photograph retrieved online

    A basic APA format structure is as follows:

- Photographer, A. (Photographer). (Year, Month Date of Publication). *Title of photograph* [digital image]. Retrieved from URL

    Here comes an example:

- Ferraro, A. (Photographer). (2014, April 28). *Liberty enlightening the world* [digital image]. Retrieved from https://www.flickr.com/photos/afer92/14278571753/in/set-72157644617030616

Appendix
词汇表

abreast /ə'brest/ adj.	并排的；并肩的	Unit 5 B
accelerate /ək'seləreɪt/ v.	加速；加快	Unit 7 A
access /'ækses/ n.	入口；进入	Unit 5 A AWL
accessible /ək'sesəbl/ adj.	易接近的	Unit 8 B AWL
accommodation /əˌkɒmə'deɪʃn/ n.	住处	Unit 6 A AWL
account for	（数量、比例上）占	Unit 4 B
accrue to	归于	Unit 4 B
accumulate /ə'kjuːmjəleɪt/ v.	积累	Unit 6 A
accurate /'ækjərət/ adj.	精确的	Unit 9 A AWL
accustomed /ə'kʌstəmd/ adj.	习惯于（做）某事的；惯常的	Unit 10 A
acquisition /ˌækwɪ'zɪʃ(ə)n/ n.	获得；收购	Unit 1 B AWL
adage /'ædɪdʒ/ n.	谚语	Unit 2 A
adapt /ə'dæpt/ v.	适应	Unit 4 A AWL
adaptability /əˌdæptə'bɪləti/ n.	适应性；可变性	Unit 2 AWL
address /ə'dres/ v.	称呼；演说	Unit 5 A
adequacy /'ædɪkwəsi/ n.	足够；适当	Unit 2 B
adherence /əd'hɪərəns/ n.	坚持；遵守；遵循	Unit 5 A
adherent /əd'hɪər(ə)nt/ n.	信徒；追随者	Unit 7 B
adhere to	坚持；拥护；追随	Unit 3 B
adjustment /ə'dʒʌstmənt/ n.	适应，调整	Unit 5 A AWL
advent /'ædvent/ n.	到来；出现	Unit 2 AWL
adversary /'ædvəs(ə)ri/ n.	对手；敌手	Unit 3 B
advocacy /'ædvəkəsi/ n.	支持，提倡	Unit 1 B AWL
aggregate /'ægrɪgət/ adj./n./v.	总计的 / 合计 / 总计	Unit 2 B AWL
aide /eɪd/ n.	助手	Unit 2 B
airtight /'eətaɪt/ adj.	密闭的，密封的；无懈可击的	Unit 3 B
akin /ə'kɪn/ adj.	同族的；相似的	Unit 7 A
algorithm /'ælgərɪðəm/ n.	算法	Unit 6 A
alienate /'eɪliəneɪt/ v.	使疏远	Unit 10 B
align /ə'laɪn/ v.	使成一线；使结盟	Unit 7 A
all-out /ˌɔːl'aʊt/ adj.	全力以赴的；竭尽全力的	Unit 10 A
allocation /ˌælə'keɪʃn/ n.	分配；配置；安置	Unit 2 A AWL
ally /'ælaɪ/ n.	盟友；同盟国	Unit 10 A
also-ran /'ɔːlsəʊræn/ n.	落选者；失败者	Unit 1 A
alternative /ɔːl'tɜːnətɪv/ adj.	可替代的；另外的	Unit 1 B AWL
aluminum /ə'luːmɪnəm/ n.	铝；铝合金	Unit 10 A
ambiguity /ˌæmbɪ'ɡjuːəti/ n.	含糊；模棱两可	Unit 6 A AWL
ample /'æmp(ə)l/ adj.	丰富的；足够的	Unit 1 A
amplify /'æmplɪfaɪ/ v.	放大，扩大	Unit 1 A
analyst /'ænəlɪst/ n.	分析师	Unit 2 AWL
anarchic /ə'nɑːkɪk/ adj.	无政府的；无政府主义的	Unit 9 B
anonymity /ˌænə'nɪməti/ n.	匿名	Unit 9 B
anonymous /ə'nɒnɪməs/ adj.	匿名的	Unit 9 AWL

商务学科英语

词汇表

单词	释义	单元
antagonistic /æn̩tægə'nɪstɪk/ adj.	敌对的；对抗性的	Unit 7 A
anticipate /æn'tɪsɪpeɪt/ v.	预期	Unit 5 B AWL
antidote /'æntɪdoʊt/ n.	克服……的良方；解毒剂	Unit 4 A
antifreeze /'æntifri:z/ n.	防冻剂	Unit 5 A
antitrust /ˌænti'trʌst/ adj.	反垄断的	Unit 7 A
apocryphal /ə'pɒkrɪfl/ adj.	真实性可疑的	Unit 7 A
appal /ə'pɔ:l/ v.	使惊骇	Unit 7 B
apparel /ə'pærəl/ n.	（商店出售的）衣服	Unit 5 A
appetite /'æpɪtaɪt/ n.	欲望；嗜好	Unit 8 B AWL
appreciate /ə'pri:ʃieɪt/ v.	欣赏；感激；理解；增值，升值	Unit 10 B AWL
approach /ə'proʊtʃ/ v.	接近；着手处理；使移近	Unit 5 A AWL
arbitrarily /ˌɑ:rbɪ'trerəli/ adv.	任意地	Unit 9 A AWL
arena /ə'ri:nə/ n.	竞争舞台；竞技场，斗争场所	Unit 2 A
articulate /ɑ:'tɪkjuleɪt/ v.	清晰地发（音）；明确地表达	Unit 5 A
assemble /ə'sembl/ v.	装配，组合	Unit 5 A AWL
assess /ə'ses/ v.	评定；估价	Unit 2 A AWL
asset /'æset/ n.	资产；优点	Unit 1 B
associate with	与……联系在一起；和……来往	Unit 3 A
atrophy /'ætrəfi/ v.	萎缩；衰退	Unit 7 B
attribute /ə'trɪbju:t/ v.	归属；把……归因于……	Unit 6 A AWL
auditor /'ɔ:dɪtə(r)/ n.	审计员；旁听生	Unit 5 A
augment /ɔ:g'ment/ v.	增强；增加	Unit 8 B
auspice /'ɔ:spɪsɪz/ n.	赞助；支持	Unit 8 B
austerity /ɒ'sterɪti/ n.	经济紧缩	Unit 4 B
authentication /ɔ:ˌθentɪ'keɪʃn/ n.	证明；鉴定	Unit 9 A
automate /'ɔ:təmeɪt/ v.	使自动化	Unit 2 A AWL
avail /ə'veɪl/ v.	利用（机会等）	Unit 6 A AWL
avert /ə'vɜ:t/ v.	避免，防止；转移	Unit 3 B
baby boomer /'beɪbi 'bu:mə/ n.	婴儿潮时期出生的人	Unit 6 AWL
baccalaureate /ˌbækə'lɔ:riət/ n.	学士学位	Unit 2 B
backfire /ˌbæk'faɪər/ v.	产生反效果，适得其反	Unit 10 A
backlash /'bæklæʃ/ n.	反冲；强烈反对	Unit 1 A
bailout /'beɪlaʊt/ n.	紧急财政援助	Unit 7 B
banquet /'bæŋkwɪt/ n.	宴会；宴席	Unit 8 A
bargain /'bɑ:gən/ n.	讨价还价	Unit 8 A AWL
bastion /'bæstiən/ n.	捍卫者；堡垒	Unit 2 A
beneficiary /ˌbenɪ'fɪʃəri/ n.	受益人	Unit 4 A AWL
bespoke /bɪ'spoʊk/ adj.	订做的；预订的	Unit 2 A
be subject to	易遭受……的；可能受……影响的	Unit 5 A
bias /'baɪəs/ n./v.	偏见 / 偏爱	Unit 2 A AWL
bilateral /ˌbaɪ'lætərəl/ adj.	双边的，有两边的	Unit 10 B
biochemist /ˌbaɪoʊ'kemɪst/ n.	生物化学家	Unit 2 AWL
blatant /'bleɪtnt/ adj.	明目张胆的；公然的	Unit 7 B

Appendix

词汇表

bolster /ˈboʊlstər/ v.	支持；支撑	Unit 3 B
booming /ˈbuːmɪŋ/ adj.	兴旺的，繁荣的	Unit 1 A
boost /buːst/ v.	促进；提高	Unit 1 B
breach /briːtʃ/ v.	违反；破坏	Unit 6 B
budget /ˈbʌdʒɪt/ v./n.	安排开支 / 预算	Unit 2 A
bulk /bʌlk/ n.	大量；大部分	Unit 8 A AWL
bungling /ˈbʌŋglɪŋ/ adj.	笨拙的；粗劣的	Unit 10 B
burdensome /ˈbɜːdns(ə)m/ adj.	累赘的	Unit 4 AWL
burgeoning /ˈbɜːdʒənɪŋ/ adj.	增长迅速的；生机勃勃的	Unit 3 B
buzzword /ˈbʌzwɜːd/ n.	时髦术语，流行行话	Unit 8 B
calculus /ˈkælkjʊləs/ n.	微积分学；结石	Unit 10 B
calendar /ˈkæləndə/ n.	日历	Unit 2 A
campaign /kæmˈpeɪn/ n.	运动	Unit 4 A
cannibalize /ˈkænɪbəlaɪz/ v.	同类相食	Unit 8 A
capacity /kəˈpæsɪtɪ/ n.	能力；容量；生产力	Unit 1 B AWL
casualty /ˈkæʒʊəltɪ/ n.	受害者；伤员，亡者	Unit 1 A
catastrophic /ˌkætəˈstrɒfɪk/ adj.	灾难的；惨重的	Unit 7 A
cease /siːs/ v.	停止，终止	Unit 1 A AWL
centralize /ˈsɛntrəlaɪz/ v.	使集中	Unit 3 AWL
chafe /tʃeɪf/ v.	发怒	Unit 9 A
chauffeur /ˈʃəʊfə(r)/ n./v.	受雇于人的汽车司机 / 为别人当司机	Unit 6 B
churn /tʃɜːn/ n./v.	搅乳器 / 搅动；恶心	Unit 2 AWL
civic /ˈsɪvɪk/ adj.	公民的	Unit 4 A
civilian /sɪˈvɪlj(ə)n/ adj.	平民的；民用的	Unit 10 B
client /ˈklaɪənt/ n.	客户；顾客；委托人	Unit 2 A
coalition /ˌkoʊəˈlɪʃn/ n.	联合；结合，合并	Unit 10 A
codifialde /ˈkɒdəfaɪəbl/ adj.	编成法典的	Unit 2 B
coherent /koʊˈhɪərənt/ adj.	连贯的；一致的	Unit 8 B
cohesion /kə(ʊ)ˈhiːʒ(ə)n/ n.	凝聚力；内聚性	Unit 1 A
collaboration /kəˌlæbəˈreɪʃn/ n.	合作	Unit 1 B
collapse /kəˈlæps/ v.	暴跌；垮掉；倒塌	Unit 4 B AWL
commitment /kəˈmɪtmənt/ n.	承诺	Unit 1 A AWL
commodity /kəˈmɒdɪtɪ/ n.	商品，货物	Unit 1 B AWL
community /kəˈmjuːnɪtɪ/ n.	共同体；伙伴关系	Unit 4 A AWL
compel /kəmˈpel/ v.	强迫，迫使；强使发生	Unit 7 B
compensate /ˈkɒmpenseɪt/ v.	补偿，赔偿，弥补	Unit 2 A
compensation /ˌkɒmpenˈseɪʃn/ n.	补偿，赔偿	Unit 5 A AWL
competence /ˈkɒmpɪtəns/ n.	竞争力	Unit 2 B
complementary /ˌkɒmplɪˈmentri/ adj.	补充的；互补的	Unit 2 B AWL
complexity /kəmˈpleksətɪ/ n.	复杂，复杂性	Unit 2 AWL
compliance /kəmˈplaɪəns/ n.	遵守；服从	Unit 6 A AWL
complimentary /ˌkɒmplɪˈmentri/ adj.	赠送的；称赞的	Unit 3 A
comply with	照做，遵守	Unit 3 B

商务学科英语

词汇表

单词	音标	词性	释义	出处
concentration	/ˌkɒnsn'treɪʃn/	n.	浓度	Unit 6 B
confederation	/kənˌfedə'reɪʃn/	n.	联盟；邦联	Unit 9 A
confine	/kən'faɪn/	v.	限制	Unit 4 B AWL
congregate	/'kɒŋgrɪgeɪt/	v.	聚集	Unit 3 AWL
consciousness	/'kɒnʃəsnɪs/	n.	意识；知觉	Unit 9 A
consensus	/kən'sensəs/	n.	共识，一致意见	Unit 1 A AWL
consortium	/kən'sɔːtiəm/	n.	联盟，联营	Unit 1 B
constituency	/kən'stɪtʃuənsi/	n.	选区	Unit 10 A
constituent	/kən'stɪtjuənt/	n.	成分；构成部分	Unit 10 B AWL
constitute	/'kɒnstɪˌtjuːt/	v.	构成	Unit 4 B AWL
contingency	/kən'tɪndʒənsi/	n.	偶然性；意外事件	Unit 3 B
contingent	/kən'tɪndʒənt/	adj.	因情况而异的	Unit 4 A
contractor	/kən'træktə(r)/	n.	订约人，承包商	Unit 6 A
coordinate	/kəʊ'ɔːdmeɪt/	v.	（使）协调	Unit 6 A
core	/kɔː/	n.	核心；要点	Unit 2 B
corporate	/'kɔːpərət/	n.	公司	Unit 2 A
correlation	/ˌkɒrə'leʃn/	n.	相关，关联	Unit 9 B
corrupt	/kə'rʌpt/	v.	使腐烂；使堕落，使恶化	Unit 7 A
cosmopolitan	/ˌkɒzmə'pɒlɪtən/	adj.	见多识广的	Unit 4 A
costly	/'kɒstli/	adj.	昂贵的；代价高的	Unit 8 A
counterbalance	/'kaʊntəˌbæl(ə)ns/	v.	使平衡；抵消	Unit 1 B
counterpart	/'kaʊntəpɑːt/	n.	对应的事物，（地位等）相当的人	Unit 6 A
creator	/krɪ'eɪtə/	n.	创造者；创建者	Unit 3 A AWL
credibility	/ˌkredə'bɪləti/	n.	可靠性，可信性	Unit 5 A
credit	/'kredɪt/	v.	归于；相信	Unit 8 B AWL
crimp	/krɪmp/	v.	使（头发）轻微卷曲；抑制；束缚	Unit 10 B
critique	/krɪ'tiːk/	n.	评论文章	Unit 9 A
crook	/krʊk/	n.	骗子	Unit 9 A
crowdfunding	/'kraʊdˌfʌndɪŋ/	n.	众筹	Unit 3 B
crucial	/'kruːʃ(ə)l/	adj.	决定性的；关键的	Unit 5 B AWL
cryptography	/krɪp'tɒgrəfi/	n.	密码学	Unit 9 AWL
crystalline	/'krɪstəlaɪn/	adj.	结晶质的；清澈的	Unit 5 B
cue	/kjuː/	n.	暗示；线索	Unit 2 AWL
cumulative	/'kjuːmjʊlətɪv/	adj.	累积的	Unit 7 B
curb	/kɜːb/	v.	抑制	Unit 4 AWL
currency	/'kʌr(ə)nsi/	n.	货币	Unit 5 AWL
cushion	/'kʊʃn/	v./n.	缓冲；放在垫子上/保护；垫子	Unit 2 B AWL
cutting-edge	/ˌkʌtɪŋ 'edʒ/	adj.	先进的，尖端的	Unit 1 AWL
data-crunching		n.	数据处理	Unit 2 AWL
decentralize	/diː'sentrə'laɪz/	v.	使分散	Unit 3 AWL
declaim	/dɪ'kleɪm/	v.	说话；抨击；大声抗议	Unit 5 A
decline	/dɪ'klaɪn/	n.	衰退	Unit 4 A AWL
de facto	/ˌdeɪ 'fæktəʊ/	adj.	事实上，实际上	Unit 6 B

Appendix 词汇表

单词	音标	词性	释义	单元
demanding	/dɪˈmɑːndɪŋ/	adj.	苛求的，强求的	Unit 8 B
demonstrate	/ˈdemənstreɪt/	v.	证明；显示；说明	Unit 7 A AWL
dent	/dent/	v.	削弱；使产生凹痕	Unit 10 B
deploy	/dɪˈplɔɪ/	v.	部署；展开；配置	Unit 2 B
deposition	/ˌdepəˈzɪʃn/	n.	沉积（物）；[律] 证词	Unit 5 B
destabilize	/diːˈsteɪbəlaɪz/	v.	使动摇	Unit 4 A
detect	/dɪˈtekt/	v.	察觉；发现	Unit 9 A AWL
dexterity	/dekˈsterəti/	n.	（手或心思）灵巧	Unit 2 B
diagnose	/ˈdaɪəgnəʊz/	v.	诊断	Unit 2 B
dimension	/daɪˈmenʃ(ə)n/	n.	尺寸；[复] 面积，范围	Unit 5 A
diminish	/dɪˈmɪnɪʃ/	v.	（使）减少，（使）减小	Unit 1 B AWL
diminishing	/dɪˈmɪnɪʃɪŋ/	adj.	逐渐缩小的	Unit 6 A AWL
disaggregate	/dɪsˈægrɪˌgeɪt/	v.	分解	Unit 4 B
disclose	/dɪsˈkloz/	v.	公开；揭露	Unit 3 B
disconcerting	/ˌdɪskənˈsɜːtɪŋ/	adj.	令人不安的；打扰人的	Unit 3 B
discontent	/ˌdɪskənˈtent/	n.	不满	Unit 1 A
disentangle	/ˌdɪsɪnˈtæŋgl/	v.	解开；解决	Unit 1 A
disparate	/ˈdɪspərət/	adj.	迥然不同的 [正式]	Unit 2 A
disparity	/dɪˈspærəti/	n.	差异，悬殊	Unit 6 A
dispersed	/dɪˈspɜːst/	adj.	分散的	Unit 1 AWL
displace	/dɪsˈpleɪs/	v.	替换，取代	Unit 5 A AWL
disproportionally	/ˌdɪsprəˈpɔːʃənli/	adv.	不均衡地；不成比例地	Unit 1 AWL
disquiet	/dɪsˈkwaɪət/	n.	担心；焦虑	Unit 1 A
disruption	/dɪsˈrʌpʃən/	n.	妨碍；扰乱	Unit 2 A
dissatisfaction	/ˌdɪsˌsætɪsˈfækʃn/	n.	不满	Unit 6 B AWL
distribution	/ˌdɪstrɪˈbjuːʃn/	n.	分布	Unit 4 B AWL
diverge	/daɪˈvɜːdʒ/	v.	背离，偏离	Unit 1 A
diverse	/daɪˈvɜːs/	adj.	不同的；多种多样的	Unit 4 A AWL
diversity	/daɪˈvɜːrsəti/	n.	多样性；差异	Unit 3 A AWL
dividend	/ˈdɪvɪdend/	n.	红利	Unit 4 A
domain	/dəˈmeɪn/	n.	领地；领域；范围	Unit 2 B AWL
dominate	/ˈdɒmɪneɪt/	v.	控制；支配	Unit 1 A AWL
downside	/ˈdaʊnsaɪd/	n.	缺点，不利方面	Unit 8 AWL
du jour	/duˈʒʊə/	adj.	当日特色（菜）的；一时流行的	Unit 5 B
dupe	/djuːp/	v.	欺骗；愚弄	Unit 3 B
durable	/ˈdjʊərəbl/	adj.	耐用的	Unit 2 B
duration	/djuˈreɪʃn/	n.	持续时间；期间	Unit 2 B AWL
dynamic	/daɪˈnæmɪk/	adj.	动力的；动态的；有活力的	Unit 2 B AWL
eclipse	/ɪˈklɪps/	v.	使黯然失色；形成蚀	Unit 3 A
ecological	/ˌiːkəˈlɒdʒɪkl/	adj.	生态（学）的	Unit 7 AWL
edge	/edʒ/	n.	优势	Unit 8 A
efficiency	/ɪˈfɪʃnsi/	n.	效率	Unit 6 A
eligibility	/ˌelɪdʒəˈbɪləti/	n.	合格；有资格	Unit 2 B

269

商务学科英语

词汇表

单词	释义	出处
eliminate /ɪˈlɪməneɪt/ v.	除去；剔除；淘汰	Unit 2 A AWL
elite /eɪˈliːt/ n.	精英	Unit 1 A
embrace /ɪmˈbreɪs/ v.	拥抱；信奉，皈依；包含	Unit 7 B
emerge /ɪˈmɜːrdʒ/ v.	出现，浮现	Unit 5 A AWL
emergence /ɪˈmɜːdʒ(ə)ns/ n.	出现，浮现	Unit 1 A AWL
empirical /ɪmˈpɪrɪkl/ adj.	凭经验的；经验主义的	Unit 5 B AWL
enact /ɪˈnækt/ v.	将……制定成法律；制定	Unit 10 A
encyclopedic /ɪnˌsaɪkləˈpiːdɪk/ adj.	渊博的；知识广博的	Unit 2 AWL
enforcement /ɪnˈfɔːsmənt/ n.	强制，实施	Unit 7 A
enhance /ɪnˈhɑːns/ v.	加强；提高	Unit 5 A
enhancement /ɪnˈhɑːnsmənt/ n.	提高，促进	Unit 2 AWL
ensure /ɪnˈʃʊə(r)/ v.	确保	Unit 6 B AWL
entrenched /ɪnˈtrentʃt/ adj.	根深蒂固的，牢固的	Unit 7 B
entrepreneurial /ˌɒntrəprəˈnɜːriəl/ adj.	创业的；企业性质的	Unit 6 A
entrepreneur /ˌɑntrəprəˈnɜː/ n.	企业家；承办人，主办者	Unit 3 A
entrepreneurship /ˌɒntrəprəˈnɜːʃɪp/ n.	企业家精神	Unit 2 AWL
ephemeral /ɪˈfem(ə)r(ə)l/ adj.	短暂的，极短的，瞬息的	Unit 5 B
equation /ɪˈkweɪʒən/ n.	等式	Unit 4 A
equity /ˈɛkwəti/ n.	公平；公正；衡平法；普通股	Unit 3 A
equivalent /ɪˈkwɪvələnt/ n. adj.	对等物；相等的	Unit 6 A AWL
errand /ˈerənd/ n.	（短程的）差事；跑腿	Unit 6 B
escalate /ˈeskəleɪt/ v.	（使）扩大；（使）恶化；（使）升级	Unit 6 B
eventually /ɪˈventʃuəli/ adv.	终究，终于	Unit 8 A AWL
exacerbate /ɪɡˈzæsəbeɪt/ v.	使恶化，使加重	Unit 8 A
exact /ɪɡˈzækt/ v.	强求；强迫	Unit 5 A
exceed /ɪkˈsiːd; ek-/ v.	超过；胜过	Unit 1 A AWL
exclusive /ɪkˈskluːsɪv/ adj.	独有的；独家经营的	Unit 8 AWL
exclusively /ɪkˈskluːsɪvli/ adv.	专门地；专有地	Unit 1 A AWL
exemplify /ɪɡˈzemplɪfaɪ/ v.	例证；例示	Unit 1 A
exemption /ɪɡˈzempʃən/ n.	免除，豁免；免税	Unit 3 B
exert /ɪɡˈzɜːt/ v.	尽力；施加（影响）	Unit 4 A
exertion /ɪɡˈzɜːʃən/ n.	运用；努力	Unit 2 B
expansion /ɪkˈspænʃən/ n.	扩张；发展	Unit 1 B AWL
expertise /ˌekspɜːrˈtiːz/ n.	专门知识；专门技术	Unit 1 B AWL
explosive /ɪkˈspləʊsɪv/ adj.	突增的；爆炸的	Unit 6 A
exponential /ˌekspəˈnenʃəl/ adj.	指数的；（增长）越来越快的	Unit 2 A
extensive /ɪkˈstensɪv/ adj.	广泛的；广阔的	Unit 2 B
facilitate /fəˈsɪlɪteɪt/ v.	促进	Unit 6 A AWL
facilitation /fəˌsɪlɪˈteɪʃn/ n.	简易化	Unit 7 AWL
facility /fəˈsɪləti/ n.	设备	Unit 5 A AWL
fad /fæd/ n.	一时的风尚；风靡一时之物	Unit 6 B
faltering /ˈfɔːltərɪŋ/ adj.	犹豫的	Unit 8 A
fantasy /ˈfæntəsi/ n.	幻想	Unit 4 A

Appendix
词汇表

单词	释义	单元
fatal /ˈfeɪt(ə)l/ adj.	致命的；重大的	Unit 7 B
feedback /ˈfiːdbæk/ n.	反馈	Unit 2 A
fickleness /ˈfɪklnəs/ n.	浮躁；变化无常	Unit 1 A
fiddly /ˈfɪdlɪ/ adj.	要求高精度的	Unit 9 AWL
firmware /ˈfɜːmweə(r)/ n.	（计算机的）固件	Unit 5 B
fiscal /ˈfɪskəl/ adj.	财政的	Unit 4 B
fissure /ˈfɪʃə/ v./n.	裂开；分裂 / 裂缝；裂沟	Unit 2 B
flexibility /ˌfleksəˈbɪlətɪ/ n.	机动性，灵活性	Unit 6 A AWL
flip /flɪp/ v.	轻弹；浏览	Unit 5 AWL
flourish /ˈflʌrɪʃ/ v.	繁荣；茁壮成长	Unit 2 AWL
fluctuation /ˌflʌktʃuˈeɪʃ(ə)n/ n.	起伏，波动	Unit 7 B AWL
flux /flʌks/ n./v.	不断的变动 / 流出；熔解	Unit 5 A
forge /fɔːdʒ/ v.	伪造	Unit 9 A
format /ˈfɔːmæt/ n.	版式，形式	Unit 8 B AWL
fraction /ˈfrækʃn/ n.	一小部分	Unit 2 A
franchisee /ˌfræntʃaɪˈziː/ n.	特许经营人	Unit 2 B
fraud /frɔːd/ n.	欺骗	Unit 3 B
fraudulent /ˈfrɔːdjʊl(ə)nt/ adj.	欺骗性的；不正的	Unit 9 A
fraught with	充满	Unit 3 B
fray /freɪ/ n.	争论；打架	Unit 10 AWL
freelancer /ˈfriːlɑːnsər/ n.	自由职业者	Unit 6 AWL
frictionless /ˈfrɪkʃnles/ adj.	无摩擦的；光滑的	Unit 9 A
fringe /frɪndʒ/ n.	边缘	Unit 6 B
fruition /fruˈɪʃən/ n.	完成，成就；结果实	Unit 3 B
fudge /fʌdʒ/ v.	回避；捏造	Unit 9 B
fuel /fjʊəl/ v.	推动；给……加燃料	Unit 1 B
full-blown /ˌfʊl ˈbloʊn/ adj.	成熟的；（花）盛开的；（帆等）张满的	Unit 10 A
gauge /geɪdʒ/ v.	测量；估计；给……定规格	Unit 3 A
gear /gɪr/ v.	使为……做准备	Unit 6 B
generate /ˈdʒenəreɪt/ v.	使形成；发生	Unit 1 B AWL
genome /ˈdʒiːnəʊm/ n.	基因组，染色体组	Unit 5 B
geographically /ˌdʒiːəˈgræfɪklɪ/ adv.	在地理上；地理学上	Unit 5 B
get carried away	得意忘形的	Unit 8 AWL
grapple with	挣扎	Unit 9 B
grounded /ˈgraʊndɪd/ adj.	有充足理由的	Unit 10 A
groundwork /ˈgraʊndwɜːk/ n.	基础；地基，根基	Unit 3 A
guru /ˈgʊruː/ n.	专家；大师；权威	Unit 5 B
halt /hɔːlt/ v.	使停住；停住	Unit 10 B
harness /ˈhɑːnɪs/ v.	利用，控制	Unit 8 B
headset /ˈhedset/ n.	头戴式受话器，耳机	Unit 3 A
height /haɪt/ n.	高度	Unit 6 A
highlight /ˈhaɪlaɪt/ v.	突出；强调	Unit 1 B AWL
hike /haɪk/ v.	提高，增加	Unit 10 A

商务学科英语

词汇表

hoard /hɔːd/ v.	秘藏	Unit 7 B
hoarding /'hɔːdɪŋ/ n.	[贸易]囤积	Unit 9 A
hobbyist /'hɒbɪɪst/ n.	业余爱好者；有某种癖好者	Unit 3 A
hostage /'hɒstɪdʒ/ n.	人质；抵押品	Unit 5 AWL
hostility /hɒ'stɪlɪtɪ/ n.	敌意；强烈反对	Unit 1 A
hotshot /'hɒtʃɒt/ n.	高手，能人	Unit 8 A
hybrid /'haɪbrɪd/ n.	混合物	Unit 5 B
identity /aɪ'dentɪtɪ/ n.	身份	Unit 4 A AWL
ignite /ɪg'naɪt/ v.	燃烧，点燃	Unit 10 AWL
illicit /ɪ'lɪsɪt/ adj.	违法的；不正当的	Unit 9 A
impartiality /ˌɪmpɑːʃɪ'ælətɪ/ n.	公平；无私	Unit 2 A
impassioned /ɪm'pæʃənd/ adj.	充满激情的	Unit 4 A
impending /ɪm'pendɪŋ/ adj.	即将发生的；迫切的	Unit 10 B
imperative /ɪm'perətɪv/ adj.	必要的	Unit 4 B
impervious /ɪm'pɜːvɪəs/ adj.	不受影响的	Unit 9 B
implement /'ɪmplɪmənt/ v.	实施，执行	Unit 3 B AWL
implementation /ˌɪmplɪmen'teɪʃn/ n.	贯彻；成就	Unit 5 A AWL
import /'ɪmpɔːt/ n.	重要性；意义，涵义	Unit 6 B
impose /ɪm'pəʊz/ v.	强加	Unit 5 A AWL
inadvertently /ˌɪnəd'vɜːtəntlɪ/ adv.	非故意地，无心地	Unit 2 AWL
incentive /ɪn'sentɪv/ n.	动机；刺激	Unit 5 B AWL
incentivize /ɪn'sentɪvaɪz/ v.	以物质刺激鼓励	Unit 1 B
inclusive /ɪn'kluːsɪv/ adj.	包括的；包容广阔的	Unit 7 A
incompatible /ˌɪnkəm'pætəbəl/ adj.	不相容的	Unit 4 A AWL
inconsistent /ˌɪnkən'sɪstənt/ adj.	不一致的	Unit 2 B AWL
incorporate /ɪn'kɔːpəreɪt/ v.	包含；吸收，使并入	Unit 7 A AWL
incremental /ˌɪnkrɪ'mentəl/ adj.	增加的，增值的	Unit 7 B
indemnify /ɪn'demnɪfaɪ/ v.	赔偿；保护；使免于受罚	Unit 9 A
index /'ɪndeks/ n.	指数	Unit 6 A AWL
indicative /ɪn'dɪkətɪv/ adj.	指示的	Unit 6 A AWL
indicator /'ɪndɪkeɪtə(r)/ n.	指标	Unit 6 A AWL
inertia /ɪ'nɜːʃə/ n.	懒惰	Unit 2 A
inevitably /ɪn'evɪtəblɪ/ adv.	不可避免地	Unit 6 A AWL
infer /ɪn'fɜː/ v.	推断；推论	Unit 2 A AWL
inflate /ɪn'fleɪt/ v.	使胀大；使膨胀	Unit 10 B
inflict /ɪn'flɪkt/ v.	使遭受（损伤、痛苦等）	Unit 1 A
infrastructure /'ɪnfrəstrʌktʃə/ n.	基础设施；公共建设	Unit 1 B AWL
infringe /ɪn'frɪndʒ/ v.	侵犯；侵害	Unit 9 A
initially /ɪ'nɪʃəlɪ/ adv.	起初	Unit 10 A AWL
initiative /ɪ'nɪʃətɪv/ n.	倡议；主动	Unit 2 A AWL
innovation /ˌɪnə'veɪʃn/ n.	创新；新方法	Unit 1 B AWL
input /'ɪnpʊt/ n.	输入	Unit 5 A AWL
insightful /'ɪnsaɪtfəl/ adj.	有深刻见解的，富有洞察力的	Unit 2 A

Appendix
词汇表

单词	释义	单元
inspection /ɪn'spekʃn/ n.	检查	Unit 6 B
instill /ɪn'stɪl/ v.	徐徐滴入；逐渐灌输	Unit 3 A
in tandem	并行	Unit 3 B
intangible /ɪn'tændʒəbl/ adj.	无形的	Unit 1 A
integration /ˌɪntɪ'greɪʃ(ə)n/ n.	融入，融合	Unit 1 A AWL
intensify /ɪn'tensɪfaɪ/ v.	（使）加剧，（使）增强	Unit 10 A AWL
intermediate /ˌɪntə'miːdɪət/ adj.	中间的，中级的	Unit 10 B AWL
interpret /ɪn'tɜːprɪt/ v.	口译；解释；诠释	Unit 2 A AWL
intersection /ˌɪntə'sekʃən/ n.	交叉；十字路口；交集	Unit 3 AWL
intertwine /ˌɪntə'twaɪn/ v.	纠缠；编结	Unit 5 B
intervene /ˌɪntər'viːn/ v.	干涉	Unit 9 A AWL
in the wake of	随着……而来；作为……的结果	Unit 3 B
intracompany /ˌɪntrə'kʌmpənɪ/ adj.	公司内部的	Unit 7 B
intricate /'ɪntrɪkət/ adj.	复杂的；错综的	Unit 10 A
intriguing /ɪn'triːgɪŋ/ adj.	有趣的，引人入胜的	Unit 8 A
intuition /ˌɪntjuː'ɪʃən/ n.	直觉	Unit 2 A
inversion /ɪn'vɜːʃ(ə)n/ n.	倒置；倒转	Unit 1 A
invocation /ˌɪnvə'keɪʃən/ n.	祈求；调用	Unit 10 A
jazz up	使变得有趣；使活泼	Unit 10 AWL
justify /'dʒʌstɪfaɪ/ v.	证明……正当	Unit 6 B AWL
lash out	猛击；痛斥	Unit 10 B
ledger /'ledʒə/ n.	总账，分户总账	Unit 9 AWL
legitimate /lə'dʒɪtəmɪt/ adj.	合法的；正当的；	Unit 3 B
level /'levl/ adj.	平稳的，平均的	Unit 6 B
leverage /'liːv(ə)rɪdʒ; 'lev(ə)rɪdʒ/ n.	影响；杠杆	Unit 10 B
levy /'levɪ/ v.	征收，收取（税项或费用）	Unit 10 A AWL
liable /'laɪəb(ə)l/ adj.	有责任的	Unit 9 A AWL
litigation /ˌlɪtɪ'geɪʃn/ n.	诉讼；起诉	Unit 3 B
lobby /'lɒbɪ/ v.	对……进行游说	Unit 7 A
logistics /lə'dʒɪstɪks/ n.	物流	Unit 8 B
loophole /'luːphəʊl/ n.	漏洞	Unit 7 B
Mafia /'mɑːfɪə/ n.	黑手党	Unit 4 AWL
magnitude /'mægnɪtjuːd/ n.	巨大；重要性	Unit 4 B
mandate /'mændeɪt/ v.	批准；颁布；强制执行	Unit 3 B
manipulate /mə'nɪpjʊleɪt/ v.	操纵；操作	Unit 9 A AWL
manual /'mænjʊ(ə)l/ adj.	手制的，手工的	Unit 5 AWL
manufacture /ˌmænjə'fæktʃə/ n.	制造；产品；制造业	Unit 2 B
margin /'mɑːdʒɪn/ n.	差数	Unit 4 B AWL
materiality /məˌtɪərɪ'ælɪtɪ/ n.	物质性；重要性	Unit 7 AWL
matrix /'meɪtrɪks/ n.	矩阵	Unit 7 AWL
matter /'mætə/ v.	要紧	Unit 4 A
mediate /'miːdɪeɪt/ v.	调解；斡旋	Unit 10 A
merchant /'mɜːtʃ(ə)nt/ n.	商人	Unit 9 A

商务学科英语

词汇表

单词	音标	词性	释义	Unit
merger	/ˈmɜːdʒə/	n.	（企业等的）合并；并购	Unit 7 B
merit	/ˈmerɪt/	n.	优点，价值；功绩	Unit 3 B
metropolitan	/ˌmetrəˈpɒlətn/	adj.	大都市的	Unit 4 A
migration	/maɪˈgreɪʃ(ə)n/	n.	迁移；移民	Unit 1 A AWL
millennial	/mɪˈleniəl/	adj./n.	千禧年的 / 千禧世代	Unit 6 AWL
minimum	/ˈmɪnɪməm/	adj.	最低限度；最小量	Unit 5 A AWL
miniscule	/ˈmɪnəskjuːl/	adj.	小字体的；极小的	Unit 2 A
misclassification	/ˌmɪsˌklæsɪfɪˈkeɪʃən/	n.	错误分类	Unit 6 B
misrepresentation	/ˌmɪsˌreprɪzenˈteɪʃn/	n.	歪曲；误传	Unit 3 B
mitigate	/ˈmɪtɪgeɪt/	v.	减轻，缓解，缓和	Unit 10 B
modest	/ˈmɒdɪst/	adj.	不太大的，不太高的，适中的	Unit 6 A
modify	/ˈmɒdɪfaɪ/	v.	修改，更改	Unit 9 B AWL
molecule	/ˈmɒlɪkjuːl/	n.	分子；微粒	Unit 2 AWL
monitor	/ˈmɒnɪtə(r)/	v.	监听；搜集，记录	Unit 5 AWL
monopoly	/məˈnɒpəli/	n.	垄断	Unit 7 A
morph	/mɔːf/	v.	改变；变化	Unit 8 A
mount	/maʊnt/	v.	组织，发起	Unit 8 A
multiplier	/ˈmʌltɪplaɪə/	n.	乘数，乘数效应	Unit 1 B
mundane	/mʌnˈdeɪn/	adj.	平凡的；单调的	Unit 2 A
mute	/mjuːt/	adj.	哑的；沉默的；无声的	Unit 5 A
naive	/naɪˈiːv/	adj.	幼稚的	Unit 4 A
nascent	/ˈnæsnt/	adj.	初期的	Unit 6 A
navigate	/ˈnævɪgeɪt/	v.	（在网站上）导航	Unit 8 B
necessity	/nəˈsesəti/	n.	必要性	Unit 6 A AWL
nevertheless	/ˌnevəðəˈles/	conj.	然而，不过	Unit 1 A AWL
niche	/niːʃ/	adj./n.	针对特定客户群的 / 商机；市场定论	Unit 2 AWL
notably	/ˈnəʊtəbli/	adv.	格外地；特别地	Unit 10 B
notion	/ˈnəʊʃ(ə)n/	n.	概念；见解	Unit 5 B AWL
notorious	/nəʊˈtɔːriəs/	adj.	臭名昭著的，声名狼藉的	Unit 10 A
nuance	/ˈnjuːɑːns/	n.	细微差别	Unit 2 AWL
nudge	/nʌdʒ/	v.	推进；用肘轻推	Unit 7 B
numerous	/ˈnuːmərəs/	adj.	许多的，很多的	Unit 10 A
obfuscate	/ˈɒbfʌskeɪt/	v.	使混淆；使困惑	Unit 5 A
obsess	/əbˈses/	v.	（使）着迷；（使）困扰	Unit 6 B
obsolete	/ˈɒbsəliːt/	adj.	废弃的；老式的	Unit 2 A
obstacle	/ˈɒbstək(ə)l/	n.	障碍，干扰	Unit 9 B
occupancy	/ˈɒkjəpənsi/	n.	占有，居住（率）	Unit 6 A AWL
offset	/ˈɒfˌset/	v.	抵消	Unit 4 B AWL
oligarchical	/ˌɒlɪˈgɑːkɪkl/	adj.	寡头政治的；主张寡头政治的	Unit 3 A
opaque	/əʊˈpeɪk/	adj.	不透明的；不传热的；迟钝的	Unit 3 A
operational	/ˌɒpəˈreɪʃənl/	adj.	经营上的；运行中的	Unit 6 A
optical	/ˈɒptɪk(ə)l/	adj.	光学的；眼的	Unit 10 B
optimize	/ˈɒptɪmaɪz/	v.	使最优化，使尽可能有效	Unit 8 A

Appendix
词汇表

单词	释义	单元
orientation /ˌɔːriən'teɪʃn/ n.	取向；方向，目标	Unit 7 AWL
ostensibly /ɒ'stensɪblɪ/ adv.	表面地，假装地，谎称地	Unit 10 B
outperform /ˌaʊtpər'fɔːrm/ v.	胜过；做得比……好	Unit 3 A
output /'aʊtpʊt/ v./n.	输出 / 产量	Unit 2 B AWL
outright /'aʊtraɪt/ adj./adv.	完全的；直接了当的 / 完全地；直接地	Unit 6 A
outweigh /ˌaʊt'weɪ/ v.	（在重要性或意义上）超过	Unit 4 B
overdraft /'əʊvədrɑːft/ n.	[金融] 透支	Unit 7 B
overlook /ˌəʊvə'lʊk/ v.	忽略	Unit 4 A
oversee /ˌəʊvə'siː/ v.	监督，监视	Unit 8 A
oversight /'əʊvəsaɪt/ n.	失察；监督	Unit 9 B
overstate /ˌəʊvə'steɪt/ v.	夸张；夸大的叙述	Unit 6 B
panel /'pænl/ n.	专家咨询组；讨论小组	Unit 5 B AWL
panic /'pænɪk/ v.	使恐慌	Unit 9 A
paradox /'pærədɒks/ n.	悖论	Unit 9 B
partisan /ˌpɑːtɪ'zæn/ adj.	党派性的；偏袒的	Unit 5 A
patent /'peɪtnt/ n./v./adj.	专利权 / 获得专利权 / 专利生产的	Unit 2 A
payroll /'peɪrəʊl/ n.	工资名单；工资总支出	Unit 7 A
penetrate /'penɪtreɪt/ v.	进入；渗入	Unit 6 A
penetration /ˌpenɪ'treɪʃn/ n.	进入，打入（市场）	Unit 6 A
per capita /pə 'kæpətə/ adj.	人均的	Unit 1 AWL
perceive /pə'siːv/ v.	察觉；理解	Unit 1 A AWL
perception /pə'sepʃ(ə)n/ n.	知觉；看法	Unit 7 A
peril /'perəl/ n.	危险；冒险	Unit 3 B
periodic /ˌpɪəri'ɒdɪk/ adj.	周期的；定期的	Unit 2 B AWL
permanent /'pɜːm(ə)nənt/ adj.	永久的	Unit 9 A
persist /pə'sɪst/ v.	坚持；存留；固执	Unit 5 B AWL
perspective /pə'spektɪv/ n.	观点；远景	Unit 5 AWL
pervasive /pə'veɪsɪv/ adj.	普遍的，渗透的	Unit 8 A
pharmaceutical /ˌfɑːmə'suːtɪkl/ adj./n.	制药的 / 药物	Unit 2 AWL
phenomenon /fɪ'nɒmɪnən/ n.	现象，事件	Unit 5 B AWL
photogenic /ˌfəʊtəʊ'dʒenɪk/ adj.	易上镜的	Unit 8 AWL
pilot /'paɪlət/ v.	试用，试行	Unit 1 B
pint /paɪnt/ n.	品脱	Unit 9 AWL
pitfall /'pɪtfɔːl/ n.	陷阱，圈套；缺陷；诱惑	Unit 3 B
pledge /pledʒ/ v.	保证，许诺	Unit 10 A
plunge /plʌndʒ/ v.	（使）突然向前倒下（跌落）	Unit 10 B
polarize /'pəʊləraɪz/ v.	（使）两极分化	Unit 7 B
populist /'pɒpjʊlɪst/ n.	民粹主义者	Unit 4 B
potent /'pəʊtənt/ adj.	强有力的	Unit 4 A
practitioner /præk'tɪʃənə/ n.	从业者；实践者	Unit 2 B AWL
precedence /'presɪdəns/ n.	优先	Unit 4 A AWL
preliminary /prɪ'lɪmɪnəri/ adj.	初步的，准备的	Unit 8 AWL
premium /'priːmiəm/ n.	额外费用，附加费	Unit 8 A

商务学科英语

词汇表

单词	音标	词性	释义	出处
preservationist	/ˌprezə'veɪʃənɪst/	n.	保护主义者	Unit 2 AWL
prevail	/prɪ'veɪl/	v.	盛行；战胜	Unit 1 B
previously	/'priːvɪəsli/	adv.	以前，先前	Unit 1 A AWL
price range			价格幅度，价格承受范围	Unit 8 AWL
primacy	/'praɪməsi/	n.	首位；卓越	Unit 8 B AWL
problematic	/ˌprɑːblə'mætɪk/	adj.	有很多问题的，难对付的	Unit 10 B
procedural	/prə'siːdʒərəl/	adj.	程序上的	Unit 4 A AWL
proceed	/prə'siːd/	v.	继续进行；开始；着手	Unit 2 B AWL
proclaim	/prə'kleɪm/	v.	宣告，公布；声明	Unit 1 B
procurement	/prə'kjʊəmənt/	n.	采购	Unit 7 AWL
productivity	/ˌprɒdʌk'tɪvəti/	n.	生产力，生产率	Unit 6 B
profitability	/ˌprɒfətə'bɪləti/	n.	盈利能力	Unit 2 A
profound	/prə'faʊnd/	adj.	深奥的；极度的；意义深远的	Unit 2 A
projection	/prə'dʒekʃən/	n.	投影；投射；规划	Unit 2 B AWL
prominent	/'prɒmɪnənt/	adj.	突出的	Unit 4 AWL
prompt	/prɒmpt/	v.	促使，导致	Unit 8 B
property	/'prɒpəti/	n.	性质，性能	Unit 9 A
proportional	/prə'pɔːʃ(ə)n(ə)l/	adj.	成比例的	Unit 9 A AWL
proprietor	/prə'praɪətə/	n.	业主；所有者；经营者	Unit 9 A
prosperity	/prɒ'sperɪti/	n.	繁荣，成功	Unit 1 B
protocol	/'prəʊtəkɒl/	n.	协议	Unit 9 B
provision	/prə'vɪʒn/	n.	（法律或协议的）条文，条款	Unit 3 B
pursuit	/pə'sjuːt/	n.	追求	Unit 4 A
qualifying	/'kwɒlɪfaɪɪŋ/	adj.	具有资格的	Unit 6 A
query	/'kwɪəri/	n.	疑问	Unit 2 A
quid pro quo	/'kwɪdprəʊ'kwəʊ/	n.	[拉丁] 补偿物	Unit 4 B
racist	/'reɪsɪst/	n.	种族主义者	Unit 4 A
radically	/'rædɪkəli/	adv.	根本上；彻底地	Unit 7 B
rail	/reɪl/	v.	抱怨	Unit 4 B
ramification	/ˌræmɪfɪ'keɪʃn/	n.	结果，后果	Unit 3 A
rampant	/'ræmp(ə)nt/	adj.	猖獗的；蔓延的	Unit 1 B
rationalize	/'ræʃnəlaɪz/	v.	使合理化；据理解释	Unit 5 B AWL
readily	/'redɪli/	adv.	快捷地；轻而易举地	Unit 8 B
reassert	/ˌriːə'sɜːt/	v.	重申	Unit 4 A
rebellion	/rɪ'beljən/	n.	叛乱；反抗	Unit 7 B
rebound effect			反弹作用	Unit 2 AWL
recession	/rɪ'seʃ(ə)n/	n.	衰退；不景气	Unit 9 A
reckon	/'rekən/	v.	认为；估计	Unit 8 A
reckoning	/'rek(ə)nɪŋ/	n.	估算，估计	Unit 1 A
reconcile	/'rek(ə)nsaɪl/	v.	调和；使一致；使和解	Unit 5 A
recoup	/rɪ'kuːp/	v.	收回；偿还；弥补	Unit 3 B
redeployment	/ˌriːdɪ'plɔɪmənt/	n.	重新部署	Unit 2 AWL
redress	/rɪ'dres/	v.	重新调整	Unit 4 A

Appendix
词汇表

referendum /ˌrefə'rendəm/ n.	全民公决	Unit 1 A
refine /rɪ'faɪn/ v.	精炼，提纯；改善	Unit 3 A AWL
refrain /rɪ'freɪn/ v.	克制；避免	Unit 9 A
refund /'riːfʌnd/ n.	退款；偿还	Unit 9 A
refundable /rɪ'fʌndəbl/ adj.	可归还的	Unit 6 A AWL
regulate /'reɡjuleɪt/ v.	管理，调整，控制	Unit 6 A AWL
regulation /ˌreɡju'leɪʃn/ n.	管理；规则	Unit 1 A AWL
reign /reɪn/ v.	统治；支配	Unit 9 A
release /rɪ'liːs/ v.	发布，发表	Unit 6 B
remedy /'remədi/ n.	补救；（通过法律程序的）解决方法	Unit 6 B
remuneration /rɪˌmjuːnə'reɪʃn/ v.	报酬，酬劳	Unit 3 B
rental /'rentl/ n.	出租，租赁	Unit 6 A AWL
repercussion /ˌriːpər'kʌʃn/ n.	反响；后果	Unit 1 A
resentment /rɪ'zentmənt/ n.	怨恨	Unit 4 A
resilient /rɪ'zɪliənt/ adj.	有弹力的；能复原的	Unit 10 B
resolve /rɪ'zɑlv/ v.	解决	Unit 10 A AWL
resource /rɪ'sɔːs; rɪ'zɔːs/ n.	资源；物力	Unit 5 B AWL
restore /rɪ'stɔː(r)/ v.	修复；归还	Unit 4 A AWL
retailer /'riːteɪlə/ n.	零售商	Unit 9 AWL
retaliation /rɪˌtælɪ'eɪʃn/ n.	报复，反击	Unit 10 A
reveal /rɪ'viːl/ v.	透露；显示	Unit 4 B AWL
revenue /'revənjuː/ n.	收入，收益	Unit 5 A AWL
reverse /rɪ'vɜːs/ v.	逆转	Unit 4 B AWL
revive /rɪ'vaɪv/ v.	使复兴；使苏醒	Unit 1 B
revolt /rɪ'vəʊlt/ n.	反抗；叛乱	Unit 1 A
rhetoric /'retərɪk/ n.	辞令，言辞；修辞	Unit 1 AWL
rigorous /'rɪɡərəs/ adj.	严密的；缜密的	Unit 7 A
robust /rəʊ'bʌst/ adj.	健壮的；强劲的；坚定的	Unit 6 A
rod /rɒd/ n.	杆；棍棒；竿	Unit 5 AWL
rumbling /'rʌmblɪŋ/ n.	咕噜声；谣言	Unit 1 A
savvy /'sævi/ n.	洞察力；了解；知识	Unit 3 B
scale back	相应缩减；按比例缩减	Unit 10 A
scramble /'skræmbl/ v.	争抢；匆忙做某事	Unit 10 A
scrap /skræp/ n.	残羹剩饭	Unit 2 A
scrupulous /'skruːpjʊləs/ adj.	小心谨慎的	Unit 9 AWL
seamless /'siːmləs/ adj.	无缝的；无漏洞的	Unit 8 B
segment /'seɡmənt/ n.	部分	Unit 4 B
segregate /'seɡrɪɡeɪt/ v.	隔离；分开	Unit 2 AWL
semblance /'sembləns/ n.	表象；外观	Unit 4 A
shady /'ʃeɪdi/ adj.	阴凉的；不法的	Unit 9 AWL
sham /ʃæm/ adj.	虚假的	Unit 6 B
shindig /'ʃɪndɪɡ/ n.	舞会；狂欢聚会	Unit 8 A
shutdown /'ʃʌtdaʊn/ n.	停止营业；停止运行	Unit 5 AWL

277

商务学科英语

词汇表

单词	音标	词性	释义	单元
simmering	/ˈsɪmərɪŋ/	adj.	升温的，持续发酵升级的	Unit 1 AWL
singular	/ˈsɪŋjʊlə/	adj.	非凡的；异常的	Unit 1 B
skirmish	/ˈskɜːmɪʃ/	n.	小冲突，小规模战斗；小争论	Unit 10 A
skirt	/skɜːt/	v.	绕开，避开（困难）等	Unit 3 B
sluggish	/ˈslʌɡɪʃ/	adj.	萧条的；懒惰的	Unit 1 A
slump	/slʌmp/	v.	暴跌，骤降	Unit 10 B
snapshot	/ˈsnæpʃɒt/	n.	（快拍）照片	Unit 8 AWL
societal	/səˈsaɪətəl/	adj.	社会的	Unit 7 AWL
solidarity	/ˌsɒlɪˈdærɪti/	n.	团结一致	Unit 4 A
source	/sɔːs/	n.	来源；水源；原始资料	Unit 5 B AWL
spearhead	/ˈspɪəhed/	v.	带头做某事	Unit 4 AWL
spectacle	/ˈspektək(ə)l/	n.	景象；场面；奇观	Unit 7 B
speculator	/ˈspekjʊleɪtə/	n.	投机者	Unit 9 B
spoiler	/ˈspɔɪlə/	n.	剧透	Unit 10 AWL
spot on			完全正确；精确的；准确的	Unit 3 B
spreadsheet	/ˈspredʃiːt/	n.	电子表格程序	Unit 2 A
spur	/spɜː/	v.	刺激；鞭策；促进	Unit 2 B
spurious	/ˈspjʊəriəs/	adj.	似是而非的；（论据、推理）不正确的	Unit 10 B
squarely	/ˈskweəli/	adv.	径直地；诚实地；正好；干脆地	Unit 7 B
stagnant	/ˈstæɡnənt/	adj.	停滞的	Unit 2 B
stagnation	/stæɡˈneɪʃən/	n.	停滞；滞止	Unit 7 B
stakeholder	/ˈsteɪkˌhəʊldə/	n.	利益相关者	Unit 2 A
static	/ˈstætɪk/	adj.	静态的	Unit 4 B AWL
straightforward	/ˌstreɪtˈfɔːwəd/	adj.	坦率的；简单的	Unit 4 B AWL
stranded	/ˈstrændɪd/	adj.	陷于困境的	Unit 4 A
strategic	/strəˈtiːdʒɪk/	adj.	战略的	Unit 1 B AWL
streamline	/ˈstriːmlaɪn/	v.	精简	Unit 6 B
strip	/strɪp/	v.	剥夺；剥去	Unit 7 B
stymie	/ˈstaɪmi/	v.	阻碍，妨碍，使不能实施	Unit 6 B
submission	/səbˈmɪʃn/	n.	提交，呈递	Unit 6 A
subsequent	/ˈsʌbsɪkwənt/	adj.	随后的，作为结果而发生的	Unit 1 A AWL
subsidiary	/səbˈsɪdiəri/	n.	子公司	Unit 4 B AWL
subsidize	/ˈsʌbsɪdaɪz/	v.	资助，补贴	Unit 4 B AWL
subsidy	/ˈsʌbsɪdi/	n.	补贴；津贴	Unit 1 A AWL
substantial	/səbˈstænʃl/	adj.	大量的；重大的	Unit 7 A
substantive	/ˈsʌbstəntɪv/	adj.	实质性的	Unit 4 A
substitute	/ˈsʌbstɪtjuːt/	n.	代替者	Unit 4 A AWL
substitution	/ˌsʌbstɪˈtjuːʃən/	n.	替代	Unit 2 B AWL
subtle	/ˈsʌt(ə)l/	adj.	微妙的；精细的	Unit 7 B
sufficiency	/səˈfɪʃnsi/	n.	充足	Unit 6 A AWL
sufficient	/səˈfɪʃnt/	adj.	足够的；充分的	Unit 2 B AWL
supplement	/ˈsʌplɪmənt/	v.	增补，补充	Unit 3 A AWL
surge	/sɜːdʒ/	n.	激增	Unit 6 B

Appendix
词汇表

词	释义	单元
surplus /'sɜːpləs/ adj.	过剩的，多余的	Unit 8 A
susceptible /sə'septəbl/ adj.	易受……影响的；易为……左右的	Unit 6 A
sustain /sə'steɪn/ v.	支持，维持	Unit 6 A AWL
sustainable /sə'steɪnəbl/ adj.	可持续的	Unit 1 B AWL
sympathy /'sɪmpəθi/ n.	同情	Unit 4 A
synthetic /sɪn'θetɪk/ adj.	人造的，人工合成的	Unit 5 B
tailor /'teɪlə(r)/ v.	调整使适应	Unit 8 B
take a chance	冒险	Unit 3 A
take heed	留意	Unit 3 B
tenet /'tenɪt/ n.	原则	Unit 4 B
tenure /'tenjə/ n.	居住权；任期	Unit 7 B
threshold /'θreʃhəʊld/ n.	临界值	Unit 8 B
tinker with	胡乱地修补；摆弄	Unit 3 A
torrent /'tɒrənt/ n.	急流	Unit 2 AWL
tout /taʊt/ v.	兜售；吹嘘	Unit 2 A
traction /'trækʃn/ n.	拖拉；牵引力	Unit 7 A
transaction /træn'zækʃn/ n.	交易，业务	Unit 6 A
transform /træns'fɔːm/ v.	改变，使……变形；转换	Unit 3 A AWL
transformative /trænz'fɔːmətɪv/ adj.	变化的；变形的	Unit 5 A
transition /træn'zɪʃn/ v.	过渡；转变	Unit 1 B AWL
transitory /'trænsɪt(ə)ri/ adj.	短暂的，暂时的	Unit 1 A AWL
transmit /træns'mɪt/ v.	传输；发射；传送	Unit 5 B AWL
treble /'trebl/ v.	使成为三倍	Unit 6 A
tumultuous /tjuː'mʌltjuəs/ adj.	嘈杂的；激动的；动荡的	Unit 4 A
turmoil /'tɜːmɔɪl/ n.	混乱，骚动	Unit 1 A
turnover /'tɜːnəʊvə(r)/ n.	人员流动率；营业额	Unit 7 A
ubiquitous /juː'bɪkwɪtəs/ adj.	无所不在的，随处可见的	Unit 6 B
ultimate /'ʌltɪmət/ adj.	极端的；最后的	Unit 5 A AWL
ultimately /'ʌltɪmətli/ adv.	最后；最终	Unit 1 B AWL
uncertainty /ʌn'sɜːrtnti/ n.	不确定	Unit 4 AWL
undergo /ˌʌndə'gəʊ/ v.	经历；遭受	Unit 6 B AWL
undermine /ˌʌndə'maɪn/ v.	破坏；挖掘地基；逐渐削弱	Unit 5 B
underutilized /ˌʌndər'juːtəlaɪzd/ v.	未充分使用	Unit 6 A
unfettered /ʌn'fetəd/ adj.	无拘无束的	Unit 1 A
unilaterally /ˌjuːni'lætərəli/ adv.	单方面地	Unit 10 B
unreservedly /ˌʌnrɪ'zɜːvɪdli/ adv.	毫无保留地，完全地	Unit 1 A
unscrupulous /ʌn'skruːpjələs/ adj.	肆无忌惮的；不讲道德的	Unit 3 B
unscrupulously /ʌn'skruːpjələsli/ adv.	无道德原则地；不客气地	Unit 7 AWL
unspecified /ʌn'spesɪfaɪd/ adj.	未指明的；未详细说明的	Unit 10 B AWL
untrustworthy /ʌn'trʌstˌwɜːðɪ/ adj.	靠不住的	Unit 4 A
upheaval /ʌp'hiːv(ə)l/ n.	剧变；动乱	Unit 1 A
uproar /'ʌprɔːr/ n.	喧嚣；吵闹；骚动	Unit 10 B
utilization /ˌjuːtəlaɪ'zeɪʃn/ n.	利用，使用	Unit 6 A AWL

商务学科英语

词汇表

utopian /juːˈtəʊpɪən/ adj.	乌托邦的	Unit 4 A
valid /ˈvælɪd/ adj.	有效的	Unit 1 A AWL
validate /ˈvælɪdeɪt/ v.	证实，验证；确认；使生效	Unit 3 A AWL
valuation /ˌvæljuˈeɪʃn/ n.	估价	Unit 6 A
varied /ˈveərɪd/ adj.	多变的；各式各样的	Unit 1 B AWL
versus /ˈvɜːsəs/ prep.	对，对抗；与……相对	Unit 2 A
vet /vet/ v.	审查	Unit 3 B
viability /ˌvaɪəˈbɪləti/ n.	可行性	Unit 2 AWL
vigilant /ˈvɪdʒələnt/ adj.	警惕的，警醒的；警戒的	Unit 3 B
vision /ˈvɪʒ(ə)n/ n.	视力；眼力	Unit 1 B
visionary /ˈvɪʒ(ə)n(ə)ri/ adj.	有远见的	Unit 7 B
volatile /ˈvɒlətaɪl/ adj.	不稳定的	Unit 9 AWL
vulnerability /ˌvʌlnərəˈbɪləti/ n.	脆弱性；易损性；弱点	Unit 10 B
wannabe /ˈwɒnəbi/ n.	（名人）崇拜模仿者	Unit 3 B
warp /wɔːp/ v.	使变形；使有偏见；使乖戾	Unit 7 B
wary /ˈweərɪ/ adj.	谨慎的，警惕的	Unit 1 B
weigh in	加入比赛	Unit 9 B
windfall /ˈwɪndfɔːl/ n.	意外之财	Unit 1 A
woe /wəʊ/ n.	问题；苦恼；悲伤	Unit 8 A